Invitation to the Theatre

BRIEF SECOND EDITION

Invitation to the Theatre

BRIEF SECOND EDITION

George Kernodle
UNIVERSITY OF ARKANSAS

Portia Kernodle

Harcourt Brace Jovanovich, Inc.

NEW YORK   SAN DIEGO   CHICAGO   SAN FRANCISCO   ATLANTA

ISBN: 0-15-546923-1

Library of Congress Catalog Card Number: 77-92752

Printed in the United States of America

Acknowledgments

Cover: *Pacific Overtures.* New York, 1975. Photo Van Williams.

Text:

The authors wish to thank the following for permission to reprint material used in this book.

ATHENEUM PUBLISHERS, INC., for material from *The Persecution and Assassination of Jean-Paul Marat as Performed by the Inmates of the Asylum of Charenton under the Direction of the Marquis de Sade,* by Peter Weiss; and *Equus,* by Peter Shaffer.

CALDER AND BOYARS LTD. for material from *Marat/Sade,* by Peter Weiss.

J. M. DENT & SONS LTD. for material from *Under Milk Wood,* by Dylan Thomas. Reprinted by permission of J. M. Dent & Sons and the Trustees for the Copyrights of the late Dylan Thomas.

ANDRE DEUTSCH, LTD. for material from *Equus,* by Peter Shaffer. Copyright © 1974 by Andre Deutsch.

FABER AND FABER LTD. for material from *Waiting for Godot,* by Samuel Beckett, and *Murder in the Cathedral,* by T. S. Eliot.

SAMUEL FRENCH, INC., for material from *The Adding Machine,* by Elmer Rice. Copyright, 1922, 1929, by Elmer Rice; copyright, 1923, by Doubleday, Page & Co.; renewal copyright, 1949, 1950, 1956, by Elmer Rice.

ELAINE GREENE LTD. for material from *Death of a Salesman,* by Arthur Miller.

GROVE PRESS, INC., for material from *Waiting for Godot,* by Samuel Beckett. Translated from the original French text by the author. Reprinted by permission of Grove Press, Inc. Copyright 1954 by Grove Press.

HARCOURT BRACE JOVANOVICH, INC., for material from *Murder in the Cathedral,* by T. S. Eliot. Copyright, 1935, by Harcourt Brace Jovanovich, Inc.; copyright, 1963, by T. S. Eliot. Reprinted by permission of the publisher.

WILLIAM HEINEMANN LTD., PUBLISHERS, for material from *On the Art of the Theatre,* by Gordon Craig.

HOUGHTON MIFFLIN CO. for material from *J. B.,* by Archibald MacLeish.

NEW DIRECTIONS PUBLISHING CORP. for material from *Under Milk Wood,* by Dylan Thomas. Copyright 1954 by New Directions Publishing Corp. Reprinted by permission of New Directions Publishing Corp.

RANDOM HOUSE, INC., for material from *Actors Talk About Acting,* by Lewis Funke and John E. Booth. Copyright © 1961 by Random House, Inc.

THE SOCIETY OF AUTHORS for material from *Man and Superman,* by George Bernard Shaw. Reprinted by permission of The Society of Authors for the Bernard Shaw Estate.

THE ESTATE OF GERTRUDE STEIN for material from *Mother of Us All,* by Gertrude Stein.

THAMES AND HUDSON LTD. for material from *Actors Talk About Acting,* by Lewis Funke and John E. Booth.

THEATRE ARTS BOOKS for material from *On the Art of the Theatre,* by Edward Gordon Craig. All rights reserved. Used with the permission of the publisher, Theatre Arts Books, New York.

THE VIKING PRESS, INC., for material from *Death of a Salesman,* by Arthur Miller. Copyright 1949 by Arthur Miller. Reprinted by permission of The Viking Press, Inc.

Preface

Changes in the theatre world since the first Brief Edition of *Invitation to the Theatre* was published, in 1971, have made a new edition desirable. Not only have new trends appeared in the 1970s, but the experimentation of the 1960s can now be seen in a new perspective. The contemporary theatre has absorbed from that rebellious decade much that is worth keeping, and it has made several new syntheses of traditions and forms that used to be considered quite separate: of Western realism with Oriental conventions, of modern dance with classical ballet, of popular rock music with grand opera, and of spoken drama with dance and music.

The very definitions of theatre are changing, with less emphasis being placed on literal illusion and more on symbolic role-playing, trance-like states of consciousness, and psychotherapy. Hence in a new prologue, "What Is Theatre?," we consider how and why actor and audience are held in a magic spell by a dynamic performance and how different theatrical conventions create illusion on different kinds of stages. In a new epilogue, "The Pleasure of Your Company," we discuss briefly the private joys of actor, playgoer, and amateur critic and the public values of different types of theatre: commercial or free-enterprise theatre, small experimental groups, community and college theatres, and a civic institution with a resident theatre company.

At the suggestion of a number of instructors who have used the first Brief Edition, we now present the major types of plays in the order in which they became important in history. We begin with Greek tragedy, which set the pattern for serious drama in the Western world, and continue with comedy, romance, realism, and the recent dramatic forms. In the discussions of each kind of play, we cite examples drawn from recent productions on stage and on screen; and many illustrations of scenes from these productions are provided.

Our thanks are due to Grigoris Daskalogrigorakis for giving us the benefit of his understanding of the work of experimental theatre groups in New York City. We are also grateful to the following individuals for their careful examinations of the first Brief Edition and their suggestions for its revision: Vincent L. Angotti, University of South Dakota; Joe Bella, Montclair State College; Saul Elkin, State University of New York at Buffalo; Edward Pixley, State University of New York at Oneota; Arthur H. Saxon; Franco Tonelli, University of California at Irvine. Finally, we are especially indebted to A. Cleveland Harrison, Auburn University, for his comments on the manuscript of the present text.

George Kernodle
Portia Kernodle

Contents

The Theatre of Romance   95

 The Theatre of Realism   125

 Realism Transformed   151

 The Theatre of Disruption   179

Invitation to the Theatre

BRIEF SECOND EDITION

Prologue

What Is Theatre?

What is theatre? It is so many things that this entire book can give only a partial answer. The patterns that shape drama—conflict, confrontation, crisis, resolution—are patterns of life itself, and every human being, like the actor, plays roles. In Shakespeare's *As You Like It*, Jaques says:

> All the world's a stage,
> And all the men and women merely players:
> They have their exits and their entrances;
> And one man in his time plays many parts.

Yet life in the world and life on the stage are not the same. Everyone knows that the theatre, with its false front and painted canvas, its masks and its disguises, is illusion created by sleight of hand. But everyone still is glad to make believe, to participate in the deception that deceives no one, because the theatre offers rich, deep experience. The theatre relates us to the great archetypal patterns of human purpose and destiny, the patterns expressed in the great myths. It is an extension of life.

Like religious conversion, the theatre brings the joy of enlightenment, a new health, a revelation that makes order of confusion and doubt. Bernard Shaw called on the theatre to take itself seriously as "a factory of thought, a prompter of conscience, an elucidator of social conflict, an armory against despair and dullness, and a temple of the Ascent of Man."

Andrei Serban, the brilliant young New York director, has said, "Theatre is a manifestation of the essence of life." That essence is more than pleasure in entertainment, more than role-playing, more than any personal emotion of love, hate, anger, or jealousy. The essence of life is a deep sense of wonder and awe, of a common human destiny.

That final revelation, that enlightenment that can triumph over confusion and doubt, is achieved in the theatre from an explosive situation. For the very center of the theatrical experience is the confrontation between two unstable, unpredictable elements: the living actor and the living audience.

Actor and Audience

Like a primitive god in a fearful mask, the actor brings into our presence the "other world": the unknown, the strange, the uncanny. In our familiar prayers we speak to a vague, distant god, but here in the temple drama the god speaks to us. In mythology we hear about gods who were active in a far-distant past; here the god suddenly becomes present and starts an action that will involve the audience in his destiny. The audience would be safe if the god spoke only set ancient phrases, or better yet if the god were a statue and priests brought prayers and offerings to him in a traditional ceremony. Familiar ritual is peaceful and reassuring; the world of awe, values, and mystery is held at a precise, measured distance. But this strange actor-god is close, often very close, and he is safe to watch only because the audience knows he will stay in his conventional playing area, start and stop at conventional signals, and speak not directly from the gods or even in his own person as an actor, but will repeat imaginary lines of a created character. To quiet the fear of the unknown, however, two other things are necessary—the stage with familiar patterns, and the play, which is more real than everyday life because it seems improvised, a spontaneous happening before our eyes and yet a work of art, carefully planned and rehearsed.

No other art rests on such a dynamic yet fragile relationship between the artist and the public. Some creations are fixed in form forever, like the pyramids. The emperors and saints in the Byzantine wall mosaics stare down on our transitory world with a serene perfection unchanged for the last thousand years. Only in the theatre does the performer work directly with the audience. Dancers and singers build the audience up to ecstasies of applause though composer, choreographer, and conductor keep the creation in tight control. Actors lead the audience to create the play afresh every night, to accept the "illusion of the first time." They may rehearse with the director for weeks and fix every nuance of inflection and every movement, yet the play is an abstract ghost of a play until the live audience is there, hanging on every word, held fast by the electric current that runs from actor to audience and back again to the actor. Sometimes an actor feels he is pulling an audience heavy as lead; sometimes the excitement is so high he feels himself flying through the air. The laughter of an audience, an intoxicating joy to the actor, is only the most obvious response; the actor feels every little change of tension in the house. A poet may now and then see a few people reading his poems; a painter can watch people looking at his pictures in a gallery. But the performing artist in each terrifying moment sees and hears his audience concentrate their pleasure or dislike.

Why is the audience so enthralled by the performer? Why does theatre, in many forms, captivate an audience, carry them in imagination out of themselves? Why do people enjoy a performance not only when it makes them laugh but even when it makes them weep or fills them with terror? One answer is that the audience is not just a collection of individuals, with their normal reactions. The members of an audience arrive as individuals, but sitting close together in the dark theatre, hypnotized by the lights and movement on the stage, feeling the spell of the actor, they become a theatre crowd. A person is not the same in a crowd as when alone: the feelings he has in common with the rest of the crowd are greatly intensified; he loses much of his separate identity and skeptical judgment and gains a new force.

The actor leads the audience as a conductor leads an orchestra, setting time and rhythm, giving the music a sweep from one mood to another, through suspensions and climaxes on to a final conclusion. The actor is like a lively revival preacher, swaying the congregation in joyful waves of agreement; or like a dynamic political speaker, leading an army in an imaginary battle of words. When the politician is a Hitler, the crowd becomes a mob united in an evil spell of hatred. If crowd psychology cannot unite an audience, for good or for evil, the spell is broken and the event is flat or chaotic. On several historic occasions a divided theatre crowd has broken into riot.

Moviegoers and television viewers are not united in the same way as the audience for live theatre, but they do form a crowd. The moviegoer feels his own responses, especially laughter, reinforced by the responses of others. He does not applaud or feel any other interrelationship with the actors on the screen. He knows that these pictures were taken in short sequences and rearranged in this order by an editor. The television drama, though it is now rarely broadcast live, derives a sense of immediacy from the live newscasts or talk shows that come before and after. But far more important than these token contacts is the idea of a nation-wide audience, seeing and listening. We may read a poem or a book privately, even surreptitiously, but there is nothing private about a drama on the screen. We project ourselves into the wider audience and become part of an imaginary crowd.

For the audience, the good performer is a gifted charmer who comes into the spotlight trailing clouds of fame and glory, set out in full glamor by expert costumers, makeup artists, hairdressers, and publicity writers— an embodiment of the color and distinction lacking in the drab lives of the audience. That charm is brazenly exploited in night clubs and especially in the Paris music halls and casinos and the super shows of Las Vegas, where feminine nudity is set off by spangles and feathers and spectacular scenery.

Tinsel, feathers, and sex can divert an audience briefly, but the important personalities of the theatre have far more than cosmetic appeal. They may become identification figures, expressing our deepest wishes and dreams, giving each generation a sense of its own identity. James Dean, young movie star of the 1950s, gave such a compelling image of the lonely "rebel without a cause" that through him a whole generation of young Americans saw themselves. In the sixties the Beatles were the rage and brought in not only a new style of music but new ways of dressing and living. On a much more serious level of accomplishment, with a smaller but no less devoted group of admirers, we have the great interpreters of drama—among them Laurence Olivier, John Gielgud, Katharine Hepburn, and Irene Worth—as well as the great singers of opera and the great dancers, men and women who have won their status as objects of near-worship by talent, skill, and tireless training.

But only in small part does the influence of charm and superb performance explain the dynamic relationship between actor and audience. As we study primitive people over the world and the earliest evidence of history, we find all the arts deeply involved with the sacred history of the tribe, presenting images of the gods and ancestral heroes in sculptured figures, masks, dramas, songs, and dances. Like the primitive *shaman*, who puts himself into a trance, flies up to heaven, brings back a magic herb, and makes a song and drama of his spiritual journey for the benefit of the whole tribe, the actor is an intermediary between the invisible godhead and the human audience. In the twentieth century, the actor may create a trance powerful enough to open the soul to an ecstatic state of consciousness. Like the tribal priest, who initiates the youth in a ritual of symbolic death and resurrection, he may give the audience a sense of being reborn in ancient mysteries powerful enough to cure the agonies of the soul. In playing a role, the actor creates an image of a human being struggling to establish his own identity and his relation to the world he lives in, an image of human destiny.

The Performance Place

The great performer can bring an audience together anywhere—in street or field—yet to have continuity the theatre must be an institution. Out of the youth rebellion of the 1950s and 1960s came a strong interest in finding places for performance other than the regular theatres, in using the informal atmosphere of an old garage or warehouse to gain the spontaneity of a "happening," where there is no sharp distinction between performer and audience. But the same kind of experiment can be made in a flexible room of a theatre building that permits different arrangements of chairs and playing areas, and that has good lighting equipment, and, perhaps, a floor with sections that can be raised and lowered for a variety of levels. In such a room, sometimes called a "little black box," some aspects of spontaneous performance can be institutionalized.

Theatres are now built in three major forms, and although almost any play may be adapted to any of the three, each was invented for a different purpose and has its own set of conventions. The simplest form is the *arena* or *theatre-in-the-round*, with the audience in a circle or rectangle surrounding the playing area. It is the form of the natural setting of most primitive villages, and when the village was small enough all the people sat or stood in a circle close around the performers. For sports events and dramatic war games, the ancient Romans built arenas seating many thousands. The small arena is popular today because it brings the spectator close to the actors. Lights, furniture, or rugs mark the separation of audience space from playing area. Since there is no front curtain, the bringing of the house lights down and the lights on the acting area up is the convention that indicates the beginning of the play.

P–1 A well-equipped, fairly large arena theatre, seating 752 in steeply banked rows: The Arena Stage, Washington, D.C.

P–2 A throne with formal entrances and an upper stage serves as the symbolic backing for a thrust stage that allows audience seating on three sides. Set up in the Presbyterian Assembly Hall for the Edinburgh Festival, the stage accommodates a production of Lindsay's *The Satire of the Three Estates*. Directed by Tyrone Guthrie. Drawing by Richard Leacroft, from Helen and Richard Leacroft, *The Theatre*. Courtesy of Methuen and Co., London.

The second form of theatre, which is called variously *thrust, apron,* or *open* stage, seats the audience around three sides of an open platform. At the back of the platform is usually a scenic symbol containing two or more entrance doors. The origin of this form was a temple stage with sacred doorways through which figures could enter from the "other world" of gods, demons, ghosts, and ancestors. On the Japanese Noh stage to this day, ghosts, spectres, and demons play their moments on earth on a temple platform in front of a sacred pine tree painted on the back wall. The Greek theatre had a formal marble structure with doorways where the gods could enter and high niches where they could appear and speak. The stage of Shakespeare's time had behind its thrust-stage platform a formal two-story symbol of the king and his realm. Most of Shakespeare's characters were human, but the ghost in *Hamlet,* the witches in *Macbeth,* and the fairies of *A Midsummer Night's Dream* could enter the human world from the symbolic architectural setting. We like the thrust stage for several reasons. It brings actors and audience closer together in a more dynamic relationship than does the *proscenium* theatre, which we will describe next. Yet it permits more scenic and lighting effects than are possible on the arena circle. It may be used for the same kinds of realistic plays that are at home behind a proscenium, but it appeals to us most because, like its transcendent ancestor, it easily suggests the symbolic, the mysterious, and the metaphysical (Figure P–2).

The third form of theatre today is the *proscenium* stage. It was invented in Europe in the sixteenth century, and independently in Japan in the seventeenth century when a new bourgeois merchant class wanted to see a complete painted picture, framed and revealed by a front curtain, creating the illusion of the streets, houses, and rooms of the world they

P–3 A large nineteenth-century example of the traditional proscenium theatre: Covent Garden Theatre, 1804. The stage set—for Sheridan's romantic *Pizarro*—includes realistic detail painted on easily changed wings and backdrops. Radio Times Hulton.

knew. One full setting was shown at a time, but machinery was soon developed to change the painted wings and backdrop a dozen or more times. Although the Kabuki, the merchants' illusionistic theatre of Japan, has kept some dynamic relationships with the audience, notably by means of the runway or "flower path" that brings the entering actor right through the audience to the stage, by the twentieth century the picture stage in the West had gone all the way to realism and confined all the action behind the curtain line. In the proscenium theatre, the members of the audience, all facing the same way, watch the play as through a peephole. The convention of the missing "fourth wall" between stage and audience requires the actor to be completely immersed in his character and to make no contact with the audience (Figure P-3).

Since its beginning, the proscenium theatre has dominated the West, and it is still the standard form used by the theatre establishment. It has been under attack for decades, however, and most new theatres are more open. The new National Theatre of England, which opened in London in 1976, has three theatres: proscenium, thrust stage, and a small flexible stage.

The Battle of Conventions

Much of the turmoil and experimentation in the theatre in the twentieth century has been a battle between conventions. The proscenium stage provides a peepshow view of a very solid, materialistic world. Those who have wanted the theatre to deal with religious themes, the fragmentation of the mechanized city, the terrors of the unconscious, or higher states of consciousness have thought it necessary to break out of the rigid limits of the proscenium stage and its conventions.

Theatre conventions, usually defined as rules of the game, are sometimes called "agreed-on falsehoods." Twentieth-century innovators who want a more dynamic theatre than the missing-fourth-wall idea permits are not deserting truth. All theatre is convention, that is, make-believe. If the audience accepts the convention, the illusion depends on the skill of the performer. A puppet may show some truths about human nature more clearly than an actor can. A mask may show more divinity or royalty than an actor's face. In the early church drama, monks played all parts, human and divine, male and female. For God's voice, three monks might chant in unison to represent the Trinity. In Shakespeare's day choir boys often performed plays, taking all the parts, young and old, male and female, and Shakespeare's company followed the convention of using boys for female roles. The Japanese Kabuki was founded by an actress, but when the noble Samurai began quarreling over the favors of the actresses, the shogun ordered the women off the stage. Since then the Japanese have been proud of the elegant femininity of their male specialists in female roles. Often artificiality itself becomes an art.

As our view of history and our acquaintance with other cultures has widened, we have wanted to produce Shakespeare, the Greek tragedies, and plays of the Orient with some of the conventions of the stages for which they were written. The Chinese stage in particular has offered an exciting alternative to the weary round of proscenium plays. The first play put on in the West in the Chinese manner caused gales of laughter at the childlike conventions—a property man shaking bits of paper snow from a box as the actor cries, "How cold it is!" or putting a cushion on the floor for the actor to kneel on or a row of cushions for his death scene.

The Chinese classical stage seems the complete opposite of the Western. It is a thrust stage, with only a symbolic back curtain decorated with a painted or embroidered dragon, symbol of a supernatural blessing of long life (Figure P-4). The Chinese use the simplest form of make-believe to solve the problems that offer such difficulty in Western staging. Where the Western theatre struggles to indicate time and place in casual dialogue or by elaborate changes of setting, the Chinese actor simply tells the audience when and where the action occurs, what has happened in the past and between scenes, and what he is thinking but not saying to the other characters. He has a few symbolic properties handed him by the property man: a whip with tassels for a horse, two flags painted with wheels for a chariot. A cloth painted as a fortified gate and hung from a pole held up by two attendants serves as the city gate to be besieged by an invading general. A small orchestra sits on the stage throughout the play, accompanying songs, creating background music, providing incidental sounds, as well as underscoring each step, movement, and formal phrase of the actor.

So many different conventions have been borrowed from the Chinese, Greek, and Shakespearean stages, and so many new conventions have been invented, that it takes a sophisticated playgoer to understand just what is being done in a particular production. Sometimes it is necessary to explain the new devices to the audience. For example, more than one director of *Our Town* has found that the audience, not knowing that the play was written to be staged in the Chinese manner, without scenery or elaborate lighting, has thought that the producer was too stingy to provide scenery.

Both in forms of theatre and stage conventions we have had to accept coexistence. Though we try to temper our innovations with some care for the traditions of the past, we have no hope of returning to any one form of the past, or any hope of establishing one new form as *the* form, or indeed

P–4 The classical Chinese platform, or thrust, stage, with audience on three sides. Property men and an orchestra assist on stage during the arrival of a general and his chariot at the city gate. Drawn by Claude Marks.

any wish for such results. At the risk of confusing the audience, we will continue to invent variations of old conventions, and we will continue to create new spaces for performing. While part of the audience will prefer familiar institutions where they can relax in comfort, knowing what to expect, many will be eager to see something new. In their choice of conventions, workers in the theatre will continue to be sensitive to the *kind* of play they are producing.

Kinds of Plays

Each kind of play presents a different attitude toward life, a different way of answering some of the age-old questions that are still very pertinent to our lives today. Tragedy, the oldest literary form, the one that gives us our model of what we mean by "dramatic," still fascinates us, as it did the Athenians of 2500 years ago and Londoners at the glorious time of Queen Elizabeth I. A great tragedy exalts the spirit with pride, for it shows a man daring to pursue his spiritual destiny in the face of a challenging universe. Some plays present the miscalculations and frantic schemes of human beings in such a farcical way that we laugh heartily and see what fools we are to take life so seriously. That attitude is our heritage from the rough and bawdy Romans. Another kind of comedy provides more thoughtful laughter as we see sophisticated characters making a game of their disagreements, trying to impose logic and philosophy on the changing patterns of human relationships. This "high comedy" is the special gift of the cultivated gentlemen of the seventeenth and eighteenth centuries. The romantic play, the favorite entertainment of the nineteenth century, with its variants in opera, dance, and musical comedy, invites us to forget the drab, everyday world and follow the charming paths of romance into the dream world of the primitive unconscious. About a century ago the realists told us to stop dreaming, to start solving the problems of humanity in its physical and social environment, to take a serious, scientific attitude as we watch man, this creature of animal drives, trying to rebuild himself and his world. Romance and realism, though they both came as revolutionary and shocking, now shape the standard expectations of the public. Often on the stage, and even more frequently in movie and television plays, they blend together. The rebels of the 1950s, 1960s, and 1970s have found themselves opposing almost everything about the romantic-realistic tradition and creating new, freer kinds of theatre.

Though it is the actor the audience sees, enjoys, and remembers in a performance, he cannot exercise his power without a form: the pattern of an interesting role and a story or other progression in time—in short, a play. The actor may create the play himself, or in the progressive division of labor create his performance on a script written by a playwright. It must seem improvised and fresh, but it must also have a strong structure and a point of view or it vanishes with the performance, like the short songs of a village entertainer or the "happenings" so popular in the 1960s, leaving only the vaguest memories behind. The continuity of the theatre depends on a finished play, either handed down by memory, as in illiterate cultures, or written down with detailed directions for performance.

In this continuity, the theatre is like a flower and its seed. The performance is the flower, a colorful blossoming, the climax of long, unseen growth. It is enjoyed in its brief perfection and vanishes forever. But it leaves a seed—the play—from which another flower may be grown.

The reader of a play gets substance from the seed itself, especially if he knows enough about theatre to create a performance in his imagination. But a richer experience is to see the fine blossoming—an actual performance on some kind of stage, where, ideally, a talented and skilled actor, creating a role in a well-structured and well-written play, casts a spell upon a responsive audience.

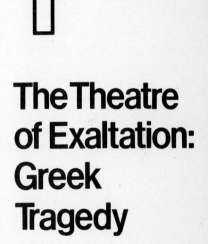

1

The Theatre of Exaltation: Greek Tragedy

SOPHOCLES' *OEDIPUS*. STATE THEATRE PRODUCTION, DARMSTADT, GERMANY. DESIGNED BY FRANZ MARTZ. PHOTO PIT LUDWIG.

The play may be as powerful as a prayer or a religious ritual in bringing human beings into contact with the infinite. Since people have had language, culture, and an idea of a destiny above that of the animals, they have used religious drama to clarify and exalt their sense of being part of divine purpose. The principal subject of prehistoric drama was the coming of the gods and their message into the life of mankind, the conflict with the evil demon of destruction and chaos, and the rebirth of the spirit in eternity. In ancient Egypt each new king performed the central role in a coronation drama celebrating the victory of the young god Horus over the evil spirit Seth and his own rebirth as son of the Divine Spirit. When the king died, either the new king or his priest performed a drama before his tomb every day at sunrise to celebrate the resurrection of the spirit and its journey to the eternal stars. Egyptian drama, though it influenced Greek drama, was completely forgotten in modern times, and only recently have scholars begun to piece together the fragmentary accounts.

The Greeks moved the mythological drama to the human plane, keeping the gods in the background and putting at the center a human hero who sets himself against the old customs of the gods. The occasion for this new approach was the Dionysian festival celebrating the resurrection of living spring out of dead winter. After a wild, ecstatic procession bringing the statue of Dionysus into his theatre, the Greeks added a very serious new form, *tragedy*, which combined the pain and humiliation of sacrificial death with the exaltation of resurrection. Tragedy was profoundly religious, yet it put the emphasis on human beings and the values of this world. In the first age of skepticism, and in the first democracy, the Greeks believed that an individual could question the gods, though death might be the punishment. In accepting the defeat and death of a great hero or heroine, the audience felt pride that someone had challenged the universe and measured the human reach against the infinite.

Comedy seems to spring up everywhere and to take many shapes and patterns as it accommodates all kinds of popular entertainment. Tragedy, on the other hand, was invented at one time and one place—Athens in the sixth and fifth centuries before Christ. While any clown could add to the repertory of comic tricks, tragedy was a deliberate artistic invention, made by selecting literary and choral elements that logically fitted together to make a strong unity.

As it has found its way to all parts of the world, tragedy has gained the highest prestige of any dramatic form. It has seemed the most universal, carrying its appeal to ages and countries far from its origin. It is the model of what we mean by "dramatic"—compact and unified, with logical development from one episode to the next. It presents a strong conflict leading to a full confrontation between two forces, the decisive victory of one, followed by accommodation and recognition. Tragedy offers some of the best acting roles. The Greeks called Thespis, who performed the first tragedies, the first "actor," though comic actors had been around for centuries. In modern times an actor or actress may win popularity in comedy or melodrama, but does not have the highest prestige until proved in tragedy. With its suggestion of both human decision and symbolic destiny, it is a challenge to both director and designer. It appeals to students of both literature and philosophy, and many of the world's great philosophers have written tragedy.

The Tragic Vision

That a serious drama of defeat and death should give pleasure to the audience is a paradox that never ceases to amaze students of drama. Each tries to find his own explanation. Tragedy asks several profound questions: What is man's relation to the world, to himself, and to God? What is the meaning of evil and suffering, of choice and responsibility? How can man be both an individual with free will and a part of society and the universe? How can a rebel yet be reconciled to the mystery at the heart of the universe?

A tragedy progresses through several phases. It is not merely the turn of fortune's wheel that lifts a man to a peak, then plunges him to disaster and ruin; not merely the irony of fate that turns hopes and promises to despair and disillusionment; not merely the miscalculation, the guilt, the tragic flaw that exposes a human being to overwhelming punishment, though tragedy may contain any or all of these. One of the strongest patterns involves making a choice and then facing the results of that choice. But often, as in Sophocles' *Oedipus the King* and many of Ibsen's plays, the choice and the deed took place long ago, and the play itself traces the long trail of consequences that must be faced.

Especially helpful for an understanding of the many possible phases of the tragic pattern is Francis Fergusson's suggestion in *The Idea of a Theatre* that they may be seen as a sequence of three P's: *purpose, passion,* and *perception.*

Purpose

In most tragedies the protagonist faces a great crisis that challenges human power to the utmost. Oedipus finds a fearful blight on the kingdom and his people turning to him to cleanse the land, no matter what the cost. In Shakespeare's *Macbeth* the promises of the witches stir ambitions that terrify the hero. Lured on in the "swelling act of the imperial theme," he knows that "to catch the nearest way" must be by murder, and though murder is against his nature, he begins the journey from which he cannot return. Willy Loman, the hero of Arthur Miller's *Death of a Salesman*, faces a terrifying failure he cannot understand. He is indignant. He has been displaced from his rightful place in the world. He demands justice—of his sons, of the past, of his long-lost brother, of the night.

Isolation is the immediate price the tragic hero pays for taking up his burden, but it is an isolation, a rebellion, that gives him identity. Beginning with Aeschylus' Prometheus, who stole fire from heaven and succored mankind in defiance of Zeus, the heroes and heroines of tragedy have taken a stand against the accepted order, whether of man or of the gods. The world may ultimately destroy them, but not before they have had their say. Theirs may be a limited freedom, but out of the solid rock of necessity, they hew a space for freedom. It is a perilous freedom, gained at a terrible price, but for a moment the hero or heroine holds it, becoming one with the gods, exercising choice and free will, transcending the finite even while sinking, lost in the infinite. The end is defeat, but that particular battle for that one little plot of freedom will never have to be fought again.

Sometimes a tragedy is simply a study of the heroic pioneer who blazes the trail for the benefit of the next generation, succeeding partially and dying in the battle in order that those who come after may succeed fully. In 1945, as the plans for the United Nations were being laid, an impressive movie about Woodrow Wilson showed his struggle to establish a League of Nations in 1919. Wilson was destroyed not merely because he miscalculated the response of American senators but because as a pioneer he was inevitably ahead of his time.

Passion

Before they reach a reconciliation, most tragic heroes or heroines undergo tremendous suffering or struggle in which they question the basis of their own being and see the foundations of the world shaken. Terrifying enough when there is the utmost faith in the benevolence of a deity, the glimpse over the edge often comes when the hero is in the strongest conflict and acutely aware of the hideous cruelty in the world. Ultimately, most protagonists find religious meaning in the universe, but not until they have fully faced the indifference, the malignity, and the devastating play of chance and accident.

Perception

Tragedy is most significant in its final phase, when meaning becomes clear, when the sacrifice is followed by resurrection, when the trial reaches judgment and sentence, when the isolated hero is reconciled to the world, having learned through suffering to be both an individual and a part of the mysterious larger entity. At last the world that seemed capricious, malignant, and unjust is revealed as moral, meaningful, and ordered, though finite man may never completely understand that order.

On the simplest level, the hero faces the result of his own actions. Even the melodramas of the nineteenth century show the fitness of retribution. In the opera *Rigoletto,* the hunchback jester, plotting to kill his enemy, kills his own daughter. Most tragedies, though more subtle and complex, suggest that the hero had it coming. There is assurance that life is not meaningless chance, that results have causes, and that fate in its indirect way has a dependable moral order. There is relief when the trial is over and the verdict is clear.

Aristotle suggested not a ritual purging but a metaphor of medical purging as an explanation of the effect of tragedy. He defined the proper reactions to tragedy as pity and terror and added that by pity and terror tragedy effects "a catharsis of such emotions." The literal meaning of catharsis is "purging" or "purification," but since no one knows exactly what Aristotle meant, the word has become the most discussed term in dramatic theory; it has been variously interpreted to mean every kind of emotional release, from the repose of "all passion spent" to a cleansing from all selfish and petty emotions.

The reconciliation of the tragic hero or heroine may take either a metaphysical or a psychological form, or both. Tokens of a wider justice break into the tragic world in many ways. The Furies in Aeschylus' *Oresteia,* Mephistopheles in Goethe's *Faust,* the Ghost in *Hamlet,* and the witches in *Macbeth* are vivid examples of supernatural forces that find an immediate echo in the psychological. In *Oedipus* the oracles and the uncanny old soothsayer are very important, and the gods in many Greek plays are brought directly on stage as symbols of forces beyond human control. Romantic writers are skillful in building up an atmosphere of terror and superstitious dread that suggests impending disaster and unaccountable fate. For some writers of the nineteenth and twentieth centuries, the environment is all-important, and its inescapable influence is suggested by fog, storms, floods, and decay and disease.

In psychological terms, the reconciliation in tragedy is with the self. All pretense has been removed as proud assertion is exhausted. At the end of Sophocles' tragedy, Oedipus has passed beyond Freudian conflict with his father and ambiguous ties with his mother. He has even worked out his self-loathing by blinding himself. He finds his identity and accepts responsibility for his deeds. Broken as he is, he takes up his burden with great dignity and serenity. In the deep humility of suffering, the tragic hero often discovers a new bond of sympathy with all suffering humanity.

The Classic Age of Tragedy

Tragedy was the invention of the Greeks. In their Golden Age, the fifth century before Christ, they produced four of the world's greatest dramatists, new forms of tragedy and comedy that have been models ever since,

1-1 Night performance of a Greek tragedy in the ancient theatre at Epidaurus. The chorus takes a formal position in the large circular orchestra. Euripides' *Hecuba*. The Greek National Theatre Company, 1955. Photo by Harissiadis, Athens.

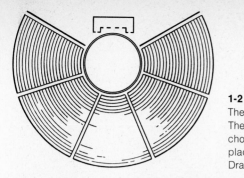

1-2
The general plan of the ancient Greek theatre.
The actors entered from the *skene*, to meet the
chorus in the circular *orchestra*, or dancing
place, almost surrounded by the audience.
Drawn by Don Creason.

and a theatre to which every age returns for rediscovery of some basic principle. At that time the Athenians had just rid themselves of a series of dictators and established the world's first important democracy. When the Persian armies invaded Europe, the Athenians led the confederation of little city-states and drove them back. They rebuilt their burned city in marble and made Athens the artistic as well as the political center of Greece.

On top of the fortified rock, the Acropolis, the Athenians built the Parthenon, a beautiful temple to Athena, the goddess of wisdom, but down by the roadside on the southern slope, available to everybody, they built the theatre, a shrine to Dionysus. The center of the theatre was a round space called an *orchestra,* or "dancing place," because the drama was derived from the dithyramb, danced and chanted by a chorus. The theatre could seat seventeen to twenty thousand people. The rows of seats, built up the slope of the hill, almost completely surrounded the orchestra; spectators in the first rows could almost touch the performers in the orchestra. The earliest plays centered on an altar in the orchestra and had only one actor, who carried on a dialogue with a chorus of fifty. But soon two more actors were added, and the actors' dressing hut, or *skene,* was moved up to the edge of the orchestra so that its three formal doors could serve for entrances in the action—hence the term *scene*. Eventually a raised stage was built, but in classic times the actors were not separated from the chorus.

Since it grew up amid primitive religious rites, with masks and ceremonial costumes, and made use of music, dance, and poetry, the Greek drama was at the opposite pole from the modern realistic stage. In fact, probably no other theatre in history has made fuller use of the intensities of art. The masks, made of painted linen, wood, and plaster, brought into the theatre the primitive atmosphere of gods, heroes, and demons. Though our nineteenth- and twentieth-century grandfathers thought of masks as very artificial, today we appreciate their exciting intensity and can see that in a large theatre they would have been indispensable. If they allowed no fleeting change of expression during a single episode, with a change of mask between the episodes, they could give for

1-3 Tragic masks of the Greek theatre. The large, dignified masks made a strong facial expression visible in a vast theatre. Between episodes they could be changed to indicate a change of emotion. Drawn by Martha Sutherland.

each episode in turn more intense expression than any human face could. When Oedipus came back with bleeding eyes, the new mask could be more terrible than any facial makeup the audience could endure, yet in the sculptured intensity more beautiful than a real face.

The Chorus

Most essential of all intensities, and hardest for us to understand, was the chorus. It is easy to see that during the episodes played by the actors the chorus could provide a background of group response, enlarging and reverberating the emotions of the characters, sometimes protesting and opposing, but in general serving as ideal spectators to stir and lead the reactions of the audience. We are familiar with such group response in the crowds of our romantic plays and the choruses of our operas. More difficult to imagine is the treatment of the choral odes. Since the action of most tragedies is complete without the odes, the modern reader either skips them or supposes that they served as some kind of lyric punctuation, like intermissions between the acts of a play. They include philosophical reflections on the meaning of human destiny and poetic references to ancient gods and heroes. They have usually been translated in such dignified, old-fashioned language that in presenting a Greek tragedy some directors have the chorus speak formally in a half-chant, standing in static groups, or moving slowly to express lamentation, sympathy, shock, or despair.

1-4 *Above:* Chorus reacting to an actor. Sophocles' *Oedipus at Kolonos*. The Greek National Theatre Company at Epidaurus, 1966. Photo by Harissiadis, Athens. *Below:* Chorus in a formal semicircular gesture of horror. Sophocles' *Oedipus at Kolonos*. The Greek National Theatre Company at Epidaurus, 1958. Photo by Harissiadis, Athens.

1-5

Dionysus with his chorus of
women stirring his opponent
to a state of destructive frenzy.
A modern, seminude, spirited
interpretation of Greek tragedy.
Euripides' *The Bacchae*.
Eastern Illinois University production,
directed by Glendon Gabbard, and
costumed by Cindy Russell.

But we now know that the choral odes were complex performances, with sung or chanted words, musical accompaniment, and vigorous, sometimes even wild, dances and symbolic actions that filled orchestras sixty to ninety feet in diameter. At first the playwrights used choruses of fifty but later set the number at fifteen. We know that the playwrights had a sophisticated audience and highly trained performers, for each of the ten tribes of Athens entered a dithyramb of fifty men or boys in the annual contest, rehearsing them in song and dance for weeks. In the plays the

1-6 Dionysus (in a bull mask) in a formal scene with the chorus. Euripides' *The Bacchae*. Texas Tech University production, directed by Ronald Schulz, designed by Clifford Ashby, and costumed by Larry Randolph.

chorus sometimes expressed simple horror or lament. Sometimes it chanted and acted out, in unison and in precise formations of rows and lines, the acts of violence the characters were enacting offstage. When Phaedra rushed offstage in *Hippolytus* to hang herself from the rafters, all fifteen members of the chorus performed in mime and chant the act of tying the rope and swinging from the rafters. Sometimes the chorus related or reenacted some parallel incident of history or legend that clarified the situation of the play. Sometimes the chorus put into specific action what was a general intention in the mind of the main character; for example, when Oedipus resolved to hunt out the guilty person and cleanse the city, he spoke metaphorically, but when he was offstage the chorus invoked the gods of vengeance and danced a wild pursuit.

Three Great Tragic Dramatists

The three great writers of Greek tragedy had different visions of the destiny of man. Aeschylus, the earliest, caught the heroic mood of an Athens that had just defeated the invading Persians and was reshaping old institutions and loyalties for a new age of responsible public life. Sophocles reflected the ideals of the golden time of Pericles, when men of intelligence and reason were striving for a well-balanced life in a world where blind chance and old political loyalites were constant sources of danger. And Euripides wrote at a time when the old ideals were fading, as Athens was drawn deeper and deeper into war with Sparta. In a world of torture, madness, and violence, he denounced old superstitions and offered a deep compassion for the suffering of defeated mankind. While Aeschylus' characters are superhuman—Titans, gods, and primeval kings struggling to bring order out of primitive darkness—Sophocles' characters are very human, searching for private identities in the midst of public duties, and Euripides' characters are neurotic individuals, bursting into uncontrolled violence in response to the evil around them.

Of Aeschylus' characters, the most memorable is the great Titan Prometheus, bound and tortured on a mountain peak. Seeing into the future, he shouts his defiance to the upstart Olympian god, Zeus. He knows that raw power must eventually be reconciled with wisdom or it will breed upstart power forever. Though we do not have the last play of the trilogy, we know that it showed the reconciliation of power and wisdom and that, like a number of Greek tragedies, it had a triumphant ending. While Oriental philosophers taught that man is bound to the endlessly turning wheel of desire and pain and that his only hope is to escape from the wheel, Aeschylus believed that by thought and heroic

1-7 The homecoming of Agamemnon. Chorus of old men at the left. Aeschylus'
Agamemnon. The Greek National Theatre Company at Epidaurus, 1966. Photo by
Harissiadis, Athens.

effort the wheel itself could be changed, that even the gods could grow
and learn.

Where Prometheus strove for a new order in heaven to replace crude
force, the three plays of Aeschylus' *Oresteia,* the only Greek trilogy that
has come down to us, trace the emergence of a new social order on the
human plane. After a series of horrible murders in a guilt-ridden royal
family, the goddess Athena comes down to help replace private hatreds
with public order. In the first play, the *Agamemnon,* the queen, Clytemnestra, and her lover, Aegisthus, conspire to murder the king on his
triumphant return from Troy. Clytemnestra has not been able to forget
that her husband had sacrificed their daughter Iphigenia in order to get
favorable winds when he set sail ten years before. The guilty pair think
that their act of revenge will bring peace, but in the next play, *The Libation
Bearers,* Orestes, goaded by his sister Electra, murders his mother and her
lover. These avengers, in their turn, find no peace, for the Furies, primitive underground spirits of vengeance, come to punish Orestes. If history
is nothing but neurotic violence in answer to violence, what hope is there
for mankind? The last play, the *Eumenides,* finds the solution. Orestes flees
to the shrine of Apollo, but Apollo cannot free him and he must take his
case to Athena, the direct representative of Zeus. Knowing that a solution
cannot be imposed from the outside, she establishes a new human institu-

tion, trial by jury, to hear the case and consider the motives rather than order punishment by the old rules. Even so, the jury is divided and needs divine guidance. Orestes is acquitted, but the old forces and instincts cannot be suppressed or destroyed—they must be transformed. Athena, goddess of wisdom, persuades the Furies to become *Eumenides*, "beneficent ones," and to dwell in open caves near the city, helping to preserve justice in Athens—a solution at once political, psychological, and metaphysical.

Aeschylus' story is a bloody tale of violence and vengeance. How is it that the humanists who are horrified at the amount of violence on the television and movie screens do not condemn these plays but revere them as classics? Is it all right for Clytemnestra in a primitive age to use an ax on her husband and his lady friend and not right for cowboys in the pioneer West to shoot it out with cattle thieves? Actually there are major differences in the treatment of violence. The modern screen shows a great deal of physical cruelty, then bright-colored blood and gore. The violence is for sheer excitement and the satisfaction of the simplest impulse to hit back. Until all the bad guys drop dead, the audience is ready for more and more action, rarely looking beyond violence. But in the Greek theatre the murders were never shown on stage. They were described, vividly, by an official messenger, or revealed as the murderer looked on his victim, wheeled in on a platform machine called the *eccyclema*. The Greeks were more interested in reaction than in simple action. Furthermore, all the elements of performance increased the aesthetic distance, creating an atmosphere of beauty rather than of simple shock: the open-air theatre, the sacred shrine, the marble *skene* with its stately formal doorways, the padded, larger-than-life actors, the large sculptured masks, the musical accompaniment, the chanting of much of the poetry, the formal odes of the chorus, and the constant reference to religious and philosophical principles. But most of all, Aeschylus shows how man can move out of the primitive age of violent revenge into a more civilized age of justice and order, with public trials before a jury. In Aeschylus' vision of history, human beings are not hopeless victims of their primitive emotions but are capable of transforming their emotions by spiritual understanding and of mobilizing them in support of public institutions of justice.

At the center of any discussion of Greek tragedy is Sophocles, for he has the clearest vision of men and women struggling mightily against fate, suffering greatly, and facing defeat with dignity. Though religion is always in the background, it is clear that the decisions and choices are made by human beings. Sophocles' heroes are kings and leaders whose fate involves the health of the state, but their struggles are the inner conflicts of solitary souls.

In Sophocles' *Antigone*, the heroine has to make a dreadful choice. When her newly crowned uncle issues orders on pain of death that no one is to bury the brother who had attacked the city, while giving all honors to the body of the brother who had defended it, Antigone makes up her mind that she will disobey him. She must perform the religious rites due the dead. Creon is furious that a member of his own family would defy his orders. But to Antigone, political expediency and even death mean nothing when measured against the spiritual value of love. She has faith that the laws of the gods are beyond time. By the end of the play, Creon himself has become a tragic figure. His son and the old soothsayer tell him he is wrong, and the citizens do not uphold him. Relenting at the last minute, he tries to save Antigone, but it is too late: she has already hanged herself in the prison cave. His son kills himself, and then his wife commits suicide. The broken man is finally humbled before the gods, awed by the tragic consequences of his miscalculation. We are perhaps even more touched by the anguish of the man or woman who learns too late than by the heroic will of the religious martyr.

Where Antigone sees everything, makes her choice, and faces her punishment, Oedipus sees nothing. He was the famous problem-solver who guessed the riddle of the Sphinx and delivered the city from that pest. In gratitude, the citizens, who had just lost their king, made him king and married him to the queen. But now they have a new problem for him to solve, a blight on the city that can be cleansed only by discovering the murderer of the old king and driving him out of the city. In one sense the play is an exciting detective story: as prosecutor, the king interrogates each witness, piecing the story together until he realizes that he himself is the guilty one. The play is rich in irony as each witness, believing he is reassuring Oedipus, reveals one more bit of evidence leading to the awful certainty that Oedipus had, unknowingly, killed his own father and married his own mother. It does not matter that the audience knows the story already. More terrible than simple surprise is this suspense of watching Oedipus come nearer and nearer to the appalling discovery and then seeing him respond to it.

In the nineteenth century Oedipus was regarded as the victim of a malevolent fate, already announced in a series of oracles. Oedipus had no chance, waking to suffering that came on him from the past. But for the twentieth century the tragedy of Oedipus has new meanings. Above all, it is a study of the search for identity, an agonizing concern of our age. It is the need to find out who he is that drives Oedipus on. His wife begs him not to ask, not to believe the soothsayer, insisting that the world is chance and nothing can be predicted. Yet what she tells him only proves how right the earlier oracles had been. Freud used the phrase "Oedipus com-

1-8

Tragic hero enhanced by a large mask, a costume that adds size, and boots that add height. Sophocles' *Oedipus*. Stratford Festival production, directed by Tyrone Guthrie, with costumes and masks by Tanya Moiseiwitsch.

plex" to describe a son's conscious antagonism toward his father and unwholesome dependence on his mother; it is startling to realize that in Sophocles' play Oedipus does not have an Oedipus complex. He has gone all the way to patricide and incest without knowing it, and only by facing his guilt can he make the mature adjustment that Freud prescribed.

Unlike Sophocles, Euripides shocked his first audiences; they considered him too sensational in depicting abnormal states of mind. He used exotic foreign melodies and dwelt on the sordid topics of betrayal, cruelty, murder, and incest. But in later centuries he became the most popular of all the Greek dramatists, and in modern times he has had the greatest influence. He portrayed the skepticism, rebellion, and desperation of an Athens drifting away from the high ideals and the religious devotion of earlier times. The democracy broke down in political corruption as the war with Sparta dragged on, and disease, superstition, and hysteria were rife in the crowded streets of Athens. Some Athenians could joke about the war and corruption; the comic poet Aristophanes lashed out at it in fantastical satires that are as funny now as they were at the end of the fifth century B.C. But Euripides could not laugh. He was haunted by images of Medea in hatred killing her own children, of Agave in religious ecstasy tearing off the head of her own son, of Phaedra in madness causing the death of her stepson—of women helpless in the grip of violent emotion, goaded by the unforgivable cruelty and injustice of the world.

Euripides was shocked when Athens killed the men and enslaved the women and children of a small island that wanted to be neutral. Then when he saw Athenians building a fleet to conquer Sicily—an ill-fated expedition that led to the defeat of Athens—he produced a play about ancient victims of Greek aggression, *The Trojan Women,* the most famous of all antiwar plays. The women of Troy, in noble anguish, leave their burning city to be slaves to the arrogant conquerors. As the ultimate cruelty, the Greeks kill the little son of Hector and deliver his broken body on a shield to his grandmother, Queen Hecuba. A procession of doom, the play has enough indignation, enough compassion, to hold the stage today. Its different episodes are arranged with strong contrast and variety, from the half-insane Cassandra whirling a torch, gloating over her knowledge of the horrible future of her new master, Agamemnon, to the wily Helen, conniving to get back into the good graces of her husband, Menelaus.

Greek Tragedy on the Modern Stage

To see an ancient Greek play in one of the ruined ancient theatres is a high point for summer travelers. There are no performances at the Dionysian theatre at Athens, but a few hundred feet west, in the ruins of the Roman theatre of Herodias Atticus are frequent concerts and plays. The greatest adventure is to go to the beautifully preserved theatre at Epidaurus, where in midsummer companies from Athens or other cities perform the ancient plays in modern Greek several times a week (Figure 1-1). Equally exciting are the Greek plays played in Italian in the old Greek theatre in Syracuse, in Sicily, where two tragedies are produced every other year during the first two weeks in June.

An unearthly intensity of voice and movement was achieved by the director Andrei Serban in his production of *Fragments of a Trilogy,* based on scenes from *Electra, The Trojan Women,* and *Medea,* under the auspices of that very experimental Off Broadway theatre La Mama Experimental Theatre Club. The *Trilogy* played several times in New York and, during a period of five years in the seventies, in more than forty festivals in fifteen countries. Serban used not a word of English, but phrases from the Greek and Latin versions of the tragedies and sounds and syllables that belonged to no language. The audience was brought into a dark room with only cushions and a runway around the sides of the hall. *Medea* was played in darkness except for one beam of light down the middle of the room. During Medea's passionate solo, only a pinspot lighted her face. Most extraordinary was the use of voices—crying, singing, wailing, cursing to

1-9

Masks of Agamemnon and
Clytemnestra. Andrei Serban's
production of *Agamemnon*
at Lincoln Center, 1977. Photo
by Joseph Abeles.

primitive melodies and sound patterns composed and drilled by Elizabeth
Swados. For *The Trojan Women* the hall was fully lighted, with the audience sitting around the edges, or standing and now dodging the fast-
moving carts carrying the captive women, now watching wild attempted
flights on the runway high above. Though all portions of the *Trilogy* had
complicated patterns of energetic action and moved at a rapid, sometimes
frantic, pace, the performance was beautifully controlled and retained the
power and nobility we associate with ancient tragedy.

Even more spectacular was Andrei Serban's production of *Agamemnon* in 1977, with a chorus large enough to fill the ample space of the
Beaumont Theatre stage at Lincoln Center, a space made wider or nar-
rower as the two large sections of audience seats in the stage area were
wheeled back and forth. Nearly all the play was set to music by Elizabeth
Swados—rhythmic chanting in monotone or with a strong melody, some
passages in full harmony. Many choral passages were acted out in symbolic form, notably Agamemnon's sacrifice of his daughter, Iphigenia.
The language was partly Greek, partly the English of Edith Hamilton's
translation. In matching the wild intensities of Priscilla Smith's portrayal
of both Clytemnestra and Cassandra with the wild intensities of a highly
trained chorus, Serban has shown, in modern terms, the unity and great-
ness of the tragedies.

The basic themes and characters of Greek tragedy have inspired many
new versions, in which twentieth-century dramatists find modern solu-
tions for the old dilemmas. Jean Anouilh's *Antigone*, first produced in 1944

in Paris during the German occupation, cuts the religious basis from Sophocles' play, but makes Antigone stubbornly keep her resolve to go against Creon's decree and bury her brother's body, even as she learns that her brother was not worth honoring and that her deed can have no meaning except in her own mind. The play has had many productions in American colleges.

In using the Greek story of Agamemnon in *Mourning Becomes Electra* (1931), set in New England just after the Civil War, Eugene O'Neill made a major attempt to recapture the Greek tragic pattern. Instead of a family curse passed on from generation to generation, he used the Freudian concept of the dangers of sexual repression. The trauma of her wedding night has created in General Mannon's wife a neurotic hatred for her husband that eventually leads her to murder him, after taking his cousin as a lover. Then the son and daughter murder the cousin and drive their mother to suicide. The mixture of love and hate, envy and anger, involves the brother and sister too closely with each other and leads to the brother's suicide. Vinnie, the Electra of this play, shuts herself inside the family mansion to live out the rest of her life with her ghosts: mourning is indeed becoming to Electra. In the 1930s the play seemed a profound study of destructive psychological forces, perhaps the greatest play America had produced. Its fourteen acts were played in one evening, starting at five o'clock and running to midnight, with an intermission for dinner. When the film was made two decades later, the fourteen acts were compacted into one screenplay of ordinary length, and the story became a thin melodrama of no consequence. O'Neill had given the tale a scope that was lost in the condensation. One can understand why Aristotle demanded magnitude for tragedy.

The Modern Festival Theatre

The Greek spirit lives most vividly today in the festival theatre, usually a large outdoor structure on a hillside at a sacred or historic spot to which travelers make special pilgrimages. Since the seventeenth century, travelers from around the world have gathered every ten years in the Bavarian mountain village of Oberammergau to witness the passion play put on with religious devotion by the villagers themselves. There are Wagner festivals in Germany and special Mozart performances in Austria. England has a well-established tradition of religious plays, usually presented in the great cathedrals. Near Palmyra, New York, Mormons and their friends see the Hill Cumorah come alive with hosts of performers reenacting the visions of Joseph Smith. Outdoor pageant-dramas, or "symphonic dramas," of American history have drawn large audiences of vacation travelers over the last three decades. Of these the best-known are Paul Green's *The Lost Colony,* which has been presented annually since 1937 on the spot of the first English settlement in North America; *Unto These Hills,* the moving story of the Cherokee tribes, presented each year in the town of Cherokee near Asheville, North Carolina; and *Texas,* presented annually near Canyon, Texas. Even more popular in recent years have been numerous Shakespeare summer festivals, of which the most famous are those in the three Stratfords—England, Ontario, and Connecticut—in Ashland, Oregon, and in New York City's Central Park, where Joseph Papp's productions have drawn large crowds. While a few festivals use some element of painted scenery, most go back to the unity and simplicity of the formal architectural structure used by the Greeks.

Some of the festival theatres, especially the Shakespeare festivals, have expanded far beyond summer entertainment. The Royal Shakespeare Company took over the Aldwych Theatre in London for a year-round season, showing not only some of the Stratford summer productions but plays of all periods. Recently a winter season has been started at Stratford as well. The Stratford, Ontario, festival company has become to all intents and purposes the national theatre of Canada.

The Greeks gave us the word *theatre* and the idea of a splendid building for the whole public to watch a play of religious, historical, and national importance. They gave us the idea of a play as the high point of a religious festival, performed at a sacred shrine. They gave us the word *drama* and the idea of a play as a work of art, complete in itself, to be looked at, felt, and thought about. Along with the words *poetry* and *poem,* they gave us the idea of a performing poet, competing with other poets, presenting his own personal view of the human condition, often in conflict with the orthodox view, often in conflict with the views of other poets. They gave us tragedy and three great writers of tragedy. The Western world owes an enormous debt to the Greek example. Different as most modern plays are from those given in the Athenian theatre of Dionysus, it is hard to imagine how they could have existed at all without the splendid groundwork of the inspired ancients.

2

The Theatre of Exaltation: From Medieval Drama to Modern Tragedy

AN ELIZABETHAN SCENE ON A MODERN
THRUST STAGE. MARLOWE'S *TAMBURLAINE* AT
THE OPENING OF THE OLIVIER THEATRE, THE
NATIONAL THEATRE, LONDON, 1976.
DIRECTED BY PETER HALL, DESIGNED BY JOHN
BURY, AND LIGHTED BY DAVID HERSEY.
COURTESY OF THE NATIONAL THEATRE
COMPANY.

Classic tragedy disappeared with the fall of Rome. In fact, in the lavish days of the Roman Empire, both comedy and tragedy had been overwhelmed by spectacular shows—gladiators, animal combats, or sea fights—and by vulgar performances of comic mimes or by elegant, danced pantomimes, all produced in the enormous half-circle theatres (see Figure 2-1). The young Christian Church set itself squarely against such vulgar theatre and put an end to it. Actors, along with thieves and other vagabonds, were proscribed. For several centuries Europe had no theatre, except for a few wandering mimes and minstrels. It was a thousand years before Renaissance princes built regular theatres and produced tragedies again, but in the meantime Western Europe produced its own exalted religious drama.

Christian Drama of the Middle Ages

Curiously, it was in the Christian Church itself that the theatre made a new start, some four or five centuries after the ancient theatres had been forced to close. In the ninth century, chanted dialogue and action were added to the most sacred service of the Christian liturgy, the Easter Mass,

2-1 Roman theatre. Although it developed from the Greek theatre, the Roman theatre differed in that a raised stage and a very high scenic wall continued the structure of the large auditorium. It was used more for clowns, mimes, and spectacular dance shows than for plays. Drawn by Ethelyn Pauley.

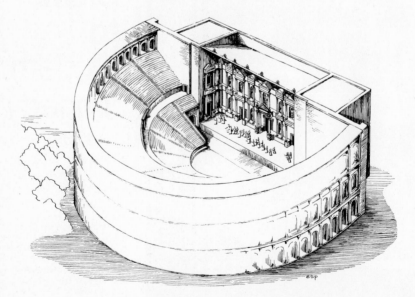

Flight to Egypt

Temptation

Salome and
John the Baptist

Annunciation

Visitation

Adoration of
Magi

Slaughter
of the
Innocents

Herod's Banquet

2-2 Eight different episodes staged simultaneously in sequence on the long platform at Valenciennes. Drawn by Martha Sutherland.

and drama was reborn. To build up to the *Te Deum*, the joyful anthem in praise of the Resurrection, some priests added a short dramatic dialogue of the three Marys coming to embalm the body of Christ. The angels show them the empty tomb and tell them to announce to the world that Christ is risen. The short drama, chanted in Latin by monks or priests, was evidently effective, for presently the Adoration of the Shepherds and the Three Kings was dramatized as part of the Christmas services, and the new drama spread all over Europe. A few churches even produced long plays for special occasions, and for five hundred years the joyful news of the Nativity, the Resurrection, and the triumphs of prophets and saints sang out in splendid chant.

Much more spectacular were the medieval religious cycles, financed by the merchant guilds for the midsummer trade fairs in the fast-growing cities of the High Gothic period (roughly from 1350 to 1550). From twenty-five to fifty separate episodes were needed to cover the whole story of the fall and redemption of man, from the creation and the fall of Adam, through the passion of Christ to the Last Judgment. Each episode needed a separate scenic unit, or *mansion*. Sometimes all the mansions were spread down a long platform (Figure 2-2) in what we call "simultaneous" staging. Sometimes the mansions were placed in a large circle surrounding the audience in a medieval variant of theatre-in-the-round. Each important character would introduce himself at his mansion, then would come through the audience to a central playing place. The most picturesque method was to put each mansion on wheels, or "pageant wagons," spreading the cycle as a long procession through the streets, each wagon stopping to perform an episode at a dozen or more places (Figure 2-3). In York some forty-eight plays were given in one long and exhausting day, while in Chester the episodes were combined into half as many plays spread over three days. Most of the audience stood in the street, while the rich had special bleachers or raised pavilions.

While the church drama remained a formal, liturgical drama, sung in Latin in the church by priests highly trained in music, the cycles of mystery plays were popular and vulgar. Not only was lively, everyday language spoken, but spectacular effects were used that would have pleased any child. Devils came out of the smoking hell-mouth amidst the beating of pots and pans. God, from his high Mandala amidst the choiring angels, sent Gabriel down for the Annunciation to Mary. The naive scenes of country shepherds, speaking broad dialects, then devoutly offering their caps, toys, and an old horn spoon to the Christ Child, were com-

2-3 A pageant wagon showing the play of the Nativity in a medieval street. As each wagon moved to the next playing place, another wagon brought the next episode, until the entire sacred history was presented. Drawn by Ethelyn Pauley.

2-4
Everyman trying to escape the call of death. The medieval morality play acted by a choral group of seven actor-dancers who play many roles without any change of the uniform, conventionalized dance costumes. The Guthrie Theatre Company, Minneapolis. Produced and directed by Robert Benedetti, and designed by Bruce Cana Fox and Robert Benedetti.

bined with the noisy anger of Herod, who carried his rage out among the audience. Shakespeare remembered the Herod of the Coventry cycle as a prime example of unrestrained acting and gave us the phrase "to out-Herod Herod." The women fight back with kitchen spoons and pans at the soldiers who come to slaughter the innocents; then Rachel sings a heart-broken lullaby over the body of her child. For the burning of a martyr or the devil not only were real flames seen, but animal bones and skin were put on the flames to make a stench. Out of these childish, realistic efforts a real exaltation emerges.

The late Middle Ages and the early Renaissance developed two forms of entertainment that provided a transition to the Elizabethan theatre. The first was the *morality play,* from which playwrights developed the art of creating long plots with sustained conflict and great variety of detail. The second was the *street show* honoring a royal visitor to a city or town—elaborately decorated structures in which actors portraying famous kings and heroes formed a silent tableau or addressed the visitor as he passed in a great procession. From these shows Elizabethan stage architects learned to combine several scenic symbols into one large structure.

Everyman (c. 1475) is the most impressive of the morality plays. In a single strong plot developed with allegorical characters, God sends Death to summon Everyman. Everyman is terrified of the journey and is not ready to present a reckoning of his life. His earthly friends Fellowship, Kindred, and Goods refuse to go with him, and Beauty, Strength, and Five Wits fall by the wayside. Only Good Deeds can go with him into the grave. *Everyman* is serious throughout, but in the sixteenth century there were many morality plays that included scenes of gaiety and satire on fashions, social life, and politics. One central character would undergo a series of tests as the Virtues contended with the Vices for his soul. Some morality plays included kings and princes as historical examples and, for all their serious moral concern, showed a great deal of humanistic tolerance for fun and revelry. From the morality form, Shakespeare learned how to show the part played by historical forces, moral duties, and private pleasures in the shaping of a prince.

Tragedy in Sixteenth-Century England

At the very beginning of the sixteenth century, learned poets and architects in Italy laboriously worked out imitations of classic (that is, Greek and Roman) comedy and tragedy and a new form of scenery designed on the principles of perspective and set behind a frame called a proscenium. At the same time managers of popular commercial theatres in Paris, Madrid, and London developed a new exalted drama out of the sprawling religious plays, the popular romantic stories in verse or prose about the adventures of King Arthur's followers and other knights, and the histories of kings and princes that had impressed the populace in the street shows or tableaux. From the diverse material of these several sources, the popular theatres kept the multiple plots, the comic clowns and servants to accompany the kings, the crowd scenes, the trials and council meetings, the battles, sieges, processions, weddings, and coronations. They kept this vivid pageant moving across a platform stage through scene after scene with scarcely an intermission, now by bringing on thrones, beds, or tables, now by using permanent doors, windows, and balconies, now by disclosing arranged tableaux behind curtains.

Romantic Tragedy

From this popular sensational drama, like modern movies in many ways, a few English poets in the late sixteenth century, the age of Elizabeth I and Shakespeare, created a romantic tragedy of heroic individuals. The great heroes of history walked out on the Elizabethan platform, defied the limits of medieval society, endured terrible suffering, expanded the

2-5 Players in an Elizabethan inn yard. The inn yard probably suggested some aspects of the Elizabethan stage. A drawing from C. Walter Hodges, *The Globe Restored*. Courtesy of Coward-McCann & Geoghegan.

bounds of the human spirit, challenged the very heavens, and met their deaths still fighting and striving. The medieval world had taught that unreasoning fortune, like a wheel, raised man to the top and then carried him on to his fall. In the medieval view, it was only by turning away from this world and seeking heaven that human beings could find meaning. But the Elizabethan hero would accept no such humility. Thomas Kyd's hero in *The Spanish Tragedy* (c. 1589) carries out his revenge though he destroys himself and many others in the carnage. The hero of Christopher Marlowe's *Tamburlaine* (c. 1587), a shepherd who conquers the world, defies every limitation, even mortality. By his determination to control his own fate, he persuades even his enemies to join him.

Mental aspiration appeals to modern audiences more than an obsession with worldly power; for this reason Marlowe's next play, *Dr. Faustus* (c. 1588), is produced more often than *Tamburlaine*. In a sense *Dr. Faustus* is merely a highly developed medieval morality play, but here the real experience, the conflict, is in the mind. By selling his soul to the devil in exchange for the removal of all human limitations for twenty-four years,

Faustus can explore all experience and search after infinite knowledge. He calls up the image of Helen, the dream of immortal beauty, and sings his paean of praise:

> Was this the face that launch'd a thousand ships,
> And burnt the topless towers of Ilium?
> Sweet Helen, make me immortal with a kiss.
>
> . . .
>
> More lovely than the monarch of the sky
> In wanton Arethusa's azur'd arms;
> And none but thou shalt be my paramour!

At the end the devil exacts the penalty, possession of his soul, and Faustus utters his curses and his remorse as passionately as he had uttered his pride and his determination to explore all knowledge. He cannot exceed God's limits. But the final impression is not of death and defeat but of the magnificent individual who dared.

This is one of the great patterns of Elizabethan tragedy: the daring assertion that expands the limits of the human spirit even as it is defeated. The impact of the deaths of Romeo and Juliet is heightened because they have snatched their moments of ecstasy in the face of the hostility of the old feudal world. Antony and Cleopatra throw away countries and continents, but who would prefer their rival, the practical, successful, calculating Octavius Caesar? Othello is another great conqueror who is defeated by the very magnitude of his emotions, who loved "not wisely but too well." Throughout the best of the Elizabethan tragedies there is this great generosity of spirit, this willingness to live and love, even in the face of probable defeat.

Shakespeare's Historical Plays

It was in his history plays that Shakespeare first worked out his subtle and complex approach to tragedy. During the patriotic years following the defeat of the Spanish Armada in 1588, when plays about English history became popular, Shakespeare wrote eight plays presenting a panorama of the Wars of the Roses, England's century of struggle to curb the fighting feudal barons and establish a strong central government. The triumphant end of the historical epic was the accession of Henry VII, the first of the Tudor family and grandfather of Elizabeth I. In the splendid pageant of national history, Shakespeare was interested in the ironies and tragic undertones of various rulers and rebels whose private ambitions and guilts so strongly affected their public careers.

Shakespeare's tragic view, suggested in these early history plays, was given its supreme expression in the great tragedies of his later years, especially in *Hamlet* and *King Lear*.

Tragic Patterns in Hamlet

Hamlet was written at a time of bitter disillusionment in the European soul. Renaissance hopes were exhausted, the hopes that had buoyed up so many Italians a century before and so many Englishmen only a decade before: hopes of reconciling Christianity and classic culture, of creating a liberated aristocracy and an enlightened state through humanistic education, and reviving art, literature, and drama for the modern world on classic models. The liberated individual, no longer closely ruled by his trade guild or his parish priest, was free to make money and to lose it, free to rise rapidly in court or market, and free to be lonely and disillusioned. The feudal order was breaking up with the concentration of power in an absolute monarch. The old religious certainties were gone, and wars over religious issues were more frequent and widespread. Individualism, encouraged by humanistic education, ran riot in ruthless murders and court intrigue. Even the heavens lost their old order as the new astronomy first banished the earth from the center of the universe, then traced the earth's course around the sun not as a circle with one center but as an ellipse with two centers, and finally caught glimpses of other planets with their own moons. The feeling of this time of change was expressed in one of John Donne's poems as "all coherence gone."

The complex dramatic form that Kyd and Marlowe had shaped out of medieval traditions served Shakespeare well. While in the comedies several different groups—servants and masters, dukes and villagers, romantic lovers and mischievous revelers—are brought together in harmony at the end, the multiple-plot scheme serves in *Hamlet* to emphasize disruption and disorder. The plots develop displacement by mirror images, where each element reflects and makes an ironic comment on the other element. Hamlet is displaced from the throne. The Elizabethan facade that so richly represents the earthly order of a throne, endorsed by the symbols of heavenly order above, stands as a solid backing of the stage. But Hamlet is out on the open platform, symbol of the free and independent individual, while a usurper king sits on the throne and from either heaven or hell comes the ghost of the dead king. The basic plot is mirrored in two other sons who must avenge their fathers: both Laertes and Fortinbras are reproaches to Hamlet, going to their violent revenges without hesitation or conscience. The immediate plot is what Hamlet calls the mousetrap, a scheme of using the players to catch the king. That plot is mirrored in three analogues as Polonius sets first Ophelia and then the queen as mousetraps to catch Hamlet. It is further echoed in the plot of Polonius to set a spy to watch his own son. Hamlet's mock madness that bursts out of control is mirrored in the real madness of Ophelia. Ophelia, the object of Hamlet's love, is seen reflected in the distorted mirror of the Queen, and Hamlet rejects her with violent disgust and bawdy innuendoes. The multiple images include three kings, three father images, two fools, two madmen, and two women in love. The play-within-a-play is a mirror of both the hidden murder and the nephew's threat of vengeance.

As many students have observed, the imagery throughout the play builds up the sense of disease and corruption. Something is rotten in the state of Denmark, and Hamlet's hope of love is blasted by the cancerous image of his mother's adultery:

> Nay, but to live
> In the rank sweat of an enseamed bed,
> Stew'd in corruption, honeying and making love
> Over the nasty sty.

Yet the mood of the play is not one of total despair. The murky night is shot through with flashes of light. Hamlet himself is keenly aware that the corruption is not normal. He affirms the ideal Renaissance vision of man's nobility in a splendid world even as he notes his own disillusionment:

> What a piece of work is a man! How noble in reason! How infinite in faculty! In form and moving how express and admirable! In action how like an angel! In apprehension how like a god! The beauty of the world! The paragon of animals! And yet, to me, what is this quintessence of dust?

At the end, order is restored after disorder, and Fortinbras stands in the center of the throne pavilion, a new king.

Tragic Patterns in King Lear

Where *Hamlet* is a play about an individual's displacement, *King Lear* is a play about the disruption and agony of a whole age. Where *Hamlet* was the favorite Shakespeare play of the romantic rebels of the nineteenth century and of the individual rebels of the early twentieth, *King Lear* is especially fascinating to those who have watched the global conflicts and revolutionary upheavals since the Second World War. The vision of an old king who turns over his authority to a set of calculating monsters who have promised him everything but who are cruel and ruthless beyond belief is amazingly pertinent today. The innocent suffer, the men of good

2-6 A permanent setting for Shakespeare's *King Lear*, suggested by the primitive forms of Stonehenge. A design by Norman Bel Geddes.

will are exiled or forced to go underground, the world is plunged into a maelstrom of domestic, political, mental, and cosmic disorder. Yet the wicked destroy themselves, and in the end a few survivors establish order and sadly take up the task of rebuilding.

The nineteenth-century poet Swinburne saw nothing but darkness in the play as Lear discovered the enormity of human cruelty, and in 1963 Peter Brook directed the Stratford production with Paul Scofield to emphasize the chaos and despair, as though Shakespeare had written for the wry absurdists of the atomic age. Yet most twentieth-century readers and audiences have found a strong line of development leading to the salvation of Lear. His gradual discovery of love and compassion gives the play a great warmth. Hamlet had only his friend Horatio, an uninvolved observer, as a companion in suffering. Lear is loved and cared for by a whole band of outcasts—the Fool, the blind Gloucester, the exile Kent, and the mad beggar Edgar. Above all, he discovers that his daughter Cordelia is as steadfast in her love as she is stubborn in her sincerity.

By studying chaos, by tracing the breakdown of the human personality and the destruction of order, Shakespeare affirms the necessity of order. Chaos leads to a new order, but at the price of an enormous waste of human potential. Macbeth and Othello were men of great deeds and noble character until their judgment was destroyed by ambition and jealousy.

The Elizabethan Stage

To the supreme examples of tragedy created by Shakespeare, the modern theatre owes an incalculable debt, but it owes almost as much to the stage on which these dramas were played. In groping for some escape from the everyday detail of the realistic theatre, playwrights, designers, and directors have learned even more from the Elizabethan stage than from the Greek or the Chinese. Though there is not a single completely dependable picture, and though the living tradition was lost in three hundred years of picture-frame scenery, enough is known about the Elizabethan stage for it to stand as a beacon. For a realistic age, to return to that stage is to enter another theatre world. There was no front curtain and no proscenium frame, no painted scenery, no pretense of creating an illusion of actual place. The action took place in the midst of the audience,

2-7 The Elizabethan public theatre, open to the sky. The final scene of *Richard III* as seen from one of the galleries. The crowd of characters, the tents and banners on the forestage, and the trumpeters on the upper stage create an elaborate spectacle. A drawing from C. Walter Hodges, *Shakespeare and the Players.* Courtesy of G. Bell & Sons, Ltd., and Coward-McCann & Geoghegan.

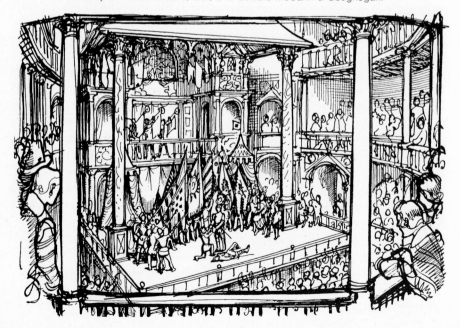

on a platform that was open to the sky and to the three rows of galleries that almost completely encircled the stage and the space for standing spectators, or "groundlings." The actor enjoyed direct contact with the audience instead of turning away in the strange pretense that it was not there. A splendid facade of two or more stories at the back of the open platform presented at least six openings, either for entrances and exits or for small scenes to be disclosed in doorways or behind small curtains. If it was necessary for the audience to know an exact place, the playwright had some character say, "This is the forest of Arden," or "What country, friends, is this?—This is Illyria, Lady," or "What wood is this before us?—The wood of Birnam." This arrangement allowed the many scenes of a Shakespeare play to follow one another without interruption for scene changes but with exciting combinations of levels and playing areas. The director would close a scene on the inner stage by means of the small curtain and immediately bring another group of actors onto the forestage or the upper stage. With the rediscovery of this flexible stage, Shakespeare's plays can now be put on with the sequence and rhythm of the original productions, without pauses for scene changes, without cutting or combining the smaller scenes, and without the distraction of a different painted setting each time a different group of actors comes on the stage.

Printed versions of the plays have been corrupted since eighteenth-century editors cut them into many separate scenes and inserted indications of place: "a room in the castle," "another part of the forest," "a corridor outside the throne room," and so on. The plays published during Shakespeare's lifetime had no indications of act and scene division, much less any indication of particular place; all Shakespeare wrote was "exeunt" for one group and "enter" for the next. Only since the 1950s have some editors gone back to the Elizabethan practice of letting one scene follow immediately after the other, just as it did on the Elizabethan stage.

The most commonly accepted picture of the Elizabethan stage, then, is of a bare platform strewn with rushes, with a penthouse roof supported by two splendid columns, and backed by an architectural facade, or "tiring house" (where the actors changed their attire). At the stage level of the facade were two doorways and an inner stage, and on the upper level were balconies and windows. The basic pattern of the Elizabethan stage was apparently derived from the throne pavilion, the arches, and the inner and upper stages of the street shows. But on the Elizabethan stage these were combined into a single formal facade as a backing for the platform of the stage. It was left to the audience to turn that background into field, forest, cave, mountain, house front, room, castle, or city gate.

It has been the fashion since the end of the nineteenth century to build "authentic reproductions" of the Elizabethan stage and to decorate them in the brown and tan half-timber style of many medieval and Elizabethan private cottages. But the contemporary references were to the splendid stage, the gaudy colors, and the painted marble columns. Further study also reveals other sources of splendor. Costumes were elaborate, and actors spent as much as princes for rich garments for the stage. Then, even though there was no painted setting, many properties could be brought on: thrones, tables, beds, shop fronts, altars, tombs, tents, caves, mountains, trees. Add many banners, pennants, and flags, and there is colorful pageantry indeed. A small group of musicians played flourishes for the processions, accompaniment for the many songs and dances, and appropriate background music: quiet, stately tunes for sad and solemn scenes, for example, or "hellish music" for scenes of terror. That plain platform and facade could present a splendid pageant of romantic drama.

Many of the modern Shakespearean festival theatres use some variation of the standard, formal, "authentic" stage (see Figure 2-9), but when only one Shakespearean play is to be produced, many designers prefer to

2-8 The Elizabethan "private" or indoor theatre used during the winter by the professional companies. A reconstruction based on recently discovered evidence. Drawn for this book by C. Walter Hodges.

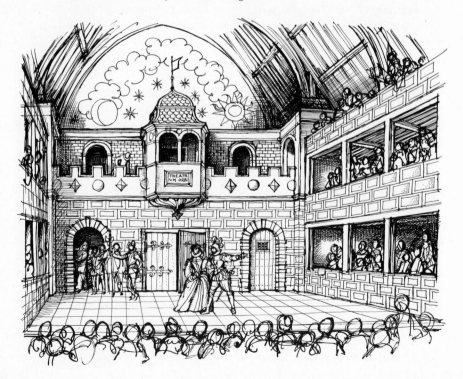

2-9 An outdoor festival theatre for Shakespeare. The auditorium is a variant of the Greek theatre, but the stage is based on early twentieth-century reconstructions of the Elizabethan theatre. The Oregon Shakespeare Festival Theatre, Ashland, Oregon, founded by Angus Bowmer. Photo Dwaine Smith.

start afresh and make a structure of steps, platforms, shapes, towers, and arches to suit the action of that particular play. With the help of modern selective lighting, they can give a playing area the atmosphere of a corridor, bower, throne, or altar and, when the action moves elsewhere, let that area retire into shadows. Thus the best possibilities of modern, medieval, and Elizabethan staging are combined. The play progresses without interruption, as small changes take place in view of the audience. Such a background creates more atmosphere than the standard "authentic" Elizabethan stage and even permits some suggestion of place, and the flexible arrangement of many levels allows more interesting grouping and movement and more effective use of modern lighting.

Neoclassic Tragedy

The Elizabethan dramatists achieved great vitality in a sprawling, complex form that owed much to the medieval theatre. Half a century later, French dramatists went to the opposite extreme and created a neoclassic tragedy that surpassed that of ancient Greece in compactness, austerity, and polish. The new classicism, in public life as well as in art, was a triumph of simplicity and order over complexity and turbulence. The expansive energies of the Renaissance had led to conflicts and tensions that set Catholics against Protestants and barons against the king. But in the seventeenth century men were tired of religious wars and emotional conflict, and gradually Richelieu brought the turbulent political forces of France under the tight control of a central power. Paris was ready for an age of reason and for a heroic drama in which violent personal forces and conflicting values were brought into controlled harmony.

Neoclassic tragedy was a triumph over the complex, romantic forms of drama. Like the London of Shakespeare, Paris at the beginning of the seventeenth century had a vigorous popular drama, mixing comedy and tragedy, kings and clowns, poetry and pageantry, blood and thunder. But by the 1630s cultivated taste in France demanded a change. The populace might continue to be entertained by street clowns and acrobats, royal processions and public executions, but men of taste gathered in small theatres to watch tragedies of man's solitary struggle with the moral dilemmas of the day.

When neoclassic tragedy arrived, with Corneille's *The Cid* in 1637, it was not a direct imitation of Greek or Roman tragedy; it was a distillation or condensation of the popular drama. Corneille took an earlier romantic Spanish play, *The Youth of the Cid,* and cut it down to a few key scenes, eliminating the giants, hermits, shepherds, princes, soldiers, and supernatural encounters. Leaving offstage all battle scenes, he concentrated on scenes between two contending characters and scenes in which a character analyzes his problems of choice. Every motive and every possible decision is carefully debated, and violent emotions are examined with utmost clarity. The Age of Reason produced not a cold debate without passion but a passionate drama of reasoning. The Cid made his choice to follow his high duty to his father's honor and his king, even if that meant dueling with and killing the father of his love. At the end he has the devotion of both his love and the king—a triumphal ending. Yet the play is called a tragedy for the serious recognition of the pain and sacrifice of individual feelings demanded in the triumph of a new era.

While Corneille stressed the triumph of the will in plays that provoke admiration rather than pity, Racine showed the appalling failure of the will. His heroes—or rather his heroines, for he specialized in feminine psychology—fall helplessly into evil, finding tortuous justifications and rationalizations until time and their own deeds bring destruction. Racine's first great triumph, *Andromaque* (1667), presents four people, children of the heroes of the Trojan War, involved in conflicts, each torn between two demands. The two offstage deeds, a betrayal and a murder, lead to a series of violent denunciations on stage. Ten years later, in 1677, Racine closed his career in the public theatre with *Phèdre,* which has

2-10 The neoclassic stage of Paris in the middle of the seventeenth century. The characters in their "antique" costumes are copied exactly from an early edition of the play. The setting is a free reconstruction from several sources. Racine's *Andromaque*. Drawn by Martha Sutherland.

provided the foremost acting role in classic French theatre, just as Hamlet is the foremost English role. It is an even more terrifying study of tragic destruction than *Andromaque*. Phèdre, in love with her stepson, Hippolytus, is spurned by him. In vengeance, she tells her husband, Theseus, that Hippolytus has attacked her. Theseus calls on the god Neptune, who sends a sea monster to destroy Hippolytus. In clear, careful debate, Phèdre analyzes her own emotions, loathing herself for her degrading passion, seeing herself caught in the fatal net, turning her frustration into destruction. Yet she remains a public figure, a queen of dignity and grandeur. The final effect is one of majestic sadness, for the violent passions and convoluted turns of the mind are all expressed in the most polished poetry, the most carefully selected impersonal diction, and the most perfectly proportioned and balanced episodes.

Scenery and costume took the audience back to a conventionalized world, far from the Baroque architecture and the lace, satin, and velvets, the petticoat breeches and wigs of seventeenth-century France. The setting was a simplification of the stage setting framed by a proscenium that

2-11
A neoclassic role as interpreted in the nineteenth century. Elisabeth Rachel wore rather austere Grecian draperies for her most famous part, the title role in Racine's *Phèdre.* Museum of the City of New York.

was introduced in Italy in 1507, more than a century before. Two or three *wings* at the sides, painted as dignified columns of a private room in a palace, led to the *back shutter* (Figure 2-10). By modern standards the "antique" costumes seem rather elaborate: Roman tunics with elaborate embroidery for the men and soft "nymph" robes for the women. The men, and sometimes the women, wore capes, plumes, and seventeenth-century wigs. But compared to the elaborate wigs of the audience and the costumes of the opera, these were simple enough to seem "classic."

It is helpful to consider how very different *Hamlet* would be if it had been written in neoclassic form. There would be no comedy, of course, none of Hamlet's bitter wit, no subplot or wide panorama of people, no public scenes, no songs, no players, no gravediggers, no ghost. The action would be concentrated on a few characters—Hamlet, the king and queen, and possibly Ophelia—who would all be drained of individuality and whose amazingly vivid diction would be reduced to a uniform, stately language. All the minor characters would be abstracted into four confidants. Hamlet would have Horatio to talk to—there would be no soliloquies, of course. The king could not have a prime minister, like Polonius, but instead would have a friend-attendant. The scenes of Hamlet refusing to kill the king at prayer, ordering Ophelia to a nunnery, and confronting the queen could all be retained, but each character would have his confidant present—the play would have to be impersonal even in intimate scenes. No throne would be visible, for not the public act but the private decision would be important.

The romantics of the nineteenth century despised neoclassic tragedy as cold and overrefined and compared it to the dead-white plaster casts made from ancient sculpture. But the twentieth century turns back to it with great respect for its ethical concern, its self-examination, its debates on moral issues, its direct scenes of personal conflict. From Henrik Ibsen's tight realistic plays of the nineteenth century, set in one Victorian living room, to Jean-Paul Sartre's *No Exit* (1944), a fantasy about three people confined in one room in hell, to Arthur Miller's *The Price* (1968), a family conflict over the past that takes place in the attic, modern drama has made frequent use of the compact neoclassic form. Far more than the Greeks, who used the elaborate effects of the chorus, the neoclassic playwrights proved that an austere presentation of characters in climactic action, with all preliminary episodes, all physical action, and all public events left offstage, can be very powerful drama.

Modern Tragedy

It is easy to see the magnitude of tragedy in other periods—Greek, Elizabethan, and neoclassic—but can tragedy seem exalted in the twentieth century? Many critics say no, and one of them, George Steiner, has written a book called *The Death of Tragedy*. If tragedy is a heroic vision of humanity celebrating the triumph of spiritual nobility over physical defeat and death, how can it exist in an age that finds no heroism, but only submission and conformity? In a pragmatic age that emphasizes scientific study of the facts and the practical solving of problems, how can there be room for tragedy? What is tragedy but a record of the unsolved problems of the past and a glorification of the failure to solve them? Instead of brooding about the terrifying gap between the vision and the reality, practical people will get on with the immediate goal of making the world better and let the infinite—if it exists—take care of itself.

Still, whatever brash front is assumed, the need for tragic drama continues to exist. After all the cures of the doctor, there is still disease; after all the sessions with the psychiatrist, anguish and defeat still come to the healthiest minds; and cosmic loneliness finds even the busiest man. Even if man's power were to increase until he could shake the planets from their course, still his achievement would fall short of his dream. Disappointment, defeat and death, the inescapable pain and terror, are with us as surely as they were with Sophocles and Shakespeare—two very fortunate, successful, well-adjusted men. The reality can never equal the vision. The truly scientific man will seek some new equation that will accommodate the discrepancy between the hopes of mankind and the reality. He will turn to tragedy.

Three Kinds of Tragic Characters

Three kinds of tragic characters have emerged in the Western struggle to change the environment, and all three have led their authors beyond simple scientific materialism: the hero who is ahead of his time, the heroic little man who salvages a modicum of choice, and the frustrated rebel who turns destructive.

Tragedy was not congenial to social reformers of the late nineteenth and early twentieth century. Though they rejected the easy optimism of the Victorian age, they felt that in the long run science and reason could build an environment that would be fit to live in. They thought that tragedy would only encourage a defeatist attitude. Still, when they looked at the appalling slums of the new industrial cities, they realized that the job of rebuilding could take generations and that, in the meantime, the individual in such an environment would be defeated no matter how hard he struggled. In this belief they found a modern tragic hero—not a hopeless victim but an individual who sees what is wrong with society and gives his life in the effort to change it. There is no reconciliation or justice in the hero's defeat, as in classic tragedy, but instead the audience takes on the guilt of the injustice and the responsibility for rectifying it. While radical social thinkers have disapproved of classic tragedy, they have accepted the concept of the hero who is ahead of his time.

The greatest hero of this kind is Joan of Shaw's *Saint Joan,* written in 1923, soon after Joan of Arc was made a saint and nearly five hundred years after she was burned at the stake as a heretic. Shaw presents her as the focus of great historical forces that were about to shatter the rigid patterns of the feudal system and to usher in the national state and the Reformation. Joan is crushed by the powerful institutions she had threatened, but Shaw gives her tragic grandeur as she refuses to recant and faces the fire. In the long run what she stood for won out, and the church finally canonized her. Shaw adds an epilogue to show that the ghosts of her enemies, come to congratulate her, would still be horrified if she threatened to perform a miracle and come back to life. He believed in the power of the institutionalized environment, but also in the power of the creative individual mind.

Far more deeply tragic, however, are plays that assume that progress

2-12 Tragedy of the little man. The setting takes its multiple playing areas and its open platform from the Elizabethan stage. Miller's *Death of a Salesman*. New York, 1949. Directed by Elia Kazan and designed by Jo Mielziner. Photo Graphic House.

will never solve all social problems and that a man must struggle to define his own individuality, even in the midst of unsettled and contradictory social forces. In the twentieth century, the tragic heroes are those who assert their will in a difficult environment. Not Promethean defiance of the ruler of the universe but rather a very modest insistence on choice gives the modern individual heroic stature. The shred of heroic goodness discovered by John Proctor at the end of *The Crucible* is "not enough to weave a banner with, but white enough to keep it from such dogs."

Arthur Miller's *Death of a Salesman* (1949) heads the list of plays that achieve tragedy on the modest modern scale by finding dignity in the struggle of the little man. Miller treats Willy Loman, the salesman, with respect. Willy's wife, Linda, says,

> I don't say he's a great man. Willy Loman never made a lot of money. His name was never in the paper. He's not the finest character that ever lived. But he's a human being, and a terrible thing is happening to him.

> So attention must be paid. He's not to be allowed to fall into his grave like an old dog. Attention, attention must be finally paid to such a person.

As disaster threatens, Willy fights back. He demands some explanation for his failure. He goes over the past to ask whether he was wrong in bringing up his sons to aim for the top, to be "well liked." He talks repeatedly to the image of his long-lost brother Ben, who made a fortune in diamonds and lumber, and wonders whether he himself was right to build his life on sales slips, appointments, and appearances. Willy does more than follow the crowd, and when he fails it is truly tragic.

Most critical discussion has centered on Willy's decision to kill himself in order to make his son Biff "magnificent" with the insurance money. To the end Willy is faithful to his false dream of success. Some critics say that in a tragedy the main character must arrive at perception. Maxwell Anderson declared that the central experience of tragedy is the main character's discovery of something about himself or about the world that makes him a better person. But Miller thought it more important to show Willy steadfast, ironically happy in his death, than to show him realizing that his whole life had been a mistake. Mistaken or not, Willy is committed to his dream and dies for it. The other characters gain the perception and clarify the issues. In the Requiem at the end, each one has his say. Biff, at last sure of his own identity, declares, "He had the wrong dreams. All, all wrong. He never knew who he was." Curiously enough, Charley, the friend next door who had no patience with Willy's worship of success, is the one who defends Willy's dream: "Nobody dast blame this man. A salesman is got to dream, boy. It comes with the territory." The wife has the final word, and it is a question: "Why?" That question can never be answered because the life of a human being is always a mystery.

Miller gave his next play, *The Crucible* (1953), a more traditional pattern of tragedy, even creating a poetic language of seventeenth-century speech. He was frightened for his country during the anti-Red hysteria of the early 1950s, when Senator Joe McCarthy led the witch hunt for spies and "Reds," intimidating Washington officialdom and stirring the whole country to persecute anyone who could be suspected of being "subversive." Miller gained a classic distance by dramatizing the similar hysteria of the witch trials of Salem in 1692, when a community was driven by its fears and the accusations of adolescent girls to hang more than a score of its citizens as witches. The play's main couple, John and Elizabeth Proctor, are excellent heroes for a modern tragedy. Not very articulate, not at all interested in rebelling, they only gradually discover the strength to be themselves. Finally, John cannot face hanging and agrees to confess to witchcraft. But when it comes to signing his name to the confession, like

Saint Joan he balks. He will not accuse others and he will not debase his name. He tears up the paper and turns toward the scaffold. His wife will not plead with him to save his life. As the drum rolls for the execution, she turns her face into the dawning sunlight and cries, "He have his goodness now. God forbid I take it from him!"

In some ways Blanche Du Bois in Tennessee Williams' *A Streetcar Named Desire* (1947) is a restless victim of a difficult environment. She is already badly damaged, a wanderer from the old plantation system. She finds refuge for a moment in the slums of New Orleans, where her sister lives with her apelike husband, Stanley Kowalski, and has adjusted to the life of an animal. But Blanche has visions of finer things, and she tries to rescue her sister and herself. For a moment Blanche hopes to marry Mitch, the gentlest of Stanley's rough friends, and find a secure corner in the cave. But her past finds her out and destroys that dream. Refusing her chance for a merely sexual relationship with Mitch, Blanche keeps her dream of something finer, fighting to the last, choosing to remain herself and to be carried to the insane asylum rather than to be like her sister.

Stanley Kowalski, especially as sensitively played by the young Marlon Brando, also has a touch of the tragic. He sees his home invaded by a difficult intruder. He suffers under her insults, and in raping and destroying her, his wife's sister, he knows he risks breaking up his own marriage. But he has his own kind of integrity to defend. The intensity of the conflict, with important values involved on both sides, gives the play considerable stature as a tragedy. It involves choice, struggle, questioning, suffering. Many of Williams' characters—Chance in *Sweet Bird of Youth,* Big Daddy in *Cat on a Hot Tin Roof*—refuse to drift on in evasion and ignorance. They wrest identity and meaning even from their pain. As Chance finally stops running away and faces the mob he knows is determined to castrate him, he says, "Something's got to mean something."

Not all modern tragedy centers on the hero who is ahead of his time or the one who clings to the right to choose, to whom "attention must be paid." Some modern tragedies are concerned with the destructive hero. Ibsen's *Hedda Gabler* (1890) is a study of a destructive woman. Hedda's Victorian society offers no outlet for intelligence and energy except complete submission to the desires of men and a smothering motherhood. Even her interference in the life of the young genius who is in love with her turns into a sordid shooting in a brothel, not the magnificent suicide she expected. She is completely in the power of the very "respectable" Judge Brack, but she can still say no. She kills herself. The fascination of the play is in the power of destruction.

That love itself could be destructive amazed and fascinated a number of playwrights. In August Strindberg's *The Father* (1887) the mother deliberately destroys her husband, and in *Miss Julie* (1888) the restless young noblewoman, unable to resist her coachman, gives herself to him and then kills herself. In Eugene O'Neill's *Desire Under the Elms* (1924), a melodrama (rather than a tragedy) about the violent greeds and lusts seething on a rocky New England farm, Abby kills her own baby to prove that she is not just using her young lover, her stepson, to get possession of the farm. Her lover is furious and sends for the sheriff. Yet at the end he returns to share her fate—an assertion of love and understanding and reconciliation with destiny that has much in common with classic tragedy.

O'Neill's later tragedy about his own family, *Long Day's Journey into Night*, which was not produced until 1956, three years after his death, is a deep, beautiful study of that perverse need of human beings, in their shame, envy, and self-reproach, to destroy those they love. O'Neill's *A Moon for the Misbegotten*, another study of suffering and lost hopes, with a compelling mood of longing and melancholy, deals poignantly with the personal tragedy of the eldest son of this family and of the earthy, warm-hearted Irish girl who loves him but cannot save him from his own weakness and despair. The play had a brilliant production, the first on

2-13 Modern tragedy. Realistic detail in foreground, setting of abstract realism designed by cutting down from reality. O'Neill's *A Moon for the Misbegotten*. New York, 1973. Directed by José Quintero. Photo by Martha Swope.

Broadway, in 1974, with Jason Robards as James and Colleen Dewhurst as the girl (Figure 2–13).

The vision of destruction indicates a radical change from the attitude of those late nineteenth- and early twentieth-century thinkers who assumed that reality is good and believed in the great myth of progress. But what if the hope of progress is itself a romantic delusion? What if nature is man's enemy and the scientific pursuit of reality is bound to destroy the old faith in human values?

If this is the case, if truth is inhuman and things of the imagination are lies, then one answer is "long live the lies." Several dramatists began to talk about life-lies and to defend the illusions even if they were delusions with no relation to the real world. Ibsen, in the middle of his career, reversed his attitude toward the disclosure of truth. In *Ghosts, An Enemy of the People*, and several other plays, he had portrayed stupid, venal people trying to prevent the exposure of the truth; but in *The Wild Duck* (1884) he showed the disastrous results that ensue when a misguided realist insists on telling a happy husband that his wife has been the mistress of her employer and that their daughter is not his own.

The yearning for illusion, for an impossible faith in defiance of reality, is given a romantic treatment in Peter Shaffer's tragedy *The Royal Hunt of the Sun*. Pizarro, the conqueror of Peru, is a disillusioned, cynical old man, yearning for immortality of some kind. An illegitimate peasant, bitter about his struggles to rise in the world, he has little respect for the church and for the Christians he is leading and feels drawn in sympathy to the Indian emperor Atahuallpa, who believes that his father, the Sun, will resurrect him if he is killed. Pizarro almost believes this too, so strong is his desire to find some faith. But when he is forced to kill the emperor and the Sun does not resurrect the body, Pizarro is left desolate in his grief for the man he had come to love like a son. The objective reality is only death—a dying Spain gorged with gold and a blighted Peru, its men slaughtered or enslaved. Achievement is empty. All faith is a delusion, and only a bitter, compassionate sorrow is left.

Poetry in Modern Tragedy

Unlike tragedy in earlier periods, modern tragedy has made little use of poetry. In Ireland and Spain poets have taken the vivid poetic language and the folklore of the peasants to build exciting tragic scenes. Early in the century John Millington Synge produced a somber one-act tragedy, *Riders to the Sea* (1904), which survived because of its sustained mood and rhythmic prose. Some people have been challenged to produce the poetic

2-14 A peasant tragedy with poetry, songs, and symbolism. Lorca's *Blood Wedding*. Indiana University production, directed and lighted by Gary Gaiser and designed by William E. Kinzer.

tragedies of the Spanish poet Federico García Lorca, who moved from fairly realistic plays to more poetic forms. In *Blood Wedding* (1933), besides poetic dialogue, he used choral rituals in the wedding and death scenes and the Requiem, and a number of symbolic and supernatural commentators. But Lorca was killed by Franco's forces and his plays remain isolated examples, too exotic for the general public.

It remained for the twentieth-century religious drama movement to combine aspects of the medieval religious plays with the suffering and exaltation of Greek tragedy in a modern poetic idiom. The most striking example is T. S. Eliot's *Murder in the Cathedral,* written for the 1935 festival at Canterbury Cathedral in England. It dramatizes the martyrdom in 1170 of Thomas à Becket, Archbishop of Canterbury. From the Greek theatre Eliot took the pattern of a heroic, divine or saintly character set against a chanting chorus of women whose spiritual problems are involved with his. For the soliloquies and confrontations of Becket, he used the sharp stanzaic and rhetorical forms of medieval and Shakespearean verse. To the chorus of Canterbury women drawn to witness the martyrdom, he gives his most vivid free-form verse. They feel the significance of the martyrdom as a ritual sacrifice of the seasons:

> Winter shall come bringing death from the sea,
>
> .   .   .
>
> And the world must be cleaned in the winter, or we shall have only
> A sour spring, a parched summer, an empty harvest.

What is expressed in abstract rhetoric by the main characters is physically sensed by these fearful women:

> I have smelt them, the death-bringers, senses are quickened
> By subtle forebodings .   .   .
>
>   .   .   .
>
> What is woven on the loom of fate
> What is woven in the councils of princes
> Is woven also in our veins, our brains,
> Is woven like a pattern of living worms
> In the guts of the women of Canterbury.

Religious intensities of a more bitter mood, using words, voice, and dance movements, were achieved in the productions of Jerzy Grotowski's Polish Laboratory Theatre, which will be discussed in Chapter 8 with other recent developments in theatre.

The Tragic and the Serious in the Movies

The movies have not shown many tragedies, even if we use the term loosely, to apply to any serious play that ends in disaster or death for the principal character. Most good films of this kind have been adaptations of stage plays, and in some of them the ending has been altered to leave a more cheerful impression. Still, more and more often in the last three decades, a complex dramatic situation has been allowed to reach a natural solution, whether favorable or unfavorable to the protagonist. This is partly due to the fact that, since television took over the entertainment of the masses and the movies became a minority art, optimism and cheer are no longer obligatory, and films can be more adventurous. Many plays, notably those of Tennessee Williams, have been filmed with their tragic endings intact.

The youth rebellion of the fifties and sixties has been reflected in some serious films. The first notable film about rebellious youth was *Rebel Without a Cause* (1955), in which James Dean began his brief career and immediately reached stardom as the ideal image of his restless generation. The phrase "rebel without a cause" fitted perfectly their unfocused kind of rebellion, and the film made a touching plea for compassion. When youth rebellion took form in the early sixties, it often had a hopeful coloring, in life and on the screen, with love-ins, new rock music, and flower power. But as the Vietnam War became more involved and hopeless and the military-industrial complex more powerful and threatening, the motorcycling, leather-jacketed, pot-smoking heroes and heroines of the films took on an aura of desperation and doom. The establishment was against them, yet they had to assert themselves; they must search for their authentic selves by living in their own way; they must find fresh innocence even in a world of violence. When the establishment could turn on them such overwhelming power, their petty law-breaking seemed negligible.

Alice's Restaurant (1969) gave a fairly happy picture of the life of a commune, though there were problems with the local police and a draft board, and the commune did not last. But *Easy Rider* (1969) and *Midnight Cowboy* (1969) showed a more tragic fate for rebels. And the trend showed in other films. The four survivors of *The Wild Bunch* (1969) set out to kill a few enemies, but when the whole Mexican bandit army is thrown at them, they are seen as victims by the movie audience, not murderers. In *Butch Cassidy and the Sundance Kid* (1969) the two adventurers seem mild in comparison with the hostile power they stir up. The naive youth trying to rob a bank in *Dog Day Afternoon* (1975) is not a criminal but a confused rebel, bargaining with an army of police to see both his male lover and his wife before he makes his last run. The driver in *Taxi Driver* (1976) stirs a hint of tragic pity and terror as he is swept up in the hideous violence of city streets. Even in the psychedelic rock opera *Tommy* (1975), Tommy, in bringing release and freedom as from an angel floating in bright-colored clouds, also releases the forces of destruction.

The best of the films of rebellious youth is *Easy Rider*. It has historic overtones as a reversal of the old American dream of adventurers taking to the open road, looking for space and freedom in the West. In *Easy Rider*, the long-haired rebels take to the open road on motorcycles, looking for space and freedom, riding eastward from California to the New Orleans Mardi Gras. The open space and the beautiful mountains and high plains are still there, but small-town America has an irrational fear of the freedom and life style of long-haired youth. In one town the wanderers are beaten by the rednecks, and after a disappointing glimpse of the Mardi Gras, they are killed by "respectable" citizens. Their doom was inevitable from the first. In the world of drawn-out war in Vietnam, of proliferating weapons, of international plots and assassinations, of ruthless competition and overkill, there is no room for the relatively innocent. The film has tragic implications not only for rebellious youth but for America, the traditional land of freedom, open space, and variety.

More comic and more sentimental is *Midnight Cowboy*, but in it, too, the principal characters reach a tragic doom on the road. The young Texas adventurer Joe Buck (Jon Voight), in many ways an innocent, goes to New York to be God's gift to lonely women. But even the women exploit him. He is lost until he finds the companionship of a wily city rat, Ratso (Dustin Hoffman). But the city rat, like the city itself, is decaying and falling apart. Ratso dreams of getting to the sunshine of Florida. Joe almost kills a man and steals his money so that the friends may start out for Miami. As they are getting in sight of the city, Ratso dies and the lonely Joe takes him in his arms.

These are not great heroic figures, and their lawlessness and violence is often childish. But they are searching for some kind of integrity and fresh innocence in an extremely difficult world. They are trying to find some meaning in life. Knowing that, we can accept their failure and destruction.

The plays and films of the absurdists and their successors introduced some new approaches to tragedy, but we will consider those in a later chapter. We turn now to comedy, to show how the theatre has provided compensation for the painful truth that is the substance of tragedy.

3

The Theatre of Laughter: Farce and High Comedy

omedy is far more complex than tragedy and harder to define. The word is used for many different kinds of plays and for a wide range of attitudes toward them, from delight in the broad slapstick of farce to sophisticated enjoyment of high comedy, ambiguous satisfaction in stinging satire, and even enthralled absorption in romantic plays that stir no laughter at all. We see ourselves reflected in a comic character, we come to like him, and then, paradoxically, we rejoice to see him beaten. We project ourselves onto the stage and yet at the same time remain detached, watching from a distance. In some ages, all plays, whether their subject matter was comic or tragic, were simply called comedies. The word "play" itself implies something that is done for sheer pleasure.

The Ways of Comedy

Laughter, that noisy cachinnation, that convulsive explosion of air and sound so like—and so different from—the barking of a dog, has never been fully explained. It brings sudden relaxation and deep pleasure. It seems involuntary and private; yet it most often occurs in social groups. It occurs when a person suddenly recognizes something left over, something that does not fit his usual expectations, something "funny." For incongruity is at the heart of comedy. Henri Bergson, in his essays *On Laughter*, tells how we laugh at the conflict between living and the rules we try to impose on it. Whenever the mechanical becomes encrusted on the living, it is thrown off in laughter.

From very early times, festivals and holidays have been special occasions for breaking the normal pattern and returning to a tradition of disorder, freedom, and license. A temporary ruler is crowned in mock pomp to preside over the revels, and at the end of the festival his throne is torn down in wild, destructive glee. According to one myth, the New Year holiday was a time for returning to an earlier age when a trickster god ruled the world, before the later, more serious gods invented hard work and strict rules. In Rome the Saturnalia in December was the reign of the early god Saturn and a time of release from all duties and expectations. Men dressed as women, and servants ordered their masters about. Another myth gave the New Year festival an even more ancient tie by recognizing an incongruity in the very nature of the creation, since the lunar calendar can be fitted into the solar calendar only if some four days— holidays—are left over. Some mythologies held that creation gave form only to a finite island floating in the waters of chaos. During the new-year gap of four days, more of the surrounding primeval waters of chaos flowed

Razullo   *Cucurucu.*

3-1 The spirit of comic acting. The masked actors of the *commedia dell' arte* depended as much on their singing, dancing, acrobatics, and slapstick as on the words that they improvised around an agreed-upon story. Note the platform stage in the background. Engraving by Callot.

into the circle of the year, renewing health and vitality. As people put on outlandish disguises to run, jump, race, dance, and act the holiday roles of revelry, they partook of that vital renewal. In the wild but ordered release of the festival, in singing satiric songs, in beating and cheating a scapegoat, in crowning and deposing a mock king, and in erecting and destroying festive buildings, the revelers found an outlet for the spirit of disorder that can never be eradicated from human nature.

For the civilized man or woman, comedy is the symbolic expression of the ancient festivals. On many levels comedy makes an attack on all forms, rules, and systems, but it is a controlled rebellion. It may point the way to improvement, but it more often shows a way of accepting the world as it is, of living with both order and disorder, rule and rebellion. The audience can stand, if not with the gods, at least with Puck in *A Midsummer Night's Dream,* to look down in amazement and delight at the foolishness of men and women and the perversity of the universe.

> Shall we their fond pageant see?
> Lord, what fools these mortals be!

Puck knows that the delusions of the night can be corrected in time.

> Jack shall have Jill;
> Naught shall go ill;
> The man shall have his mare again, and all shall be well.

Traditions of Comedy

Different periods of the past have fostered particular kinds of comedy. In ancient Greece Aristophanes found ready to his artist's hand a festival of spring fertility processions, with songs and dances, competitions and contests, installation of a ruler of the festival, ridicule and expulsion of intruders and obstructors, and a final ritual wedding and feast. Through that time-honored medium, he expressed his bitter anger at the Athenians for allowing their democracy to be controlled by dictators of the war party and for letting their education, law courts, philosophy, and literature be corrupted by irresponsible leaders of cults and fads. The spring festival was a privileged time, and even the war party could not censor the drama. Many Athenians still thought free speech important, and Aristophanes was not silenced when he wrote the most fantastic, and the sharpest, satires the world has ever known. In *The Knights* he even lampooned the current dictator, Cleon, as an amateur sausage-peddler selling baloney to the public. In *Lysistrata* one woman puts an end to the war by persuading the women on both sides to enforce a sex strike until their husbands make peace. *The Clouds* deals hilariously and sharply with the intellectuals who dwell in the clouds. Although Aristophanes' plays laugh at the struggles of little men faced with difficult public problems, they also carry the assurance that little men can do something about them.

After Athens was overrun by Alexander the Great and then by the Romans, the citizens were no longer free to take an interest in important public questions. The topical satire of Aristophanes gave way to the neat plots of Menander. Later, in Rome, Plautus developed from Menander's situation drama a farcical comedy that has been the standard entertainment for the tired businessman ever since.

The medieval period developed its own little farces, about a clever lawyer tricked by a simple-minded shepherd in *Patelin,* for example, or about wives dominating and cheating their husbands. Such robust tales even intruded into the great religious cycles, as we have seen. Like the sculpture in a medieval cathedral, which included grotesque gargoyles and homely scenes of everyday life, the religious plays included both low and high characters and many elements of comedy. Medieval drama and art made a great contribution to the comic tradition, showing Shakespeare not only how to use comedy in serious plays but how to add the grim, the grotesque, and the demonic to both serious plays and comedies.

The Renaissance saw two great achievements in comedy. The first was a romantic type of comedy in which idealized young ladies and knights, engaged in the loves and intrigues of an aristocratic court, are surrounded by a variety of colorful comic characters. The appreciation of comic characters as enjoyable and even lovable was a result of the new humanistic respect for individuality, explicitly taught at the beginning of the sixteenth century in Erasmus' *Praise of Folly*. Without that attitude Shakespeare's humorous characters, from jesters, clowns, and bumbling rustics on up to the wise, playful, fat knight, Sir John Falstaff, would never have been conceived; even to this day some overserious moralists cannot love them or indulge them in their foolishness. The second Renaissance achievement in comedy was a realistic satiric comedy made popular by Shakespeare's young friend Ben Jonson. Disillusioned and bitter, Jonson attacked man's "humours," or obsessions, with savage anger and took delight in exposing their greed and other vices as well as their gullibility and stupidity. His *Volpone* (1606) and *The Alchemist* (1610) still amaze and delight audiences as dramas of sharp castigation. In both plays the gulls deserve to be cheated, as there is nothing outrageous they would not do for power or money. A modern version of *Volpone*, called *Sly Fox*, set in nineteenth-century San Francisco, was a successful vehicle for George C. Scott in the New York season of 1976–77.

The high comedy of the latter part of the seventeenth century (the "Restoration Period" in England) took some of the best aspects of both kinds of Renaissance comedy—the sharp, disillusioned view of reality from Jonson, without his bitterness, and the charming, cultivated young

3-2
Farcical action. Plautus' *Haunted House*. Texas Tech University production, adapted directed, and designed by Clifford Ashby, and costumed by Larry Randolph.

lovers and the amiable fools from the romantic comedy. Before we examine this highly developed social type of comedy, we must consider the basic, more universal type—farce.

Farce, or "Low" Comedy

What this world needs is a good laugh. After a wearing day, the busy man wants a scene of horseplay to relax him, and he turns on the television to watch a lively comedian. The Romans on their holidays went by the thousands to see a clownish servant in a red wig and a wide-mouthed mask, who would be chased all over the enormous stage and beaten vigorously, yet would always be ready with a clever remark and a new scheme for getting the money or the girl. The Renaissance clown Harlequin made his sword into a "slapstick" of two strips of wood, which gave a maximum of sound with a minimum of damage to the rump. For three centuries children and adults have screamed with delight as the puppet Punch turns on his nagging wife Judy, on the whining cat, and finally on the devil himself, and gives them such a fast, noisy beating that it seems that the puppet heads will splinter.

Curiously, our loudest laughs are at someone else's pain. A good farce is excruciatingly funny. It provides popular entertainment by turning the difficulties, restrictions, frustrations, and embarrassments of life into laughter. It relaxes the audience by first tying it into new knots of tension, then exploding the tension into guffaws and roars of delight.

Elements of Farce

Farce is based on a threefold compact between the audience and the play. One term of that compact is the realism; the audience must recognize themselves in farce, whether the actor is Woody Allen, a circus clown in fantastic costume, or Mr. Magoo in a cartoon. The second element is the built-in irony of a false situation as the playwright carefully lets the audience know that it is all a mistake or a lie. He shows the putting on of the disguise, the concocting of the lie, or the beginning of the mistaken identity. In actuality, it is painful to see a husband deny his wife and upbraid her, but not in Plautus' *Menaechmi* or Shakespeare's version of the same play, *The Comedy of Errors*, because the audience knows it is not really the husband but his long-lost twin brother. Suicide is no laughing matter, but the funniest scene in Alan Ayckbourn's *Absurd Person Singular* (1974) is one in which a woman doggedly sets about killing herself. The audience knows that she has no very good reason for suicide and that she will not succeed, but it is hilariously funny to see her try and to see other characters in the play completely unaware that she is trying.

The third element is the comic treatment created by the director, the designer, and the actor. The actor may contribute a squeaky or reedy voice, a nasal tone, a peculiar inflection, or a monotone to reinforce the comic quality of a character. In broad farce, actors do not hesitate to use lisping, stuttering, limping, and tics. Madame Arcati's sudden jumps and squeaks are the funniest things in *Blithe Spirit*. A floppy hat, an old-fashioned stripe, or a garment a bit too large or too short may give just the needed incongruous touch. Incongruity can make a disguise quite hilarious. The man dressed as Charley's aunt repeatedly forgets and shows his trousers and smokes a cigar, rousing screams of terror in the audience as he almost gets caught by the girls. Moments of undress or threats of exposure cause violent laughter because they come close to breaking our strong taboos. Bright-colored underclothes heighten the effect and at the same time prevent any actual exposure.

More important than such comic qualities are the intensities of the performance. Speed is the most obvious farcical intensity. Play anything fast enough and, as long as it carries the audience with it, it will be funny. Charlie Chaplin's Monsieur Verdoux counting money at superhuman speed can never be forgotten. Chase scenes, whether of the couples running around the restaurant tables in *The Matchmaker* or of automobile thieves fleeing over curb and cliff in the silent movies, are high points of delight. Beatings, fights, struggles, pratfalls—all create an enormous amount of energetic action. To speed, farce usually adds the intensity of sound—startling noises, crashes, collisions, explosions. At the end of the first act of *The Matchmaker* the young men are jumping with delight because at last they are to run away from the store. Thornton Wilder adds a whole battery of sounds as the tomato cans in the store below explode and cans and debris fly up through the trap door. Emotions in a farce are exaggerated to the fullest intensity. In a serious play sorrow and pain are suppressed and indicated by half-hidden tensions, but not in farce. Audiences receive great pleasure from seeing crying on the stage. While their empathy is enlisted, their own tension is released by the actors' squalling. The various intensities—speed, energy, noise, physical action, and exaggerated expression of emotion—all illustrate the basic quality of low comedy. Characters must be convincing, yet played with such single-minded, demoniacal obsession that the audience's empathy spills over into laughter.

Farce also makes use of many mechanical patterns: duplications, repetitions, sequences, reversals, delays, surprises, interruptions, and sudden breaks in pattern. Identical twins, two brothers or two servants

3-3 Farce with romantic charm. Hiding, listening, deceiving. Wilder's *The Matchmaker*. Barter Theatre production, Abingdon, Virginia, 1977.

dressed alike, or two people who find themselves in the same predicament, can be a source of endless amusement as they move in unison, in opposition, or in sequence. Duplication of movement is so funny that in serious plays the director takes great care to see that two actors do not by chance sit, turn, or step in unison. Duplication with variation is highly entertaining. Sometimes it is deliberate and derisive, as when one character apes another to make fun of him or express anger. Sometimes the variation depends on incongruity, as when a short and a tall person are made to look alike or act alike. Sometimes the sequence of repetition is continued with several examples, and it is just a step to a Gilbert and Sullivan chorus, "and so do his sisters and his cousins and his aunts." To see a dozen Keystone Cops tumble out of a car too small to hold them and scramble after a suspect, all falling over the same obstacles, rolling downhill and piling up in a ditch, was one of the delights of moviegoing in the "Golden Age" of film comedy. To see a dozen secret, scheming adventurers surprise one another in a hotel is one of the delights of the farces of France's Georges Feydeau. His *Hotel Paradiso* (1894) and, even more, *A Flea in Her Ear* (1907) are perennial favorites, revived again and again.

The Popularity of Farce

In spite of its enemies, farce has been the most popular of all theatre forms for more than two thousand years. Literary critics have attacked it as trivial and vulgar, and highbrows of all periods have despised it for its use of physical action. Puritans and fanatics have despised it simply because it is funny. Being dead serious is supposed to be more profound, and entertainment is "diversion," a turning away from important things. Yet year after year, night after night, the broad laugh has been as indispensable a part of the lives of millions of people as their food and sleep. On the movie screen, Peter Sellers' Pink Panther can strike again and again, with ingenious variations of a few ludicrous situations, with dire catastrophe and hilarious recovery, without tiring an enthusiastic public; on the television screen Monty Python has survived for years on his special variety of imaginative foolishness.

There are at least three reasons why farce continues century after century to delight its audience. In the first place, it is a release of pent-up dormant life, like the arrival of spring. The two boys in *The Matchmaker* break away from the store in Yonkers. They go downtown to the big city; they kiss some girls, take them out to a restaurant, and almost get arrested. The old merchant himself gets into unexpected adventure and brings home a wife and a much more tolerant disposition. It is as important to thaw out his tyranny and stinginess as it is to thaw the frozen ground before new things can grow.

A second reason for people's pleasure in farce is that it brings the great reassurance that all the great clowns have brought, the reassurance that a person can take it. The clown takes his beating and survives; by his wisecrack and his comeback he proves his spiritual superiority to his fate. The clown has always been the butt, the victim, the fall guy, the little fellow that something always happens to. He is all of us, unlucky, put upon, mistreated. But he refuses to give up. He never admits defeat. He can always show his indifference to pain, and sometimes, just sometimes, he has a chance to snatch his own victory from his overwhelming enemies.

It is that superb aplomb in the midst of disaster that makes the best moments of the great clowns so memorable. At one moment in the film *A Night at the Opera,* the Marx brothers are frantically fleeing along the galleries high up in the backstage rigging in the opera house. The next moment they are serenely sailing through the air on the tie ropes as the scenery flies up and down around the performers. Or they pretend to be part of the performance, just out of reach of their pursuers. Who can forget the gravity of Charlie Chaplin as a rookie soldier in *Shoulder Arms,* left on the field marking time alone after the rest of the squad has marched away, or his quiet assertion in an early short film, *A Night Out,* when, as he is being dragged away by the collar, he picks a daisy and smells it? It is very painful to keep a bit of individuality in a regimented world, but the clown does it. We may also remember Chaplin's unquestioning absorption in his job on a swaying ladder as he cleans the street sign each time the ladder brings him by, or the same carefree bravery as he walks to the other side of the room to keep the house from toppling over the cliff in *The Gold Rush.* In *The Kid* he is a proud society man refusing to bow down to poverty and rags, twirling his cane, taking off his fingerless gloves with elegance, reaching for his cigarette case (a sardine can), and carefully tapping his choice of the butts he has picked up. Charlie Chaplin in the midst of hostile surroundings can blithely follow the life and logic of his own mind in complete disregard of his enemies. While he is sweeping a pawnshop, a rope on the floor suddenly becomes in his mind a circus tightrope, and he an expert tightrope performer beloved and applauded by the crowd. While fleeing through an enormous house, he suddenly stops before a vast birthday cake to play pool and golf with bits of the frosting, making every shot count. In farce, the world may be reeling and humanity hostile, but the clowns possess what has been called the "incalculable strength of the weak."

Farce delights in the reverse of the noble virtues. Instead of heroic defiance, courage, ability to meet any sudden danger, to overcome any obstacle, to conquer all enemies, the comic hero shows total ineptitude in practical matters, fear, and submission. Yet with unconscious ingenuity he wins in the end. In Woody Allen's film *Love and Death* (1975), in part a parody of Tolstoy's *War and Peace,* the simple little man, trying to live up to the part of a military hero, is repeatedly put down but never conquered, even when he is dead and his ghost dances off through the trees to some clowns' paradise.

Besides giving us strength to free the spirit and to hold the chin up, farce has a third function. It makes an important philosophical synthesis. It is a device for accepting the basic incongruity of everyday living, for spanning the ideal and the real without denying either. Farce accepts the discrepancy between the finite and the infinite; it affirms the infinite as it laughs at us for being bogged down in the finite. In particular, it accepts both the pattern and the impulse to break the pattern. Ultimately, farce does not demand revolutionary change. It has no wish to abolish the rules, the officers, the policemen, the parents, the wives, the jobs—the conformity that gives structure to our daily lives. But it does expect to bend the rules, to get around the officer, to vary the conformity. It reaffirms order in the universe as a whole, but it suggests that on the lower levels there may be considerable incongruity. In the very successful farcical movie

M*A*S*H (1970), and in the long-running television serial based on it, the frantic, overworked doctors in a field hospital are completely conscientious. Not for a second would they neglect their constantly arriving, wounded patients. But when a brash young woman administrator arrives, determined to enforce strict rules, they must undermine her authority. After they hide a microphone under her bed and broadcast the sounds of her lovemaking over the whole camp, they are allowed to leave the camp for a brief rest and also get permission to bend the rules and do their work in their own way. It is not surprising that many famous comic figures have come in contrasting pairs—Don Quixote and Sancho Panza, the young, idealistic Prince Hal and the old, disillusioned Falstaff, the clever slave and the stupid slave of Roman comedy, Pierrot and Harlequin, Mutt and Jeff, Weber and Fields, Amos and Andy, Laurel and Hardy. These are symbols not only of the affinity of different social classes but also of the companionship of incongruous temperaments.

In some aspects, farce presents life in the glow of ideals impossible to realize. It shows the youth leaving home to go out and kill the dragon and rescue the enchanted maiden but running back into the house before the dragon quite gets him. Farce emphasizes the realistic details that the truly romantic story omits. As the dragon charges with breath of flame, your sword sticks in the scabbard. As you lift the veil of enchantment, it catches on a nail and rips. As you mount the stairs to her tower, you bump your head on a beam. As you slowly move in to kiss her, you are interrupted by a sneeze. In true romance such things never happen. Your clothes always fit and look right. You never have to worry about money or weather or law and order. But in farce your friend with the money is late, the rain shrinks your clothes, and the policeman puts handcuffs on you. No one believes you or understands you, least of all when you speak the plain truth. Farce makes the fullest demonstration possible of the breakdown of communication. Romance can soar with poetry into celestial clarity, but farce has to stumble along on the clumsiness of prose.

To many romantic rebels, society is an establishment designed to crush the individual. In the world of farce, society is a conglomeration of selfish individuals, clumsy institutions, and foolish customs. In your youth you are hemmed in by parents and policemen, but half the time they are busy or stupid, and you can get around them. When you grow up, your work, your family, and the causes you are committed to would absorb every last minute of your life if you let them. But you can escape. In a universe of incongruity, the accidents can work for you as well as against you. If you are stopped in your flight because someone has locked the gate, you find that the demon pursuing you has fallen into an open manhole.

It's a mad world, my masters, and a laugh is the one way of accepting it, better relaxation than wine, women, or song. Without the relaxation of farcical laughter, human beings would long ago have torn themselves and their neighbors apart.

High Comedy

Comedy is not limited to the antics of farce or to the enchanted dreams of romance. It can also create a vision of well-dressed people matching wits and exploring human relations in a world of fashion and sophistication. In this drawing-room comedy, or high comedy, business deals are made, political intrigues are sketched, plots are foiled, secret scandals are revealed, liaisons and marriages are arranged—all kinds of exciting situations develop through the witty conversations and wily maneuvers of urbane, charming people who are enjoying the social games immensely. In actual life, at any social level, conversation is usually one-sided, over-weighted with trivia, halting, disconnected, and dull, but in high comedy every line sparkles as it hits the mark precisely in the constant excitement of retort and repartee. High comedy shows an experienced adult picking his way skillfully and confidently among the pitfalls of a complex social

3-4 High comedy. Strong conflicts become part of a social game in elegant, upper-class surroundings. Coward's *Present Laughter*. New York, 1946. Photo Vandamm.

world and maintaining his individuality while outwardly conforming to the expectations of the group.

One of any person's greatest ambitions, often the reason he or she works so hard for money or fame, is to be accepted in society, to "arrive," to know the language and manners of the in-group. After the adolescent has freed himself from his parents (the subject of countless farces) and has established his independence, with at least a minimum of financial and professional security, he is ready to find his role in social gatherings where he will hear not only casual gossip but comment on everything from current fashion and human behavior to the latest developments in institutions and ideas. Much high comedy is concerned with the social education of both old and young. It is no wonder that several high comedies have been called "schools"—*School for Husbands, School for Wives, School for Scandal.*

Civilized society does not exist until women can freely participate as equals of men. A mixed society adds warmth to intellectual discussion and permits the impersonal appreciation of the opposite sex. In the theatre, high comedy did not develop until women became important as characters, until Moliere and Shakespeare brought them in to confront men, outwit them in deception, and stand up to them proudly and independently. Ever since Congreve's women set a classic precedent in laying down the law to their men, playwrights have put a proud, independent woman at the center of nearly every high comedy. Unlike romance, where the woman waits for the man to pursue, high comedy often allows the woman to go after the man.

Attraction, good manners, independence—to keep these three in balance at a proper distance requires a high skill in the social game. In some encounters the game requires a mask, a protective disguise that disarms the opponent by covering hostility with a smile. One of the most famous scenes of charming hostility is the garden scene in Oscar Wilde's *The Importance of Being Earnest* (1895), in which the two girls who think they are engaged to the same man slug it out verbally with more devastating blows than any prizefighter ever landed. They never lose the smile that keeps communication open or the elaborate phrase that keeps it on a generalized level above the particular or personal. When Gwendolen, the city girl, praises the garden, she adds, "I had no idea there were any flowers in the country." That gives Cecily, the country girl, her chance. "Oh, flowers are as common here, Miss Fairfax, as people are in London." Gwendolen retaliates: "Personally I cannot understand how anybody manages to exist in the country, if anybody who is anybody does. The country always bores me to death." Cecily is ready to answer with, "Ah! This is what the newspapers call agricultural depression, is it not? I believe the aristocracy are suffering very much from it just at present. It is almost an epidemic amongst them, I have been told. May I offer you some tea, Miss Fairfax?''

But the protective disguise is the negative side of high comedy. High comedy also offers positive joys, which are experienced by the characters and shared by the audience. One of these is to make a game of "the others.'' Instead of masking hostility, tease the fools, draw them out. It helps them to see their faults and follies. George Meredith thought that the function of the "Comic Spirit" was to correct the faults of mankind, but through gentle laughter, without the "pain of satiric heat" or the "bitter craving to strike heavy blows." In *An Essay on Comedy,* he wrote of this Comic Spirit as a "sunlight of the mind.''

A second joy in high comedy is to laugh at oneself, a very hard thing to do, but satisfying when one has managed it. Such acceptance requires the self-knowledge of maturity, the confidence of being an individual able to play a role in society. Still another delight in high comedy depends on disillusionment, a full awareness of the limitations of human existence. It brings a triumph of balance, spanning the inner and the outer, the self and the others, independence and interaction, self-respect and friendship or love.

High Comedy in the Seventeenth Century

Though there were glimpses of it in ancient comedy and in minor scenes in Shakespeare, high comedy was the achievement of the seventeenth century, the first great age that produced a *society,* a class of cultivated people with the time and the inclination to devote themselves to human relations and to the forms and manners that make a society possible. After a century of humanistic education, with its emphasis on classic comedy and on the social graces of good manners, eloquence, and wit, Europe was ready for attitudes of sophistication and maturity. In Paris and London a number of men and women, gathering in the salons, at the royal court, at the coffeehouses of the town, and in the walkways of the parks, set about exploring urbane, subtle, complex, and civilized patterns of human behavior. They created a new concept of ladies and gentlemen and produced a new kind of comedy.

Like the twentieth century, the seventeenth century was trying to achieve a sane, comic view of life in a period of shattering disillusion. For more than a century religious wars had devastated France, Germany, and England, until everyone was weary of fanaticism and ready to try to achieve toleration and stability.

It was no accident that modern science and the new comedy were born at the same time. Both required a certain detachment, a separation of man as objective observer from man as a subjective holder of values, beliefs, and feelings. Detachment grew out of the painful and disillusioning recognition of increasing complexity in the world: several religions in conflict, many suns in the skies, new continents across the seas. The first reaction to that multiplicity was bitterness and anguish, much like the bitterness and anguish of the twentieth century. We have noted how that anguish found expression in Shakespeare's *Hamlet* and *King Lear*. At the same time, comedy explored gaiety in detachment. Shakespeare's clowns captured that gaiety in a form we can still enjoy, while the masked comedians of the *commedia dell' arte* made Pantalone, Harlequin, and Pulcinella popular in both court and town. By the virtuosity of their singing, dancing, acrobatic acting, broad slapstick, and witty repartee, they taught Europe to laugh at confusion. Ben Jonson found a form for the new bitter laughter through his comedies of "humours" or obsessions, and it was not until the middle of the century that a better balance was achieved. Though not expecting any more of human nature than Jonson, the later generation of playwrights learned to accept the fact that man is an earth-bound creature and to look on fools with indulgent amusement.

The Achievement of Moliere

Where Jonson was bitter, Moliere was urbane. He showed plenty of fanatics completely devoted to their monstrous obsessions and young people who eventually managed to get around them. Like Jonson, Moliere took his plots from Plautus, but what was low-comedy intrigue in Plautus here becomes more complex and subtle. In Plautus the clownish servants had to trick the old fathers, but in Moliere the deception, usually played with affection and kindness, becomes a game of juggling with the basic illusions of life. The Miser will have his children marry only for money, the Bourgeois Gentleman only for title, Orgon in *Tartuffe* only for piety, the Imaginary Invalid only to bring a doctor into the family.

Moliere brought interesting women into his farcical plays—wily old housekeepers or matchmakers—to trick the old men when necessary and to shake some sense into both old and young when their contentions passed all bounds. The Miser can be teased and indulged and led along by his obsession. The Imaginary Invalid is deceived not by a simple lie but by elaborate indulgence of his concern with his health: his brother and the able housekeeper arrange to have him initiated as a doctor so that he can prescribe for himself. They win more freedom not only for the young couple but for the old man by freeing him from his fears and his foolish dependence on doctors.

3-5 A farcical scene formalized by even spacing and elegant costumes. All but the accused and the true thief are standing. Moliere's *The Miser*. Indiana University Theatre production, directed and designed by Richard Scammon.

The young girl also becomes much more important in Moliere than she had been in earlier comedy. In Plautus she was merely the prize for the young man or his servant when they had gotten around the old man; sometimes she did not even come on stage. But Moliere often told the story from her point of view and made her the active schemer. In *The School for Husbands* (1661) the young girl makes her jealous old guardian carry messages to her young man, and in *The School for Wives* (1662) the ingénue and her sweetheart tell the helpless guardian frankly that they are deceiving him. The scenes are just as funny as any classic farce scenes, but the women provide variety and complexity and add a light touch to the teasing that moves the plays toward high comedy.

Finally, in *The Misanthrope* (1666), Moliere moved fully into high comedy and did not bother to include the low-comedy scenes on which the other plays depend for much of the fun. Here he presents an adult couple, free from all restrictions, exploring their relationships with other free adults. Célimène is the center of attraction of many beaux, with whom she points out, in malicious character sketches, the shortcomings of their friends. With triumphant, smiling wit, she outdoes her rival in double-edged attack. The overhonest Alceste, who falls in love with her, objects violently to her enjoyment of the social group. Unable to see that his own obsession with sincerity is a fault, he despises flattery and even politeness. The girl refuses, at the age of twenty, to leave society and go off to a

3-6 Farce, formality, and fantasy. Moliere's *The Imaginary Invalid*. Eastern Illinois University production, directed by Gerald Sullivan, designed by Clarence Blanchette, and costumed by John Keough.

3-7 A stylish modern production of Moliere. The setting is based on three-dimensional Renaissance wings and painted backdrop. Moliere's *The School for Husbands*. New York, 1933. Designed by Lee Simonson. Photo Vandamm.

desert with him. They separate forever, unable to achieve a workable relationship.

In a comedy of Moliere, the audience senses, and the characters sometimes do also, that each person must have absolute trust and respect for the other as an independent being or there can be no real human relations, only lies and deception. A century before Jefferson and half a century before Locke, Moliere was defining the basic equality of all human beings and the independence of every individual. His plays constitute a social declaration of independence, though his deep skepticism made him realize that full respect for independence is not often achieved.

The Golden Age of High Comedy

Moliere was a pioneer in the intricate maneuvers of high comedy, but it remained for the witty playwrights writing for a small group of London sophisticates in the years following the restoration of the monarchy after the rule of Oliver Cromwell to achieve the full realization of high comedy

3-8 Farcical deception becomes self-deception. *Dr. B. S. Black*, an adaptation of Moliere's *The Doctor in Spite of Himself*. Spelman College of Atlanta University production, adapted and directed by Carlton W. Molette II, designed by Louis Maza, costumed by Barbara Molette, and lighted by Charles Walker.

3-9 Comedy on the Restoration stage. A forestage almost as large as the Elizabethan stage was combined with Italian perspective scenery of wings and backdrop. Candles and oil lamps lit the audience almost as much as the actors. Notice the music box above the proscenium. Drawn by Ethelyn Pauley and Martha Sutherland.

in the union of two proud and independent people. In their plays, the comic crudeness of the unsophisticated characters and the comic wiliness of the fops and giddy women are foils for the maturity of one central couple, who learn to play the roles of free, well-adjusted adults, discarding their masks of hostility and caution for the joys of love and partnership.

The characters in Restoration comedy begin where most of Moliere's couples end, free from family restraints. They are free from serious political and economic affairs and ready to devote their wit and their leisure to the game of human relations. That game includes gossip, intrigue, flirtation, and a great deal of discussion of social behavior. To most Victorian readers and playgoers these gallants and ladies seemed artificial, if not downright wicked, but a few nineteenth-century writers defended them just because they were free from such important matters as morality and duty. Charles Lamb pictured the characters of Restoration comedy in a "Utopia of gallantry," removed from all responsibility, and William Hazlitt was delighted by their sparkling uselessness.

The early twentieth century regarded Restoration society as artificial because it enjoyed dressing up, showing off, and expressing both love

3-10 A painted backdrop for a street scene for the 1936 revival of Wycherley's *The Country Wife*. The actors are on the shallow forestage next to the footlights, with chandeliers above and at the sides. Directed by Tyrone Guthrie and Gilbert Miller and designed by Oliver Messel. Photo Vandamm.

and hate with politeness and wit. Presumably it is more natural and honest in the twentieth century to be churlish and ill-mannered. Audiences in the 1920s praised Restoration comedy because it was naughty and disillusioned and made fun of the puritans, taking special delight in the rough escapades of William Wycherley's *The Country Wife* (1675), with its double-entendres and gleeful leers. Present-day audiences are not much disturbed by the naughtiness; on the contrary, they find in the best plays of Etherege, Congreve, and Sheridan important and subtle studies of the complex relationships of men and women. Taking sex for granted as an easy relationship, the best Restoration plays are concerned with the more difficult relations that involve pride and self-respect.

The first fully developed hero of Restoration comedy, Dorimant in Sir George Etherege's *The Man of Mode* (1676), samples the casual relations of sex, insisting on freedom and variety only because he is determined eventually to find someone who is not so casual. When one mistress tries to hold him by his vows of love, he casts her off with indignant irony, saying, "Constancy, at my years! You might as well expect the fruit the autumn ripens in the spring . . . youth has a long journey to go, madam: should I have set up my rest at the first inn I lodged at I should never have arrived at the happiness I now enjoy."

In such an atmosphere there would seem to be little hope of finding a woman of wit and spirit who could interest a man for a lifetime. But the dramatists created a vision of such a woman—rich, independent, proud, sophisticated, but unspoiled by the shallowness around her. William Congreve's Angelica in *Love for Love* (1695) accepts the world as it is and revels in the joy of the game. She insists, "Would anything but a madman complain of uncertainty? Uncertainty and expectation are the joys of life. Security is an insipid thing, and the overtaking and possessing of a wish, discovers the folly of the chase . . . the pleasure of a masquerade is done when we come to show our faces."

Love between two proud, intelligent, independent people is bound to be difficult, and a great many of the best comic scenes between lovers, from Shakespeare's Katherine and Petruchio and Beatrice and Benedick to the couples in the modern musicals *Oklahoma!* and *My Fair Lady,* are built on antagonism that is both exasperating and enjoyable. Congreve gave his most famous couple, Millamant and Mirabell of *The Way of the World* (1700), several encounters where gaiety ripples in the very words and rhythm of the scene. For more than two centuries famous actors have interpreted these roles, and in 1976 at Stratford, Ontario, Maggie Smith as Millamant made the haughty lady glow and the lines sparkle. But the most famous stage duelists in love are Sir Peter and Lady Teazle in Richard Brinsley Sheridan's *The School for Scandal* (1777), which is also frequently revived. For all Lady Teazle's high spirits, she is very fond of her gruff old husband, and for all his anger with her, he finds her irresistible when her fiery temper is up. Though she bests him in battle, he thoroughly enjoys it: "There is great satisfaction in quarreling with her, and I think she never appears to such advantage as when she is doing everything in her power to plague me." Like his high-comedy descendant, Henry Higgins, of Shaw's *Pygmalion* and the musical version *My Fair Lady,* Sir Peter has much to learn in order to be a better husband. He must learn a little humility and gain a sense of humor. He does finally laugh at himself in one of the funniest scenes in the play. When he discovers his wife behind a screen in the rooms of the young man he had thought perfect, he is outraged. The social gossips, of course, tease him without mercy, and he drives them from the house in a lively low-comedy scene. But when his two close friends begin to laugh at him, he cannot drive them out but must laugh at his own predicament, if grimly. After that he begins to see his wife in a new light, and he forgives her.

Social Comedy in the Twentieth Century

After Sheridan in the eighteenth century, English high comedy was largely superseded by sentimental comedy and made no other notable appearance until the 1890s, when Oscar Wilde shocked and amused the public with his shrewd, witty plays, one of which, *The Importance of Being Earnest,* was mentioned earlier. George Bernard Shaw, too, in play after play showed idealistic people learning to be practical. In *Caesar and Cleopatra* the middle-aged Caesar teaches the young Queen Cleopatra how to manage people. Violet in *Man and Superman* will not let her young man defy his wealthy father by acknowledging her as his wife. "We can't afford it," she says. "You can be as romantic as you please about love, Hector; but you mustn't be romantic about money."

Shaw's great contribution was to widen the scope of high comedy beyond the personal relationships of lovers, parents, and friends to show characters involved in social, political, and philosophical problems. His *Major Barbara* starts as a drawing-room comedy of family relationships but moves out of the drawing room to a Salvation Army shelter to show Barbara's work in offering food and salvation to the poor, then to her father's factory as she decides that it is more important to offer a purpose in life to those who are no longer poor. In his witty discussion of poverty, wealth, power, and religion, Shaw anticipated by half a century the time when the world would try to use power to abolish poverty and money to help individuals find a higher spiritual life.

The most popular writer of high comedy in this century was the English author Noël Coward, who was also an excellent actor, director, and composer of musical plays. In the 1920s and 1930s, and into the 1940s, when high comedy was no longer a dominant form, he wrote sophisticated plays with witty dialogue, especially tracing the mixtures of anger and attraction in marital relationships. Several of his works, among them *Private Lives* (1930), *Design for Living* (1933), and *Blithe Spirit* (1941), have become comedy classics, frequently revived on the university or the professional stage, and a revue based on the musical works was a popular production in the early seventies.

After its great period of popularity in the 1920s, sophisticated comedy began to seem out of place in the modern world. In the 1930s the two extremes of fascism and communism were threatening by revolution and war to put an end to democracy and the liberal tradition. A fanatical devotion to some great cause seemed to be the order of the day, and those

3-11 Thoughtful laughter. Complex human relations are involved with love, death, art, and medicine. Shaw's *The Doctor's Dilemma*, with Raymond Massey. New York, 1941. Photo Vandamm.

who wanted civilized detachment or independence were lost. In 1934 Robert Emmet Sherwood, who had written delightful high comedies about ancient Rome and postwar Vienna, wrote a very effective play, *The Petrified Forest*, half comedy, half serious drama, about the death of a cultivated English liberal hitchhiking through the petrified forests of Arizona. The liberal, convinced that his urbane world is gone, invites the modern gangster to kill him, leaving his insurance to a young girl who wants to escape to Paris. S. N. Behrman wrote several drawing-room comedies in the thirties. When the war came, he tried to dramatize his hope of preserving the values of tolerance and detachment even in difficult times, but his very title, *No Time for Comedy*, shows his dilemma.

Americans have never felt completely at home in the parlor; they are more apt to work out their social problems on the job. Hence American social comedy is often more melodramatic, full of intrigue and action, or more satiric than the London tradition. For four decades American audiences looked to George S. Kaufman and his several collaborators for satiric comment on new fads and interests. Though usually quite ridiculous, the Kaufman characters were treated with sympathy and affection. Most memorable are the lovable American screwballs in *You Can't Take It With You*, first presented in 1936 and revived many times, notably on the New York stage in 1965. The play was also a favorite for college productions in the country's bicentennial year.

New and Old Elements in High Comedy

To the revolutionary youth of the 1950s and 1960s, high comedies seemed leftovers from a different age. In the midst of racial conflict, antiwar demonstrations, and campus confrontations, what possibility was there for toleration, mutual respect, playful wit, or friendly teasing? Yet looking back we can see that the elements of a new high comedy have appeared. Like the high comedy of the seventeenth century, the new form is born out of bitter disillusionment, out of the blackest despair. But where the tradition inherited from seventeenth-century London and Paris was reticent, indirect, and polite in its manner, the new American form is frank, cruel, and devastating.

Several of Edward Albee's plays are cases in point. There is so much hatred and vituperation in *Who's Afraid of Virginia Woolf?* (1962) that nobody called it a comedy. The London critic Kenneth Tynan scolded the actors and the audience for the laughter. The movie version, with moonlight scenes and many closeups of the serious faces of Richard Burton and Elizabeth Taylor, drew less laughter. The movie camera often softens comic effects by forcing the audience to identify with one character at a time. When the author directed a revival in 1975, the two, three, or four people playing at bitter games and scoring verbal hits provoked vigorous laughter. In the course of their games, all four characters learn more about themselves and learn to accept their limitations.

The play is saved for comedy by the wit and the underlying tenderness, troubled but genuine. These are lacking in the vicious verbal encounters of the bitter couple in John Osborne's *Watch It Come Down* (1976), and the result is not comedy but painful "demolition," as the title of the play implies.

Albee's *A Delicate Balance* (1966) is even more obviously a high comedy than *Virginia Woolf*. It begins on a note of mystery as another couple arrives to stay indefinitely, fleeing a nameless terror that suddenly drove them from their home. But the host and hostess have their own

3-12 High comedy. A middle-aged couple—the woman at far left and the man at far right—try to maintain their integrity despite the threatening demands of family and friends. Albee's *A Delicate Balance.* New York, 1966. Photo Alix Jeffry.

family problems. The wife's alcoholic sister is staying with them, and later their daughter arrives, having failed in her fourth marriage. The house is too crowded, and when conflict bursts out, all are forced to consider the limits of people's demands on one another. The main concern is that of most high comedies: how to relate to other people and still respect both their independence and one's own.

In *Seascape* (1974) Albee gave high comedy a delightful touch of fantasy to make a comment on marriage and evolution, animal and human. He starts with a middle-aged couple as they picnic near the shore, half longing to give up the effort of civilization and go back under the sea, where, they say, it all began. They confront a couple of lizard-like creatures just emerging from the sea to begin their evolutionary climb. When the sea creatures see what pain and confusion civilization can be, they start back to the sea, but the human couple persuade them, and themselves, that no one can turn back.

Most high comedies have been written about contemporary people, though we regularly present the high comedies of the past in period costume. But in 1966 James Goldman wrote an excellent high comedy about twelfth-century England. *The Lion in Winter* has been quite popular in colleges, and it provided brilliant movie roles for Peter O'Toole and

3-13 New patterns of high comedy. Conflicts of love, hatred, and rivalry in a context of important public events. Katharine Hepburn as Eleanor of Aquitaine and Peter O'Toole as Henry II in *The Lion in Winter*, 1968. Avco Embassy Pictures Corp.

Katharine Hepburn as King Henry II and his queen, Eleanor of Aquitaine. The rivalry and hatred between the two, who love each other, is expressed in the bitter language of a ruthless modern age.

Even race relations can occasionally be seen in their comic aspects. Understandably, most race plays have emphasized strong, uncompromising conflict. But a note of genuine high comedy appeared in Ossie Davis's *Purlie Victorious* (1961), which satirizes the stereotype of old Captain Cotchipee and indulges in the verbal fantasy of bloody retaliation. In the vein of true comedy, it assumes that the two races will somehow learn to get along. While the romantics would try to ignore or obliterate differences, Davis's characters, by acting out their conflicts in play, learn to accept their differences and to regard one another with humor and respect. The musical version of 1970, called *Purlie*, celebrated that wisdom in song.

Neil Simon, the most prolific and the most popular American writer of comedy of our day, won his first successes with light farcical comedies. In *Barefoot in the Park* (1963) his struggling young couple are trying to hide their urban difficulties from conventional small-town parents. Simon has since veered to high comedy and expanded its scope into the problems of older people, into relations other than sex that bind people together. In *The Odd Couple* (1965) two men, divorced and lonely, try to keep house together and fail as miserably as any married couple. In *The Sunshine Boys* (1972) two very successful partners in a vaudeville team had suppressed their anger at their uncongeniality until they had exploded apart years ago. The attempt to bring them together again for a nostalgic revival of their famous act fails. In *California Suite* (1976), a group of four playlets, Simon shows, among other situations, a divorced couple still tied together in concern over their daughter and still feeling much of their former love. They attack each other with vituperation almost as sharp as that of Albee's characters, not only hitting back at each other with angry wit but torturing each other with all the greater accuracy since they know each other's weaknesses. They are also hitting back at the infirmities and failures of middle age—hysterectomies and prostate trouble, the decline of sexual and creative ability.

The English playwright Simon Gray has been compared to Noël Coward, but he is less direct in presenting his characters, some of them sophisticated but none as witty as Coward's. In *Otherwise Engaged* (1976) a man who has planned to spend an afternoon alone listening to his favorite records is beset by visitors making emotional disclosures and insistent demands. Each scene is the more amusing because the visitor's unreasonableness is set off by the host's calm response. When his wife returns and he learns that she is leaving him, he is not visibly moved. At the end he is again preparing to listen to his records. But his aloofness is disquieting. Is he indifferent? Is he really unmoved? What lies behind the calm exterior? The enigmatic quality of the play is not characteristic of high comedy in general, but it is in keeping with many recent treatments of personality on the stage.

In all its forms, comedy remains the great favorite of stage and screen. Farce is the staple of what the English director Peter Brook admiringly calls the ''Rough Theatre,'' the truly popular theatre. And the spirited independence, zest, and wit of high comedy ensure that form's lasting appeal to the audience that knows ''the way of the world.''

4

The Theatre
of Romance

ROMANTIC CHARM WITH A MODERN
FLAIR. A MODEL BY MING CHO LEE FOR
ROSSINI'S *BARBER OF SEVILLE*. JUILLIARD
OPERA THEATRE PRODUCTION. PHOTO
NATHAN RABIN.

Some people go to the theatre not for a serious reflection on man's destiny, for a picture of the world they live in, or even for a laugh, but for color and romance. They want exotic scenery, music and dance, and a bittersweet story of long ago or far away. They want to escape from the petty, the dull, the usual, to find release from daily frustration. They want to identify with the romantic hero, who does big things, makes exciting journeys, takes great risks. Where the ordinary man fritters his life away in thwarted impulses, tentative efforts, irrelevancies and delays, the romantic hero lives life to the fullest. He makes no compromises, appeases no one. Every issue is clear and of the utmost importance. Chance brings him great opportunities, and he takes full advantage of them. In defeat he goes down fighting, sure that his cause is just and that some day the evil will be overcome.

It is an axiom of the romantic theatre that no one is tongue-tied or clumsy. Romeo pours forth his soul to Juliet in the inspired verse of Shakespeare or in gorgeous operatic song. Gravity and other laws of the universe are ignored as skaters swing around curves and leap over obstacles with complete power over space. Ballet dancers rise into the air and land again without a suggestion of weight or muscle. In the movie *South Pacific*, Lieutenant Cable, a perfect swimmer, pursues his lovely native girl into the water and under the water with a freedom known only in dreams. To see a romantic play is to forget the limitations of the material world and move into a world with laws and ideals of its own.

Development of the Romantic Ideals

The two great ideals of romance, developed in the Middle Ages and still of primary importance in our concepts of what man should be, are the ideals of the knight-champion and the knight-lover. Feudalism created an ideal of a knight loyal to his lord and ready at all times to fight to protect the castle. The Crusades developed that champion into the knight-errant, ready to recover the Holy Land from the infidel or to go about rescuing innocent maidens and the poor or persecuted. In a sacred ceremony, he dedicated his sword and himself to the protection of the weak and the endless fight against evil.

Under the influence of Eleanor of Aquitaine, who was for a time Queen of France, then for many years Queen of England, the troubadour poets created another version of the knight that has had even more influence on the modern world, that of the knight in love. It is no exaggeration to say that the modern concept of passionate, dedicated, transforming love was the invention of the poets of the twelfth and thirteenth centuries. Before that time, love had been a youthful adventure or a family partnership. Now the worship of woman became a new religion, with the woman on a pedestal and the man an abject slave at her feet. This "Court of Love" game, which gives us the words *courting* and *courtship* as well as *courtesy*, puts love at the center of man's life. It is one of the major attempts made to shift the emphasis in the relations between the sexes from the physical to the spiritual. It calls for the woman to be very difficult and distant. The young man gets one glimpse of her beauty and is transformed forever. He shows a long list of medical symptoms—he can't eat or sleep, he grows pale, he wanders in melancholy groves by moonlight. He may write poems for his lady or serenade her, but he actually sees little of her. She sets him difficult tasks that may take years to perform. Sometimes he pictures her as so far removed from the real world that it would be a sacrilege to win her and touch her. It may be better to yearn unhappily for the ideal than to desecrate it by turning it into reality. That dilemma has greatly complicated the psychology of love to the present day, but it has been a great inspiration to romantic art; melancholy, absence, and longing make for excellent songs.

Romantic love was invented outside of marriage. It was assumed that the lady was already married to someone else; hence the attachment must be secret. There seemed to be no chance for real love in marriage. By the strict doctrine of the medieval church, all passion, even in marriage, was a sin; marriage in feudal times was an alliance of convenience, not of choice, while true love must be free and spontaneous—a gift, not a bond or duty. It was not until three hundred years later, in Shakespeare's time, when the rising middle class was developing new ideals, that it became possible to think of romantic love in marriage. *Romeo and Juliet*, written about 1594, was the first great poetic drama to celebrate the union of love with marriage.

Dedication to love and adventure made Shakespeare's plays the first great romantic dramas. The historical plays have many romantic elements. They are full of wars and rebellions, sieges of castles, challenges and duels, threats and denunciations. There are songs and clowns, and intimate scenes alternate with splendid processions and coronations. The whole range of human experience is shown with magnificent costumes and pageantry. Shakespeare's Richard III is a scheming villain, wicked enough for a child's tale of adventure, and a young champion kills him in the end. The poetic young King Richard II is defeated and killed, but the idealistic Prince Hal, leaving his tavern revelry, comes to the rescue of his father and becomes the successful warrior-king, Henry V, who conquers

France and returns with the French princess as his bride. Shakespeare added characterization and ironies that transcend the basic plots, but one finds in his plays the eternal themes of romance.

Shakespeare's comedies are set in the faraway, never-never land of romance: the enchanted, moonlit woods of *A Midsummer Night's Dream,* where the Fairy King and Queen hold their revels and the mischievous Puck helps delude foolish mortals; the Forest of Arden; the seacoast of Illyria or Bohemia; the fabulous orchards, gardens, and courts of an Italy Shakespeare had never seen. There are handsome princes and charming ladies, wicked usurpers and envious villains spreading terrible lies, powerful magicians and magic herbs, long-lost brothers found again, and statues that come to life. It is a bittersweet world where "parting is such sweet sorrow," where "the course of true love never did run smooth," and where "present mirth hath present laughter" because "youth's a thing will not endure." It is a world of accident, chance, evil, and delusion, where everything is transitory and beauty and virtue pass too quickly. But it is also a world of faith, love, and hope, of noble purpose and high adventure.

Romance in the Modern Theatre

After the French Revolution, a new romantic movement gave fresh impetus to the old formulas and introduced new themes and characters. Following Rousseau's exaltation of the free man, the hero became a rebel against a corrupt society, either stirring up wars of liberation or seeking out high mountains or deep caves where he could question the meaning of the universe. Goethe's Faust most fully expressed the rebellious spirit of the time—the release of irrepressible yearning, the rejection of old rules, and the angry attack on all the institutions of society. Faust is torn between God and the Devil, between day and night, between creation and destruction. Magic is only one of the mysterious, irrational forces he appeals to. He wants all experience, but when he gains the love of Marguerite he destroys her and feels more lonely than ever in his guilt. In poetry, fiction, and drama, the rebel dominated the imagination. Lord Byron, most daring and turbulent of the English poets, created heroes in his own image, proud and rebellious, maimed and tortured by secret guilt.

The best solution for the romantic rebel, hemmed in by restrictive society or torn by inner conflict and self-doubt, was to embark on some great adventure far away from home. Before the theme of the Crusades had faded, the discovery of America opened up to Europeans an even greater adventure to the west. The typical motivation for leaving home is traced in a nineteenth-century novel by Emily Brontë, *Wuthering Heights,* dramatized in 1939 in a movie still popular, starring the handsome, youthful couple Laurence Olivier and Merle Oberon. The tension of resentment builds up in the poor boy as he watches from the window of his attic room in the barn to see the girl he loves escorted by the rich boy to a party he is not invited to. As he watches the party from outside, he determines to show the world his true worth. He lives to come back from America, rich and famous, to humiliate them all.

As explorers in the wilderness of a strange land, as settlers determined to start a new society, better and freer than the old, as pioneers to take and possess a whole continent, Americans have seen themselves in the romantic sweep of history, and history has been one of the strongest interests in romantic drama. Or the great adventure might be a creative challenge: to build a church or a school, to find a new cure for a disease, to capture the essence of a scene in a painting, the meaning of an experience in a poem or a play. The romantic movement glamorized the dedication of the artist. Out of the anguish of our own frustration we dream of a free, intense, romantic deed. Romantic heroes may be very much alike, with little specific characterization, but put a good-looking actor in the role and he becomes the incarnation of our romantic dreams.

Melodrama and the Romantic Play

The melodrama was the poor man's romantic play. It simplified the complex hero of the early nineteenth century, the romantic rebel with both good and bad impulses, by dividing him into two characters—a spotless hero and a deep-dyed villain. It kept the guilty hero but made the guilt false, a lie invented by the villain. Sometimes the hero himself thought he was guilty, but always at the end he was cleared by the proper papers or the villain's confession. As its name implies, the melodrama used music, not only songs and dances but background music, to accompany the emotional scenes and sometimes to set off each movement, gesture, or speech. Often long sequences were performed in pantomime, and when a group action led to a climax, the tableau would be held still for several seconds while the drums rolled. The most exciting sequence was the chase, as the heroine fled from the villain—out windows, over roofs, off bridges, through fires, floods, earthquakes, explosions, and train wrecks. To thrill the spectators, the old wing-and-backdrop scenery inherited from the Renaissance and the seventeenth century had to keep moving and make room for all kinds of platforms, steps, towers, trap doors, and trick effects. Burlesque revivals of old-fashioned melodramas amuse sophisti-

4-1 Romantic melodrama in Russia. The nobleman abducts a girl from the poor man's house. The State Dramatic Theatre production, Leningrad, 1832. From Derjavine's *A Century of the State Theatre.*

cated audiences today by exaggerating the trite sentiments and expressing all emotions in a few patterned gestures. Nineteenth-century actors had a far greater range of gestures and were completely convincing to their devoted fans. The melodrama built one of the widest popular audiences in history.

Throughout the nineteenth century the romantic play, sometimes mixed with melodrama, dominated the popular theatre. *Cyrano de Bergerac* (1897), by the French dramatist Edmond Rostand, summed up many of the best features of the romantic play, using poetry, historical costume, duels, serenades, battles, and crowds. Cyrano is a brave and dashing French soldier of the time of Richelieu and the Three Musketeers. He is endowed with unlimited strength, ability, and wit, but he has one great defect, an enormous nose. His soul is full of love for his cousin, Roxane, but he dares not speak to her of love because he is mortally afraid of being laughed at for his grotesque nose. When he finds that Roxane is enamored of Christian, a handsome new cadet in his company, he hides his own feeling and composes for Christian the letters that win her, even whispering of romance under her balcony until Christian can climb up and take her kiss. After Christian is killed in battle, Cyrano still sustains Roxane's delusion, and only years later, as he is dying, does she learn that it was Cyrano's mind and soul she loved. He bravely defies his enemies to the last: "What's that you say? Hopeless?—Why, very well. But a man does not fight merely to win. No—no—better to know one fights in vain!"

Romance in the Movies

As movies developed early in the twentieth century, they naturally followed the patterns of romance and melodrama that had been established for the stage. So many films were concerned with romantic themes that for more than three decades Hollywood was truly "the city of dreams."

Of the many romantic movies based on American history, the most rewarding have been set in the Old South—the land of cotton and magnolia blossoms, Greek-columned mansions, and the glamor of a lost cause. The first film epic, which established the importance of the art of the movies, was *The Birth of a Nation* (1915). It gave a wide sweeping view of the South during the Civil War and the Reconstruction period that followed. It is rarely shown now, because its treatment of the former slaves shames both whites and blacks. It has spectacle on the grand scale, with armies in battle and the wild rides of the Ku Klux Klan, pure women and brave men of both North and South, tender meetings and farewells, and encounters with villainous carpetbaggers.

One of the most impressive romantic spectacles ever filmed was *Gone With the Wind,* produced in 1939 and regularly shown every few years since. It has spectacle enough to please anybody: plantation scenes, battle scenes, hundreds of wounded on stretchers lined in rows at the railroad station, the burning of the city of Atlanta. But beyond this, the characters are treated in depth and perfectly acted, with Clark Gable as Rhett Butler, the English actor Leslie Howard as the Confederate officer, and sharply contrasted characterizations by Vivien Leigh as the calculating, ruthless, anti-heroine Scarlett O'Hara, and Olivia de Haviland as the sweet, compliant wife—all romantic characters set in changing tensions and conflicts.

A movie that runs even more true to the best type of stage romance, with complex characterization and an anguished, yearning hero, is the French film *Children of Paradise* (1945). It tells the story of a famous nineteenth-century mime who endures the brutal street life of Paris and suffers a hopeless love for a beautiful actress. The picture has become a classic of the screen.

Although romantic spectacle continued into the 1960s and 1970s, especially in grade B movies, it seemed routine and uninspired as the interest of the audience turned to rebellious youth and psychedelic states of consciousness. But in 1975–76, *Barry Lyndon* showed that the old romantic formula held as much vitality as ever. Produced in stunning color, the film took us back to a glamorous eighteenth century as a dashing hero was leaving an unhappy home in Ireland to meet strange adventures in picturesque scenes in England and on the continent. Here were duels, highway robbery, professional gambling, battles, hairbreadth escapes, imprisonment, disguises, all set in beautiful landscapes, farmers' cottages, and genuine palaces. The colorful period costumes and elegant manners made a sharp contrast to the casual carelessness of dress and behavior today. More sad and less heroic is the wanderer in François Truffaut's *The Story of Adele H.* (1975), based on the real story of a daughter of Victor Hugo. The mysterious Adele moves in her daze of dreams and obsessions through scenes on the Island of Jersey, in Nova Scotia, and in Barbados, always pursuing the lover who scorns her, until she no longer knows where she is wandering—a romantic image of helpless humanity lured by the unattainable.

Sheer melodrama, along with the less sensational romantic play, found a happy home on the screen. Today, in the movies or on television, it has the same appeal it had on the nineteenth-century stage. By setting a good hero against a wicked villain, it captures the most elemental sympathies. Whether the villain is a cattle rustler, a city gangster, or a Nazi or Communist spy plotting to blow up the capital, we know that the hero must come quickly to the rescue.

The great terror-disaster movies of the seventies have involved the same simple melodramatic fears, as men put aside their everyday affairs to be plunged into some holocaust—the upheaval in *Earthquake*, the man-eating shark in *Jaws*, the burning skyscraper of *The Towering Inferno*, the exploding airship in *The Hindenburg*. *The Sound of Music*, the great money-maker of the 1960s, though it had good songs and some dances, depended basically on the simple plot of an old-fashioned melodrama—armies of wicked Nazis, with spies and traitors in the fort, an exciting escape, and a wild flight over the mountains to freedom.

Grand Opera

The most highly perfected forms of romantic theatre are to be seen today in the performances of nineteenth-century grand opera and ballet. Extremely difficult, they require years of rigorous training. Although singer and dancer must give some illusion of spontaneity, everything is planned and drilled in endless hours of practice. Both the large orchestra and the performers are controlled in performance by the conductor, as the music dictates to the dancer the exact mood and each change of pace and to the singer, every inflection and nuance of phrasing and timing.

Both opera and ballet began in the aristocratic European courts of the sixteenth and seventeenth centuries. Opera began as an experiment in reviving Greek tragedy, with a stylized, intoned speech called *recitative.* In the seventeenth century the recitative came to be used for dialogue, while passionate *arias,* accompanied by an orchestra, were added for solos, duets, and even large ensembles. When dances were added and scene designers learned how to make spectacular scene changes, grand opera became the most impressive of all Baroque entertainments. The plots were as magnificent as the music and settings. Great heroes struggled with Saracens or demonic magicians until Jupiter himself descended with a heavenly host to reestablish order in the world.

Mozart and Italian Opera

In the eighteenth century the middle class began to go to the opera and to demand less grandiose music and heroes with whom they could identify. Both farce and sentimental scenes were added. At the end of the eighteenth century, Mozart was able to combine all the forms, new and old, comic and sentimental, raising opera to an expressive power it had never known. For many music lovers today, the three best Mozart operas are the high points of all music. *Don Giovanni* is an amazing achievement. The old Don Juan story is about seduction, murder, and damnation and builds to a tremendous scene when the statue of the murdered father comes to take the Don into the open jaws of hell. Mozart lets a comic servant dominate much of the opera, and his Don keeps a brash cynicism almost to the end, yet the whole range of comic and serious feelings is expressed in the most charming, graceful music. In *The Marriage of Figaro* Mozart took a fairly serious French comedy, deepened the feelings of the characters, even the rake-seducer and his lonely, sad countess, and built up to a wonderful finale of lyric self-revelation and forgiveness in what may be the most perfect blend of light and sentimental comedy ever created. In his last opera, *The Magic Flute,* Mozart included an even wider range of characters and emotions in a charming allegory. One of the gayest of all clowns, the bird-catcher Papageno, accompanies a young knight in search of ideal love and virtue. They overcome the wicked Queen of the Night, liberate the girl, and are initiated into Masonic rites of purification.

Although most operas are too grandiose to film well—the camera and microphone seem to bring us far too close to the singers—Ingmar Bergman's film of *The Magic Flute* (1975) was a great success. He used the beautiful eighteenth-century royal theatre at Drottningholm just outside

4-2 Grand opera. A spectacular setting that spans the old Roman sports amphitheatre in Verona. The triumphal scene in Verdi's *Aida*, 1971. Designed and costumed by Giulio Coltelucci. Photo © by Pagliarani Andrea/Opera News.

Stockholm and showed the audience listening to the overture and seeing the eighteenth-century scenery, then gradually led the action out into a wide range of movie settings in the same style as the theatre, using many closeups of his attractive young singers.

Mozart perfected the Italian form of opera, enabling highly skilled singers to show off their voices in a wide range of songs—solos, duets, recitative. The songs and recitative dialogue combined to tell a dramatic story. After Mozart, nineteenth-century composers had only to set to music the fashionable historical romances and melodramas of the day. For most opera fans, romantic theatre means the Italian opera of the nineteenth and early twentieth centuries, especially the works of Giuseppe Verdi. Though he wrote for opera singers, his songs sound good on the concert stage. He used the conventional forms the audience was familiar with, but his arias are extremely dramatic; they create character, express the inner emotions, change dynamically from one part of a song to another, and drive the drama forward from beginning to end.

Most impressive of Verdi's operas is *Aida*, written for the opening of the Suez Canal and first performed in 1871. Great spectacle is possible in the story of an Egyptian princess and an Ethiopian slave girl, both in love with the triumphant young general. There are large processions of military display and solemn conclaves of chanting priests, then midnight love trysts and betrayals in the lush moonlight on the banks of the Nile. Yet there are many passionate, melodic arias for solos, duets, and ensembles. In contrast, Verdi's *La Traviata,* also a favorite, is much less spectacular, indeed almost intimate. It is based on Dumas's novel *La Dame aux camélias,* or *Camille,* about an actual courtesan who fell in love, left the gay social world to join her lover, and died of tuberculosis. At first audiences did not like the opera. A realistic story in contemporary dress, it had no romantic distance. Only when it was revived years later and set in the historic past was it acceptable. In the transformation from familiar to historical, spectacle has crept in. In the production of the Santa Fe summer opera season in 1976, the splendid settings on the huge stage almost overwhelmed the actors. Today Italian opera is a great romantic spectacle of the past, sung by virtuoso singers, with elaborate, romantic scenic effects, showing us a world far removed from our everyday lives.

Wagnerian Opera

It is the other operatic tradition, the German opera created by Richard Wagner, that has had a direct influence on twentieth-century theatre. Wagner, in the middle of the nineteenth century, raised the ideal of a serious, romantic, superhuman story to its highest peak. He disliked the use of a "set song" with a definite beginning and end, which was too much like a concert piece that could be sung out of its context. His ideal was a real drama that combined all the arts, a *Gesamtkunstwerk,* or composite work of art, which moved from the opening of an act through to the end with no place for a pause. The result was a continuous, uninterrupted symphonic poem. He enlarged and enriched the orchestra and wrote the vocal parts as single strands woven with the instruments of the orchestra into a complex web. Instead of separate arias, he developed his symphonic poem with short, bold melodies, called *leitmotifs,* or leading motifs. Each motif is associated with a particular character or idea—an ingenious way of making the music carry the story and even the inner drama. A character's motif is heard not only when he is speaking but also when someone else is speaking or thinking of him.

Of Wagner's operas, the most impressive accomplishment is *The Ring of the Nibelungs,* a series of four long operas tracing a legendary story of northern gods contending with men and dwarfs for a magic hoard of gold deep in the waters of the Rhine. It includes the story of Siegfried, who kills the dragon and wakes the princess who has been sleeping within a wall of magic fire. With the rippling waters of the Rhine, the murmuring of the forest, the magic fire, the birds and rainbows, the mists around Valhalla, and the mountain castle of the gods, there is enough descriptive music to hold an audience for hours, watching the display of changing scenery, lighting, and grouping. Yet there are also joys and sorrows, and the strong-willed conflict of superhuman beings. For even the gods are swept along by passions greater than themselves. At the end Valhalla sinks, carrying the old gods down in flame and water to make way for a new world.

Some people find the highest achievement of Wagner's operas not in the complex mythology of the *Ring* but in the simple love story of Tristan and Isolde, perhaps the most powerful drama of passionate yearning ever written. Isolde is the King's bride, but she is bound to Tristan by a love potion. Their moonlight love scene is interrupted by the King and Tristan is wounded. On a lonely island the dying Tristan looks back on his life and comes to a new realization of the spiritual meaning of love. Isolde arrives and they sing their *Liebestod*, "love in death."

Wagner has had a great influence on the modern theatre both by his theoretical writing and his example; not only for particular reforms, such

4-3 Opera spectacle in the nineteenth century. Full romantic detail of trees, rocks, clouds, and sky painted on wings and backdrop, with some three-dimensional structures in the foreground. Wagner's *Götterdämmerung* at the Bayreuth Festival, 1876. Painting by J. Hoffman. Photo Richard Wagner Gedenkstätte der Stadt Bayreuth.

4-4 Modern emotions in opera. The helpless little man protests being treated as an object by a cruel, unfeeling world. Berg's *Wozzeck*. Teatro La Scala, Milan, 1971. Photo © by E. Riccagliani/Opera News.

as darkening the auditorium so that the audience could more completely lose themselves in the drama, but for the concept of total theatre, with all aspects of the production coordinated, and for the concept of an inner life of the drama. This inner life is not the words or even the plot as conceived by the playwright, but a dynamic sequence, constantly surging in rhythmic waves from the beginning to the end. The actor must follow the inner sequence, and his words, tones, and movements, as well as the accompanying music and sound effects, must follow and express that surging rhythm. Adolphe Appia, in working out his approach to settings and lighting, followed the lead of Wagner and showed how, by means of changing plastic lighting, all the visual elements could follow the same inner life.

Romantic Dance

An even purer form of romance than opera is preserved in the ballet. No other form of art so directly expresses our simplest, most frequent daydreams. Nowhere else is reality so refined and idealized. Nowhere is the

4-5 Romantic charm in ballet. *The Nutcracker.* New York City Ballet, 1972. Photo Martha Swope.

human body more charmingly displayed. But the tights and the tutu, the precise movement so perfectly keyed to the music, and the soft lighting transform the erotic into romantic yearning. All is seen behind the veil of the imagination.

Ballet movements are abstracted from movements of real life—stepping, leaping, landing, kicking, turning—but they are carefully selected and simplified. In this ideal of beauty, charm, and dignity, the back is held rigid, the head high, the toes are turned out, and the feet and hands are limited to a few precise positions. Every movement begins and ends in a set pose. Only occasionally in the solo character parts does personality or emotion or even facial expression find a place. One of the pleasures of a good ballet is the exact duplication as a line of ballerinas, dressed alike, make exactly the same movements in unison, sequence, or opposition.

The Development of Ballet

Ballet has a tradition of more than four centuries and has gone through three major stages of development: the Renaissance courts gave it pattern and stateliness, the classic academies of the seventeenth and eighteenth centuries formulated its technique, and the romantic theatre of the nineteenth century gave it soul and drama. During the Renaissance it was practiced by the aristocrats themselves, who liked to dress up and act the parts of shepherds and nymphs or Greek gods and heroes. They liked a "classic" costume, derived from a soft, diaphanous "nymph" costume such as we see in Botticelli's famous painting *Primavera* ("Allegory of Spring"). During the seventeenth and eighteenth centuries ballet became more strictly disciplined, calling for systematic training in the five basic positions of the feet and the neat and elegant positions of the head and arms. The skirt was shortened to show the elaborate foot movements, and both men and women wore a stiff bodice or tunic.

But it was the nineteenth century that made ballet the perfect expression of romance. The main theme of romantic ballet is the irresistible lure of the ideal, which draws man away from the real, often to his destruction. In the first great romantic ballet, *La Sylphide* (1832), James, a young Scotsman, sits by the fire on his wedding day dreaming of an ethereal creature, a *sylphide,* who dances with him but always eludes him. At his wedding she snatches the ring and lures him out to dance on the moors. When he tries to catch her with a witch's scarf, she dies, leaving him to discover that his earthly bride has married another man. In *Giselle* (1841), the luring spirit is the ghost of a country girl who had killed herself when she discovered that her love was a prince and that he was engaged to a noblewoman. She tries to save the prince from the other ghosts, who lure

4-6

The ballet dancer as an ethereal being from the world of dreams. Marie Taglioni, who created the first of the diaphanous charmers in *La Sylphide* in 1832, is about to lure the Scotsman James away from the world of everyday reality. Dance Collection of the New York Public Library.

4-7 Romantic drama in ballet. The prince captures the Queen of the Swans. Martine van Hamel and Vladimir Gelvan in *Swan Lake*. Restaged by David Blair for the American Ballet Theatre, 1976. Photo Martha Swope.

men into the lake, but the Queen of the Wilis orders her to lead him into wilder and wilder dances. He tries to follow her to the grave, but dawn interrupts, the Wilis fade away, and he is found and consoled by his earthly love. In *Swan Lake* (1877), for which Tchaikovsky wrote such seductive music, the hero falls in love with the Queen of the Swans, maidens who are under the spell of a wicked magician. The two lovers finally plunge into the lake, thereby breaking the spell, and are seen in an enchanted bark, united forever in the world of the ideal. These romantic stories gave opportunities for both idealized folk and classical dance, with formal lines of dancers, solos, duets *(pas de deux)*, and both small groups and large, creating an ideal world of charming ladies with perfect discipline and control. To this day a new ballet dancer has not really arrived until he or she has won acclaim in a star role of one of the great romantic ballets of the nineteenth century.

A Rival: Modern Dance

Early in the twentieth century another form of dance appeared to challenge the supremacy of ballet. The way to "modern dance" was opened by Isadora Duncan, an Irish-American girl from San Francisco, who for the first three decades of the century had the artistic world of Europe at her feet—her bare feet. As a symbol of freedom and rebellion, she threw off the slippers, tight bodices, and fixed positions of the ballet and openly defied conventional morality in her personal life. With her remarkable personality, Isadora had a great influence on the public. On both continents she stimulated great interest in "aesthetic dancing," and "interpretive dancers" in loose robes and veils floated about while a piano or small orchestra played light classical music. But no one was able to follow her with a professional group.

A company of some stability was created by Ruth St. Denis and Ted Shawn, and in the 1910s and 1920s it trouped the country with carefully prepared numbers based on local color, many with Oriental or American Indian themes. But the "Denishawn" style of dance was still too pretty and soft for some younger members of the company. In the late 1920s three broke away and started in new directions of their own. They became the founders of modern dance. Martha Graham set up her own school and for four decades remained the top performer of modern dance. Together Doris Humphrey and Charles Weidman set up a school and a performing company. From the first, these studio companies were as dedicated as religious monks, ardently working out new techniques for achieving their new form of theatre. Although they used regular theatres for their few major performances, they broke away from the scenic patterns of the Broadway theatre as disdainfully as they broke away from the techniques of the classic ballet. They refused to wear pretty costumes and flaunted their stark leotards. Instead of picture scenery, they used drapes, blocks, and abstract shapes; instead of soft string orchestras and waltz tunes, they called for percussion and harsh dissonance; instead of lightness, daintiness, and delicate poses, they offered weight, struggle, and tension. At first their performances seemed as abstract as cubist paintings, as wild and ecstatic as primitive rituals, as heavy and straining as wrestling matches. They explored the natural relation of movement to breathing, to tension and relaxation, to work and play. They were especially interested in gravity—that natural force which ballet hides or denies—and hence in falls.

Martha Graham was the most distinctive figure. "Martha," as she was called, embodied the tight nervousness of modern life with her rigid lips, stiff hands, and stark costumes, her percussive movements, with sudden jerks, sharp accents, and short, broken gestures. She did falls, she stamped her feet and clapped her hands, she walked on her knees, she crouched, she sprang, she suddenly pulled her head between her knees. If Doris Humphrey was not so startling as Martha Graham, not so angular,

4-8 Extreme intensities in modern dance. Martha Graham and Merce Cunningham in *Letter to the World*, a dance interpretation of the life of Emily Dickinson, featuring some of her poems. Photo Barbara Morgan.

not so taut and neurotic, she was just as fresh in her search for free, natural movements. In 1931 the American movement was strengthened by the visit of the German dancer Mary Wigman, who in the bitter moods of pre-Hitler Germany had developed a more somber approach to dance—stark, demonic intensity, without dependence on music, story, or surface charm.

As soon as audiences got used to the new approach to movement, they realized that the modern dancers had much to say—about modern life, but most of all about modern feelings, about revolt and independence, sympathy for the struggling masses, the vital sweep of America, religious idealism, the half-hidden fears in the depths of the soul.

By the 1960s modern dance was no longer revolutionary and rivalry between the two forms of dance had ceased. Ballet had become more popular than ever, not only in New York but throughout the country, and modern dance also flourished in a variety of interpretations. Ballet influenced modern dance and modern dance influenced ballet, and blends of the two were common. In Chapter 8 we will see how both forms have enriched the new forms of theatre.

The Musical

For the last four decades the musical has been the principal form of romantic theatre in America. Most people have called it musical comedy, but it often carries such deep emotion, such rich characterization, and even so much serious thought, that it is more than just comedy. For London and Paris audiences, American musicals surpass those of all other countries and seem the most distinctive theatrical contribution of America. Borrowing from the sentimental Viennese operetta, from the satirical Parisian comic opera and revue, even from the English Christmas pantomime, and using ideas from vaudeville, music halls, and burlesque, Americans have created a form that catches the energy and dash, the combination of skepticism and faith, the naive heart on the sophisticated sleeve that is the active image of America. Until recently serious critics looked down on the musical, but finally they have come to recognize that when story, characters, music, dance, and spectacle are all integrated in a musical, it is one of the highest dramatic achievements of the modern age.

Song and Dance in the Musical

What is amazing is that the best musicals have unity and most of the songs and dances grow out of the plot and express what the characters are feeling but could not express in any other way. When Eliza in *My Fair Lady* at last begins to pronounce her vowels correctly, she turns her practice sentence about "the rain in Spain" into a tango, and she and her two teachers celebrate their triumph in a wild release that is one of the high points of the play.

A type of song that fits the musical well and that was used very wittily by Gilbert and Sullivan is the self-introduction. The same audience that wants a drama to be indirect and implicit—to be "natural"—is delighted when a character in a musical comes right out and tells in song who he is and what he thinks, as Sir Joseph Porter in *H.M.S. Pinafore* does on his first entrance:

> I am the monarch of the sea,
> The ruler of the Queen's Navee
> Whose praise Great Britain loudly chants,

followed by the chorus "and so do his sisters, and his cousins, and his aunts," and a frank recital of his indoor training for a naval career:

> When I was a lad I served a term
> As office boy to an attorney's firm.
> I cleaned the windows and I swept the floor
> And I polished up the handle of the big front door.
> I polished up the handle so carefulee
> That now I am the ruler of the Queen's Navee.

No musical is complete without its romantic love song. It may be as direct as "O, Rose Marie, I Love You" from *Rose Marie,* or it may be sung alone, as the nurse from Little Rock sings "I'm in Love with a Wonderful Guy" in *South Pacific* and Eliza sings "I Could Have Danced All Night" in *My Fair Lady*.

Between the individual songs the musical is shaped by the big production numbers at the beginning, the middle, and the end, with choruses of singers and crowds of dancers in picturesque formations, bright costumes, and colorful settings and lighting. Spectacle is a great pleasure in itself, but it can also create a sense of community and build a social and geographical background for the main story. Put together "There is Nothing Like a Dame" for the lusty American Seabees, "Bloody Mary" for the madam, "Bali Hai" for the exotic native girls, and "Dites-moi" for the French planter's children, and you have the whole background for Lieutenant Cable's sad love and Nellie Forbush's more hopeful love in *South Pacific*. Since Eliza and Higgins come together at the end of *My Fair Lady* in a quiet mood, there can be no big production number, but just before the end Eliza's father is the center of the noisy wedding celebration as he sings "Get Me to the Church on Time."

Since the first big American musical, *The Black Crook* (1866), which combined a noisy romantic melodrama with a bevy of ballet dancers, dance has been as important as music; but for a long time dances in musicals consisted mainly of well-drilled lines of brightly painted chorus girls stepping, kicking, and whirling, or prancing the can-can. But there has been a revolution in the twentieth century as choreographers have absorbed both ballet and modern dance and have learned to integrate the dance into the plot and style of the whole show. A number of shows have been directed by the choreographers. Some ballet scenes appeared in the 1930s, but for the general public, the first real ballet that seemed completely right and overwhelmingly effective was Agnes de Mille's in *Oklahoma!* in 1943. There was dance throughout the play, reinforcing the cheerful, open-air songs. But the high point of the show was the dream ballet. Laurey's fears that she had been too independent with Curly and

4-9 Modern street violence danced to music. Bernstein's *West Side Story*. New York, 1957. Choreographed by Jerome Robbins. Photo Fred Fehl.

had become too involved with the dangerous Jud were acted out in the ballet. Here were beautiful dancing, lovely music, costumes, and lighting based clearly on the main characters and emotions of the play. After *Oklahoma!* Agnes de Mille was in great demand and a more serious type of dancing—ballet or modern—was recognized as a major part of show business. An even closer integration of dance and drama was achieved in *West Side Story* (1957), conceived and directed by the dancer Jerome Robbins.

Two American dancers, Fred Astaire and Gene Kelly, who began dancing in musicals in New York, Astaire in the 1920s and Kelly in the 1940s, found their best work in films. They were able to blend easily from dialogue into song and dance, closely integrating the song and dance into drama. For Astaire the camera caught just the right amount of movement, closely framing his solo beginnings and moving backward ahead of him, then expanding to include the larger ensembles. The simple popular songs and Astaire's own brand of popular dance—part ballroom, part theatrical tap and soft-shoe—fitted well his light, sophisticated style of comedy. Gene Kelly danced the entire drama of *An American in Paris* (1951) to the music of George Gershwin, with Paris streets for his stage in much of the film. Both Astaire and Kelly show up extremely well in the examples of musical comedies of the past shown in MGM's two nostalgic selections

4-10 A musical about dancers that is mostly dance. Bennett's *A Chorus Line*. New York, 1975. Photo Martha Swope.

from musical films of the past: *That's Entertainment* (1974) and *That's Entertainment Part 2* (1976).

Dancing is both the subject and the form in *A Chorus Line*, the theatre's surprise sensation of 1975–76. The dance director for a new musical asks each of the young people trying out not only to dance but to speak briefly about himself, giving us a cross section of youthful hopes and ambitions. Only two characters are given much story—a lonely, gay boy and the ex-wife of the director, out of a job, hoping to make a comeback by starting again in the chorus line. Though *A Chorus Line* had a very slight story, the situation of young people trying, against odds, to make careers on the stage had great appeal, and the dance routines were performed with such zest and freshness that both young and older audiences responded with enthusiasm.

The Musical Celebration of America

Above all, the musical is a celebration of America, perhaps the best celebration we have. *Show Boat* (1927) is a picture of mid-America of the nineteenth century, with its color, its gambling spirit and quick success, its restless changes and disrupted family life—a picture made sharper by its background of Negro workers and mulatto girls. One of the brightest shows of the 1930s was *Of Thee I Sing*, which opened at the end of 1931 and continued through the Roosevelt-Hoover campaign of 1932. A sharp but good-natured thrust at American elections, George S. Kaufman's satire is distinctively American. It points up imperfections with the utmost clarity, yet with that amused indulgence which makes fanatical reformers despair of America's ever reaching perfection. To show a presidential election being run as a beauty contest, campaign oratory being spiced up with wrestling, and nine Supreme Court justices hopping into a football huddle to pronounce on the sex of the President's child, is to remind Americans, as Aristophanes reminded the ancient Athenians, that a pompous politician can be as self-serving as anyone else. George Gershwin's music, alternately charming and raucous, emphasizes the irreverence and the satire.

In 1935 the great Negro folk "opera," *Porgy and Bess*, brought together a number of traditions. Dorothy and DuBose Heyward created the story of a gentle cripple, Porgy, who wins the trollop Bess from the strong man only to have her lured away by Sportin' Life, the high-stepping dope peddler from Harlem. At the end Porgy leaves home with only his goat cart to search the world for his woman. George Gershwin studied the group rhythms and melodies of the Gullah Negroes and produced the first operatic music that seemed authentically American. His songs express the

4-11 Local color in a folk opera. The main action is reinforced by the acting and singing of the chorus. In this picturesque setting every window is an acting area. Heyward and Gershwin's *Porgy and Bess*. New York, 1935. Photo Vandamm.

tenderness of love, a cheerful defiance in "I Got Plenty o' Nuttin'," a humorous reflection on Biblical stories in "It Ain't Necessarily So," and, most powerfully of all, the fears, amusements, laments, and prayers of the crowd. The opera is a celebration of American regionalism and a farewell to it, but, like any classic, it has lasting power. The revival of the show in 1976–77, as a grand opera, with all the dialogue sung as Gershwin wrote it, was a popular success in both Houston and New York.

The top musicals of the forties—the decade of giants like *Oklahoma!*, *Carousel*, *Annie Get Your Gun*, *Finian's Rainbow*, and *South Pacific*— included the sorrows of separation and death, but even when they were set in picturesque, faraway places, they celebrated American strength and faith, that great "willingness of the heart" that has always seemed so peculiarly American. And the old-fashioned, brassy *The Music Man* and the almost completely operatic *The Most Happy Fella* of the 1950s continued the tradition of big, energetic productions set in the romantic America of the past. As for the West, *Annie Get Your Gun* and *Paint Your Wagon* make most television and movie Westerns seem pale and adolescent by comparison.

America as the dream of European immigrants was dramatized in *Fiorello!* (1959) and *Fiddler on the Roof* (1964). *Fiorello!* is set in a New York City ridden by graft and corruption, where minority groups are struggling to find their place. They are led by that great little hero, Fiorello LaGuardia, the half-Jewish, half-Italian champion of the people, who went to Congress and then served for years as mayor of New York. *Fiddler on the Roof*, taken from the Yiddish stories of Sholem Aleichem, projects the immigrant back to the narrow but colorful ghetto communities of central Europe. The old father Tevye, struggling to keep a balance between the traditions of his people and the new ideas of his children, is finally driven out of his old-world home and moves to America. Early in this century such old-world backgrounds were the subject of broad comedy and ridicule, with clownish comedians presenting Jewish, Irish, and German caricatures. In the years of Hitler and the Second World War, such national dialects and customs were either avoided or treated with awed seriousness. By the mid-sixties, it was possible to look with both amusement and affection at the minorities who brought their local traditions and their high hopes to America.

Workers and labor unions would seem to be far from the romantic world of the musical theatre, but not in America. In the 1930s, the decade of the depression and the New Deal, labor and industry fought battles that did not stop short of shooting. It was a great day in 1937 when a musical revue called *Pins and Needles*, produced and acted by the International Ladies Garment Workers Union, showed a sense of humor. Its love songs

A super girlie show *(top)*. *Golden Rainbow.* New York, 1968. Directed by Arthur Storch, designed and lighted by Robert Randolph, choreographed by Tom Panko, costumed by Alvin Colt, music and lyrics by Walter Marks. Photo Joseph Abeles. Spectacle in grand opera *(bottom)*. Elaborate painted wings and backdrop. Donizetti's *The Daughter of the Regiment.* New York City Opera production, 1975. Directed by Lotfi Mansouri and designed and costumed by Beni Montresor. Photo Beth Bergman © 1975.

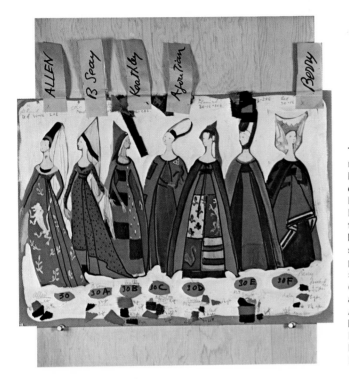

The peak of spectacular American musicals: Lerner and Loewe's *Camelot.* New York, 1960. Staged by Moss Hart, designed by Oliver Smith, lighted by Feder, and choreographed by Hanya Holm. *Opposite page, top:* the design for the inner proscenium frame and one backdrop. *Opposite page, bottom:* the same frame with a theme scene of painted backdrops and three-dimensional structures. *Left:* sketches of some of the costumes designed by Adrian Duquette and Tony Duquette. Photos Joseph Abeles. *Bottom:* musical fantasy with bright colors. *The Wiz.* New York, 1975. Directed and costumed by Geoffrey Holder, designed by Tom H. John. Photo Martha Swope.

Highly theatrical masks and make-up. *Top left:* traditional Japanese Noh mask. *Top right:* traditional Peking Opera make-up. Photos Sekai Bunka Photo. Modern imaginative make-up. *Center:* stages in the make-up of the Tortoise in Alan Broadhurst's *The Tortoise and the Hare. Bottom left:* the character Job from *The Book of Job,* adapted and designed by Orlin Corey and Irene Corey. *Bottom right:* the Lion in Fauquez' *Reynard the Fox.* Photos from Irene Corey, *The Mask of Reality* (Anchorage, Ky.: Anchorage Press, 1968).

Theatrical readings of a series of poems by Ntozake Shange *(top)*. Simply staged with only a rose as symbolic background. *For Colored Girls Who Have Considered Suicide When the Rainbow Is Enuf*. New York, 1976. Directed by Oz Scott. Photo Martha Swope. A cabaret scene in the musical *Cabaret (bottom)*. New York, 1966. Directed by Hal Prince, designed by Boris Aronson, lighted by Jean Rosenthal, costumed by Patricia Zipprodt, choreographed by Ronald Field, music by John Kander, and lyrics by Fred Ebb. Photo Joseph Abeles.

Spectacular rock-opera using elaborate machines and a choral group *(left)*. *Jesus Christ Superstar.* New York, 1971. Directed by Tom O'Horgan, designed by Robin Wagner, costumed by Randy Barcello, music by Andrew Lloyd Webber, and lyrics by Tim Rice. Photo Joseph Abeles. *Bottom:* an American musical in the style of the Kabuki Theatre of Japan. Sondheim's *Pacific Overtures.* New York, 1975. Directed by Hal Prince, designed by Boris Aronson, and costumed by Florence Klotz. Photo Martha Swope. *Opposite page, top: Black Dragon Residence*, University of Colorado production of a Peking Opera, 1970. Directed and choreographed by Daniel S. P. Yang and designed by Roger Klaiber. Costumes imported from Taiwan. Photo Daniel S. P. Yang. *Opposite page, bottom:* Titania making love to the ass's head. Shakespeare's *A Midsummer Night's Dream,* Wayne State University production, directed by Richard Spear, designed by Timothy R. Dewart, lighted by Gary M. Witt, and costumed by Judith Haugan.

Open staging in an exhibition hall *(top)*. A covered wagon scene with projections on screens above the entrances. *Hurray America!*, a bicentennial pageant. Miami, Florida, 1976. Lighting and projections by Randall Will. Photo courtesy of Randall Will, Staging Techniques. The "multimedia" approach to theatre *(bottom)*. The setting for the Humboldt State College première of John Pauley's *September Tea* (1970), which used dynamic groups of actors, pools of light, fragments of scenery, projected images, voices, and sounds. Directed by Richard Rothrock, designed by David Brune, and costumed by Ethelyn Pauley.

took such forms as "One Big Union for Two" and "Sing me a song with social significance—nothing else will do. It must be packed with social fact, or I won't love you." An excellent recording in 1962 and television revivals brought to life again the songs of a turbulent but idealistic period of American labor. In 1954 it seemed natural for a musical to be based on love and group spirit in a labor union; *The Pajama Game* was a great success in both America and England.

Though *West Side Story* seems to be the most strikingly original and one of the most harmonious of all American musicals, it is yet a summary and perfection of the whole line, giving the audience almost everything it had learned to expect. There are dances and songs of group unity for the juvenile gang, songs of love and of dreams of the future, a half-comic celebration, "America," sung by girls recently arrived from Puerto Rico, and a sardonic-comic song, "Gee, Officer Krupke," mocking the police and social workers. There are satire, violence, gang warfare, and murder, yet such an obvious love of New York, such a strong assertion of the hope that love can win over hatred, that this musical must be described as a celebration of America. The musical *1776* (1969), shrewd but sympathetic in its appraisal of the mixture of selfish interests, doubts, and idealism in the Revolutionary Fathers, is still a celebration of American traditions. With playful humor, satire, and irony it follows the uneven course of the Continental Congress to its achievement of the Declaration of Independence. It was a great favorite all over America in the bicentennial year 1976.

Film Musicals

Movie adaptations have given stage musicals the usual Hollywood formula, increasing the spectacle, adding many crowd scenes and dancers, using tourist geography—a whole island for *South Pacific*, Austrian mountains for *The Sound of Music*—and increasing the romantic identification of the audience by using many closeups of the main characters. Yet the total effect of these additions has often been to dull the impact of the music by increasing the difficulty of projecting the songs to the audience. In a movie it is more natural to sing facing the scenery and to blend the songs into the action. But then there is no way to build the song to a big climax that brings the audience to a wild burst of applause. So most songs from stage musicals, like those from grand opera, seem too large and unbelievable for real surroundings; yet when translated to the screen, they are too short and too quiet to achieve the impact they had on the stage.

The most satisfactory movie musicals have been those that were developed especially for the screen. In the 1930s, Busby Berkeley made some remarkable discoveries of what could be done with a camera for spectacular dance effects. In most of the films he directed, he used stories of backstage or nightclub life, thus giving a theatrical motivation for the music. Then he expanded the dance effects far beyond anything that would be seen in an actual nightclub or theatre. Sometimes he used large choruses, photographing them from far above, from below, from the sides, or reflected in complex multiple mirrors. Sometimes with trick lenses he built up elaborate geometrical patterns of dancers on the screen. And sometimes he created startling sequences by combining closeup shots of single dancers or parts of their bodies. He was at his best in expanding the sparkling mirror and rhinestone effects of a nightclub act, with songs and dances that were ends in themselves and had little relation to the action of the play.

In the last several decades the musical, on the stage and on the screen, has been modified in directions that move it far from the romantic glamor of the early musical comedies. The first new direction was toward the bitter, sardonic moods that seem more likely in realism. The second new direction has been toward the more open, flowing forms, the mass-group choruses, and the rhythms of rock music, of rebellious youth. Hence we will discuss *Pal Joey, Guys and Dolls,* and some of the musicals of Stephen Sondheim along with the newer moods of later realism, and *Hair, Man of La Mancha, Jesus Christ Superstar,* and *Godspell* in connection with the other freer forms of the 1960s and 1970s.

A Picture Stage for Romance

The picture stage was invented as a solid, three-dimensional architectural setting for the courts of Renaissance Italy (see Figure 4-12). For the masques and operas of the seventeenth century, scenery that could be visibly changed became the rage, and the wing-and-backdrop system began its long career. Two rows of painted *wings* led back to a painted *backdrop* (see Figure 4-13). At a signal from the prompter, a hidden stagehand at each wing would slide it offstage, revealing another wing just behind it, and at the same time other stagehands would pull up the backdrop by hidden ropes, revealing another backdrop. Thus the change could be made in a few seconds without having to drop the front curtain. The system was excellent for repertory companies, furnishing colorful painted settings at low cost.

It was only when nineteenth-century producers wanted to add realistic three-dimensional effects to the painted wings and backdrop that difficulties arose. For the changing of steps, platforms, and solid struc-

4-12 Early perspective setting of solid two-faced or angle wings. Two rows of wings on a sloping floor lead up to a painted cloth drop to give the illusion of a long street. The Tragic Scene from Sebastiano Serlio's *Architecture*, Book II, Paris, 1545.

tures, the curtain had to be lowered and the continuity of the play was broken. Nineteenth- and twentieth-century engineers devised elaborate and extremely expensive machinery—pulleys and ropes for flying heavy scenery, wagon stages, jackknife stages, turntables, and even elevator stages—to speed up the changes. But it still took so long to get a beautiful painted picture ready to disclose to the audience that opera composers sometimes wrote an intermezzo to fill the time.

During the nineteenth century the picture stage reached a peak of painted illusion. Tableau effects became the rage, especially in the popular melodramas, and as many as thirty might be used in a single play. *Ben Hur* started its great career in 1899 with as much emphasis on pictorial effect as there was in later movie productions. The first act alone had fourteen changes, each setting designed by a different painter. The chariot race was run on a treadmill by real horses and chariots, as a panorama

4-13 Climax of a seventeenth-century opera. Jupiter and his celestial court are let down in a cloud machine. Flat wings on perspective lines lead to the backdrop. Drawn from Italian sources by Martha Sutherland.

painted on cloth and attached to huge rollers moved across the back of the stage. The galley scenes that filled the stage with rows of oarsmen faded into a scene of the tempestuous sea, with a boat that sank out of sight through the stage floor, leaving Ben Hur and his captain tossing on a raft.

Similar painted settings were expected for Shakespeare, giving Shylock a very real-looking Venice and Juliet a beautiful balcony, even if the audience had to wait for long changes and Shakespeare's cinematic rhythm of many short scenes had to be broken up. It is no wonder that more and more twentieth-century producers have returned to medieval or Elizabethan stage forms, which used few or no scene changes, and let the splendor of Shakespeare appear in the costumes, the processions, and the words themselves.

Romance as Psychological Structure

Romance was under strong attack in the early twentieth century. Over-literal minds were impatient with fantasy and dismissed romance as a child's daydream of old fairy tales and legends. The avant-garde continues to despise it because its old fairy tales are charming and popular. Overserious reformers, especially the revolutionary Marxists, have attacked it as bourgeois, as another opiate of the people that, like conventional religion, distracts workers from their duty to the state and wastes their time and emotions. Realists are skeptical of romance because they think that its impossible ideals make people unwilling to face the world as it is. Does not the romantic lover, like the neurotic Tristan of Wagner's opera, dwell on unsatisfied longings until he associates his love with death?

The objection that romance is escape is no longer convincing. A fantastic parable may be the best way to understand a real situation. Since Freud, psychologists have recognized that the great romantic stories fascinate both children and adults because, like dreams, they express the patterns of the search for identity and destiny in the half-hidden depths of the mind. The person seeing a romantic play may momentarily forget the immediate problems of his life. But he wakes from his dream with his ego strengthened and a new perspective on the patterns of human aspiration and desire.

The essence of romance is freedom. Where realism is bound by fact and classicism by logic, the romantic play is bound by neither. In the classic view the individual is summed up by the one great decision he makes, and hence the classic tragedy is a very compact form, leaving out everything not connected with that decision. The free structure of the romantic plot that wanders through many episodes expresses the romantic idea of a complex, infinitely varied, paradoxical, and mysterious universe. And since it is an open universe, unfinished and unmeasured, no one act or crisis is all-important. Not one conscious decision, analyzed and debated, then final and overwhelming, but many choices made in the heat of action over a long period of time, are what shape the romantic character, who in turn gives unity to the play.

Like the romantic playwright, the dramatist of today wants to deal with a complex, baffling universe that is mystical and surreal rather than real, illogical and disconnected rather than clear. To a considerable degree he follows the structure of the romantic drama.

But before we arrive at an analysis of the work of recent playwrights, we must examine the development of the drama of realism, which dominated the stage for more than fifty years and is still important.

5

The Theatre
of Realism

NATURALISM. TENANT FAMILY ON A
RUN-DOWN FARM, AT THE MERCY OF THE
ENVIRONMENT. CALDWELL'S *TOBACCO
ROAD*. TEXAS TECH UNIVERSITY
PRODUCTION, DIRECTED AND
COSTUMED BY LARRY RANDOLPH,
AND DESIGNED BY CLIFFORD ASHBY.

Realists in the nineteenth century turned away from the far away and long ago of the romantics to a concern with the here and now, from fantasies of heroic adventure to a journalistic study of how ordinary people live, from idealistic speculation to pragmatic concern with actual problems. A few plays in the 1850s and 1860s made tentative explorations in a cheerful, shallow realism, but the main theatre fare continued to be artificial comedies, romantic spectacles, and melodramas. In 1873 Émile Zola wrote a preface to his play *Thérèse Raquin* in which he heaped scorn on the unreality and pomposity of the conventional nineteenth-century theatre, with its "medieval scrap-iron, secret doors, poisoned wine," its middle-class sentimentality, "kidnapped children, recovered documents, immodest boastings." He believed that the outmoded romantic theatre would be replaced by a new realistic theatre based on the scientific study of the actual world.

The scientific spirit of the century indeed transformed the theatre. It taught writers to be objective observers, carefully studying real people living in real places. Where the romantics conceived of their characters as embodiments of large, clear passions, the realists watched for the complex influence of environment on the basic drives. From the beginning of the nineteenth century, increasing interest was shown in biology, the study of how creatures live and grow and especially of how they react to their environment. The climax of biological study came in 1859 with the publication of Charles Darwin's *Origin of Species,* which offered the theory that all animals, including men and women, evolve from lower forms and that, by "natural selection," or "survival of the fittest," only those animals that best adapt to their environment will survive. Another powerful influence on nineteenth-century thought was the materialism that seemed an inevitable concomitant of the science, technology, and the great industrial development of the era.

The quite visible effect of these new attitudes on the theatre was the absorbing interest in properties and little pantomimed business on the stage. Objects became as important as actors. They not only documented the authentic qualities of the environment but also gave the actor a sense of reality as he interacted with the environment. Anton Chekhov, perhaps the greatest Russian dramatist, created his characters out of their little daily actions. One of the directors who worked with him wrote,

> He represented human beings only as he observed them in life, and he could not dissociate them from their surroundings: from the rosy morning or the blue twilight, from sounds, odours, rain, trembling shutters, the lamp, the stove, the samovar, the piano, the harmonica, tobacco, the sisters, the in-laws, neighbors, song, drink, from everyday existence, from the million trifles that give warmth to life.

5-1 Realism in setting, directing, and acting. The actors, seen in a box set, are absorbed in the detail of the environment, making a clear, balanced picture, but one without obvious design. Odets' *Awake and Sing*. New York, 1935. Photo Vandamm.

That last phrase—"the million trifles that give warmth to life"—might be the motto of the whole realistic movement.

The Philosophy of Naturalism

In the 1880s a deeper wave of realism, called naturalism, went much further than the exploration of daily life by probing into the violent forces that lie beneath the surface. The naturalistic realists were determined to make people face the basic facts of hunger, greed, and sex—drives it would be dangerous to ignore. A Viennese physician named Sigmund Freud insisted that if the basic drives are not given normal outlets they may emerge indirectly in distorted and destructive ways, and that the only healthy approach is to make the conscious mind aware of these hatreds and drives that have been suppressed because they are not pretty or respectable.

Naturalism was based not only on an interest in exposing the more brutal aspects of human nature but on an explicit philosophy of determinism—the belief that there is no freedom of will or choice but that all is "determined" by heredity and environment. Many plays from the late nineteenth century to the present day could be described as either realistic or naturalistic, but we will use the term *naturalism* only when the deterministic philosophy is apparent or when such basic animal drives as sex, hunger, and greed are important in the play.

Artists who were influenced by the naturalistic philosophy were determined to break through the cheerful surface of early realism, with its conventional pictures of the humble poor, and to show the hatred, frustration, and debauchery of the victims of poverty, who survive through forlorn delusions and dreams of escape. Maxim Gorki wrote one of the most powerful naturalistic plays, *The Lower Depths* (1902), to show the suffering, the hopeless dreams, and the depravity of the human dregs in one cellar room.

Champions of Strong Realism

One of the greatest objections made by serious realists to nineteenth-century melodramas and farces was that they never faced a real problem. After several acts of suspense, the missing papers were recovered, the accused hero was proved innocent, the long-lost child was found, the uncle returned with a fortune, or lightning struck the villain. No one had to face a major loss or adjust to people who had both good and bad qualities. Strong realistic plays shocked late Victorian and early twentieth-century audiences by actually facing such problems. When the Victorian idealist said, "Keep your eyes on the stars," the naturalist added, "And fall into a ditch!"

With *A Doll's House* (1879) and *Ghosts* (1881), Henrik Ibsen became the European champion of truth versus conventional hypocrisy. In *A Doll's House,* when Torvald discovers that his charming little wife, Nora, has innocently forged her father's name and that he might be disgraced by the exposure, he turns on her in anger. But when he finds that someone is willing to cover up the scandal, he forgives her. Repelled by his selfishness and hypocrisy, however, and realizing that he has never treated her as an adult, she walks out of the house to try to find herself, with a slam of the door that was heard all over the Western world. *Ghosts* made an even more shocking attack on convention by bringing the subject of venereal disease to the stage and by indicating that the leading character, Mrs. Alving, should have left her debauched husband. In the end she is faced with the horrible dilemma of giving poison to their son, whose mind has given way, or of caring for him as an idiot. Naturalistic characters must make painful choices, not merely toy with the picturesque problems of romantic heroes.

In writing about the serious problems of real people, Ibsen perfected the "well-made play" with which the French dramatist Eugène Scribe had been very successful a half-century before—a very compact play of few characters, with careful exposition, logical progression, great suspense, and strong conflict, all leading up to surprising climaxes and effective curtains. However, unlike Scribe, Alexandre Dumas the younger, and several others who used the well-made play to present such problems as the fallen woman, divorce, and financial and family crises, Ibsen used it to show men and women who rebelled against the basic attitudes of nineteenth-century society.

Much realistic and naturalistic literature was informed by a zealous determination to tear off the mask of respectability and show human nature in its brute vitality, to face facts, to expose corruption and hypocrisy. Chekhov said, "To make a man better, you must first show him what he is." European cities, after a century of industrial revolution, were a mass of slums filled with poverty, depravity, and misery. But the Victorian middle class, seemingly happy with the idealized stereotypes of its sentimental literature, refused to look. Bernard Shaw showed respectable people some of the unpleasant facts of economic life. In *Major Barbara,* for instance, he showed that slum properties, from which church-going landlords collected their rents, bred disease and crime and that society would do better to build a decent world for the workers than to depend on such charities as the Salvation Army to keep the workers from rebelling. The radicals of the time looked for a revolution, a war between labor and capital. The liberals put their hope in new laws, labor unions, schools, settlement houses, and slum clearance. Both groups welcomed the new realistic art, whether in the simpler form of realism or the grimmer form of naturalism. They believed that only by seeing actual conditions and particular cases—in painting, in novels, in plays—would the general public become aware of the problems and even recognize that slum dwellers had human feelings. Since that first enthusiasm, realistic art has helped to bring about so vast a transformation of human environment in all the industrialized nations of the world that it is no wonder that emerging nations, from Russia to Africa, regard "social realism" as the most important form of art.

In America, where the impact of industrial and urban development on literature came later than in Europe, there was some interest in realism from the 1880s on. But the greatest interest came after the First World War, in 1918, and especially in the decade of the depression, from 1929 to 1939. Sidney Kingsley's *Dead End* (1935) reinforced the hopes of the New Deal of the Franklin D. Roosevelt era and exploded the myth that the poor can help themselves. It brought together on the stage a slum alley and the courtyard of a luxury apartment house and studied the effects of these entirely different environments on each other. The play shows in detail

5-2 Realism or naturalism showing the influence of environment on character. The grouping is complex and varied, clear but not obviously designed. Kingsley's *Dead End*. New York, 1935. Directed and designed by Norman Bel Geddes. Hoblitzelle Theatre Arts Library, University of Texas.

how alley boys learn to be gangsters. An alumnus of the slums, now a famous killer returning home for the last time, teaches the boys how to follow in his footsteps, thus goading the young architect to work toward improving the housing of his slum neighbors instead of dreaming of escape with the rich. But the main progression of the play is not the story of the architect or the gangster but a succession of moods, blending together many small conflicts and discords.

Impressionism: Muted Realism

A similar emphasis on moods can be found in many other plays. Most realistic and naturalistic plays, in fact, are organized, directed, and acted by techniques that correspond very closely to the techniques of impressionism in painting and music. While we have not been in the habit of applying the term *impressionism* to realism, we can understand realism far better if we notice that painting, music, and drama responded in much the same way to the same historical developments of the late nineteenth century and that the aesthetics of impressionism in painting and music are much the same as those of realism and naturalism in the theatre. Hence we may speak of the many plays of realism and naturalism in which strong conflicts are kept muted as impressionist plays. Even those plays in which violence breaks out at some point may employ impressionistic techniques.

Impressionism was developed in the second half of the nineteenth century in reaction to the strident intensities of romanticism. Instead of choosing heroic subjects for large canvases, painters became interested in the passing moods of the local landscape, the atmosphere of various times of day, and the special qualities of jugs, tables, and fabrics. Claude Monet wanted to catch in his paintings the impression of a cathedral half lost in the haze of early morning or a bridge in a foggy London twilight. The French composer Claude Debussy was fascinated by sea, clouds, mist, and rain, by the thought of a cathedral with its chimes deep under the sea or by the local color of a Spanish town at festival time. In the 1890s he was working out a music of new harmonies, weaving many little themes into rich textures of mood and avoiding most of the conventional harmonies and expected progressions.

Now, nearly a century after impressionism reached its first flowering, the basic attitude toward life that produced it is clearer. The techniques of impressionism—in painting, the tiny dots of color, the bold brush strokes, the blurred lines that blend gardens, bridges, trees, and people into soft-focus images; in music, the overlapping sequences, the massed chords, the exotic harmonies that blend the fragments of melodies into muted discords; in the theatre, the details of setting and properties, the overlapping bits of dialogue and background sounds, the tentative gestures and movements that blend the characters and the locality into rich moods—express the belief, explicit in the plays and implicit in painting and music, that human beings have no freedom from the environment of which they are a product and helpless victim—a belief that is, as we have seen, basic to naturalism. Foreground disappears into background, melody into accompaniment, and individual decisions into unconscious natural and social forces. People may struggle to escape the environment, they may be in conflict with it in many ways, but they are themselves threads in a complex web. In impressionist plays, as in impressionist music, there is never a decisive beginning or end, never a clear-cut climax or turn, because no one is expected to make a major decision. Violence may smolder beneath the surface and even erupt offstage, but the main characters are bewildered victims who do not understand their own feelings. In presenting such passive people, the playwright weaves a complex pattern from suggestions of mood, hints of half-formed desires and impulses, and fragments of abortive action, which can be more expressive than the strong plot of a typical nineteenth-century play.

Chekhov's plays show how impressionistic patterns were worked out in the theatre. They are all mood studies of groups of people caught in situations they can do nothing about. In *The Three Sisters* (1901), the sisters fret through four acts at the dullness and oppression of the provincial town they live in and plan constantly to escape to Moscow, but they never do because they find themselves trapped by family ties and by habits they cannot change. A thousand and one conflicts arise and stir people deeply, showing slightly on the surface and sometimes catching the attention of other characters, sometimes going unnoticed in the continuous flow of little actions. At times all the characters on stage are caught by the same mood of joy or sadness, but often several characters carry on their own separate sequences. In spite of the deep melancholy of Chekhov's plays, the author insisted that they were comedies. The greatest appeal of an impressionist play is usually its combination of comedy and tragedy. Once the idea is accepted that life goes on no matter how many hearts are broken, there can be deep sympathy for failure and suffering along with laughter at the absurd context of the suffering.

Chekhov's *The Cherry Orchard* (1904) is a very touching, sad, yet funny study of a group of people trying to hold on to the moods and meanings of an old estate. Madame Ranevsky, the owner, returns to the estate after spending all her money on a worthless man in Paris. If only she will subdivide the estate and lease the lots for summer villas, she can have a good income. Her business adviser, the son of one of her father's serfs, is ready to help, but she and her brother cannot make up their minds. In Act I, arriving at daybreak, she cannot bring herself to do anything. In Act II, on a twilight walk, listening to distant music, she still cannot do anything. In Act III, at a big party, she is waiting for news that the estate has been sold. In Act IV she departs for Paris again. Around her are her brother, daughter, foster daughter, the governess, old friends of the family, the business friend who buys the estate, the former tutor of her drowned boy, and the upstart valet who is glad to be going back to Paris—all laughing, teasing, dreaming of the past and dreading the future, doing anything to avoid adjusting to a changing world. They are helpless, hopeless people, but the author looks at them with great warmth and affection. It is not surprising that Chekhov's great popularity has been in the West, where the complexity of modern life is so confusing and frustrating.

Some of the moods and techniques of impressionism appeared in America as early as 1916 in Susan Glaspell's one-act play, *Trifles*. Moods of

5-3 Realism and impressionism. Mood of nostalgia and indecision. The scene is indoors, but no visible wall divides it from the cherry orchard, a symbol which dominates the lives of the characters. Chekhov's *The Cherry Orchard.* Andrei Serban's production at Lincoln Center, 1977. Photo Sy Friedman.

frustration were not common dramatic material in the 1920s, but with the depression of the 1930s and the darkening clouds of impending war, large numbers of Americans could understand and respond to such moods. In two movies of the 1930s John Ford used the soft-focus techniques of impressionism to create a compassionate picture of groups of people struggling to escape from an oppressive background. *The Informer* (1935) traces the mute sufferings of a Dublin tough who stumbles to his death in the night fog after betraying his friend in the hope of escaping to America. In *The Grapes of Wrath* (1939) the Joad family does escape from an Oklahoma desolated by drought and depression and makes an epic journey to California, only to find itself embroiled in the struggle of the migrant farm laborers. The play that catches beautifully the depression decade's feeling of weary helplessness is Tennessee Williams' *The Glass Menagerie* (1944), a rich mood-study of a group of helpless victims, loving and torturing one another but unable to change or break away. The play will be discussed more fully in the next chapter as a blend of naturalism with romance.

Thus impressionism accepted the idea of human helplessness in a baffling world, but sought for understanding and compassion. If it could not trace any clear purpose or larger meaning in the absurd contradictions of life, it could at least discover a rich, vibrant texture in the relation of the characters to the environment. Impressionism and realism are not identical; there are realistic plays of clear decision and melodramatic action, with characters who are not helpless. But many of the principles of acting and directing realistic plays are based on principles that are found in impressionistic music and painting.

New Theatres and a New Acting Method

Impressionist plays—indeed, all the new plays of realism and naturalism—demanded not only a new kind of playwriting and acting but a new kind of theatre. No realistic play had a chance in the large nineteenth-century theatres, which were built to accommodate from two to four thousand people and included from three to six balconies. In such a theatre the large stage, on which were sometimes presented spectacular operatic scenes with horses and hundreds of people, was a vast open space with scenery consisting of painted flats and backdrops. For interiors, pieces of furniture from the property rooms were spread around the bare stage floor in conventional arrangements—a sofa here, a table and two chairs there—supplemented at times by furniture painted on the wings and backdrop. The actors expected to act close to the footlights, where their large gestures could be seen and their oratorical voices heard clearly throughout the house.

The new movement for a more intimate theatre started with a few bold, enterprising groups late in the nineteenth century and was so successful that by the 1920s practically all the new theatres in Western Europe and America were small, with at most 1,000 to 1,500 seats. Today, the newer college theatres of America usually seat three or four hundred. The idea of the intimate theatre has won out, and in spite of a hundred experiments in new directions, the realistic approach still dominates the theatre.

The first great step toward both realism and intimacy in the theatre was taken in London in 1865 when Squire Bancroft and his wife refurbished a small neglected theatre, gathered a group of young actors, and found a new director and playwright, T. W. Robertson. Robertson put his actors in the midst of real furniture and properties, real doors, ceilings, and windows, using the upstage as well as the downstage areas. He achieved a more subtle and more realistic ensemble acting than had been known before, making his sentimental scenes and everyday people very convincing by "new school" acting. His critics made fun of his "teacup and saucer" realism, however, and soon it came to seem mild and superficial.

A stronger impetus was given by the Norwegian rebel Henrik Ibsen. Although he himself founded no theatre, he furnished the inspiration for new theatres throughout the world. The first of the new "free" theatres—that is, free from commercial control—was the Théâtre Libre in Paris, founded in 1887 by André Antoine, who made his living working for the gas company. In a tiny hall, using real furniture, some of which he carted through the streets from his mother's dining room, he and a group of amateur actors made a strong impression and in a short while attracted a sizable audience. In 1889 a similar free theatre (Freie Bühne) opened in Berlin with Ibsen's *Ghosts* and soon was presenting Gerhart Hauptmann, a realistic German playwright of major importance. In 1890 London followed with the Independent Theatre, and it too found a native playwright, George Bernard Shaw, to follow Ibsen. Dublin's Abbey Theatre was at first devoted to the poetic, mythical plays of William Butler Yeats, but John Millington Synge soon gave the rich poetic language of Ireland a realistic turn. Then in the 1920s Sean O'Casey wrote some of the most powerful and beautiful realistic plays of the twentieth century.

Most important of the new theatres was the Moscow Art Theatre, founded in 1897 by Constantin Stanislavsky. Anton Chekhov was the new playwright who ensured its success. It established itself as a lasting institution and is still the principal theatre in Moscow.

In New York the intimate theatre came a little later. From 1916 to 1920, on Cape Cod, the Provincetown Players introduced the naturalistic one-act plays of their gifted playwright, Eugene O'Neill. The Provincetown Playhouse, which they established in 1919 in a converted stable on Mac-Dougal Street in New York, was even smaller than the realistic theatres of Europe, but it made an enormous impression. As an acting institution it did not last long, but soon the Theatre Guild, and even the commercial producers, adopted its ideals of honesty and realistic acting.

Like the Off Broadway theatres of recent decades, the "free" theatres started on a small scale, with ideals of acting, directing, and playwriting quite different from those of the big commercial theatres. Though short-lived, they pointed the way for others, and proved that a new audience was ready.

In the intimate theatres the proscenium arch was simplified or, in many cases, eliminated as a decorative element, leaving only a functional opening for viewing the "slice of life." Footlights, with their distasteful associations with glaring, romantic spectacle and ham acting, were eliminated or hidden under removable sections of the floor for the few times when some artificial effect might be needed. The Cleveland Playhouse of

5-4 Realism. Diagonal lines and dynamic variations of level weave the individuals into the web of environment. Inge's *Bus Stop*. Mankato State College production, directed by Ted Paul and designed by Burton E. Meisel.

1927 set the pattern for intimate community theatres, with no decorative proscenium and no footlights but only two or three plain, dark steps leading the audience, in their minds, right onto the stage.

The box setting is the basic one in realism, using three walls and a ceiling, with the illusion that the fourth wall has been removed. Though actors have occasionally supposed a fireplace and even windows in the missing wall, most groups soon found it better to ignore that wall and to keep the actors facing not toward the audience but toward the properties and action on the stage.

With changes in theatres and plays came new principles of directing: keep the actors focused on some center of interest on the stage; make full use of many different playing areas, especially the upstage areas; enrich the action with frequent use of properties and bodily reactions. The visit of the Moscow Art Theatre company to New York in 1923 left a lasting impression as the ultimate in art that hid all art. Nothing was obviously arranged, yet everything was meticulously clear. The actors seemed to have their backs to the audience constantly and to be absorbed in something behind the furniture or the other actors; no one ever moved out into a clear open space; no one ever seemed to turn toward the audience. Yet behind the casualness was such careful planning that for every important line the speaker just happened to have his face visible. Despite what appeared to be informal composition and random movement, the attention of the audience was always carried straight to the important person or action. Though each character seemed completely independent of the others, so strong was the basic rhythm that they all became part of one compelling action. There was no star, no predominant character, but rather a perfect ensemble. The foreground and background were one, and properties, costumes, doors, lamps, window curtains, and lights—no less than the actors—performed their parts.

Beginning in 1897, at the Moscow Art Theatre, Stanislavsky gradually worked out a systematic "method" for training actors to play the new realistic drama, and his method became in this century the basis for most actor training in Russia, Western Europe, and America—everywhere that realism is important. It was not enough to fill the stage with real furniture and properties and pull the actors back from the footlights for more quiet, intimate acting. The stately tread and the loud declamation or the resounding intonation of the traditional romantic actors were not suitable for the intimate theatres. It was not enough to give the actor small properties to handle. In order to give life to complex, inarticulate characters who are baffled or overwhelmed by the environment, whether the desperate slum characters of Gorki's *The Lower Depths* or the equally

5-5 Simplified realism. A back yard in New Orleans and a house with a wall omitted to show inner rooms. Hellman's *Toys in the Attic*. Indiana University production, directed and designed by Richard L. Scammon.

5-6 Strong tensions in a realistic play. Several groups of Americans in a shabby hotel in Mexico. Simplified cut-down setting, suggesting the fragmentation that comes from neglect. Williams's *The Night of the Iguana*. Indiana University production, directed and designed by Richard L. Scammon.

helpless upper-class people of Chekhov, the actor needed to find the inner life of the character, a life beyond, between, and sometimes in contradiction to, the words. He must find the "inner text" to add a complex richness to the actions, voice tones, and words.

The main reason for the success of the Stanislavsky method is the precision with which it expresses the materialistic vision of human beings trapped by heredity and environment, victims of their baser drives, their wills thwarted, unable to express their feelings even when deeply moved. Mute violence stirs through the inner being, coloring daily movements and breaking into the ordinary voice tones. Without deliberately raising the voice or asserting a gesture, the method actor can move an audience deeply by suggesting a dark, inarticulate tragedy that is held in. We will examine that method in more detail in Chapter 10.

Factual Realism on Screen and Stage

The drama, like the novel, has always relied heavily on factual material as a source. But it was the movies that first realized the possibilities of using factual material directly for informative entertainment, without "plot," with real people in real life situations as actors, and with minimal arrangement of the filmed scenes.

The Film Documentary

While Hollywood was producing Cecil B. DeMille's colossal spectacles, superromantic films with Rudolph Valentino, and equally unreal pictures about the social games of wealthy people, Robert Flaherty created the documentary, a type of film that had enormous influence not only on movies but on television, epic theatre, and other forms of stage drama. In 1922 he filmed *Nanook of the North*, showing the daily life and trials of a real Eskimo family. He created an even more compelling documentary in *Man of Aran* (1934), showing life on an isolated island off the coast of Ireland. Flaherty's photography and editing made these studies of real life as absorbing as any fictional film.

Three memorable documentaries of the 1930s studied wide problems that challenged public policy in the days of Franklin D. Roosevelt and the New Deal: the misuse of water and land and the decay of cities. *The Plow That Broke the Plains* (1936), *The River* (1937), and *The City* (made for the New York World's Fair of 1939–40) were impressive and beautiful films.

Documentary realism is a staple of television. Every important political event is the subject of a "special report" that provides background material and a summary and analysis of the event itself. Extensive accounts of interesting geographical areas, scientific discoveries, space flights, personalities in the public eye, significant historical events are brought visually into the home. The viewer is bombarded with factual material, much of it with suspense, confrontation, and other dramatic elements, even if it does not tell the story of a fictional character.

In the 1970s many political and social problems were treated in documentary movies—evils in mental hospitals and nursing homes, racial injustice, political chicanery, corruption in business, labor problems. The callous judgment of Washington policymakers and American leaders in Vietnam, and the mindless and heartless cruelty in the conduct of the war as it dragged toward its anticlimactic end, were presented vividly in the documentary *Hearts and Minds* (1974).

A much better documentary, more searching and more carefully prepared, though it used material of less immediate interest to Americans, was Marcel Ophuls' *The Sorrow and the Pity* (1972), a four-and-a-half-hour film dealing with the fall of France in the Second World War and the actions and attitudes of French citizens under the German occupation. It is developed by an interweaving of interviews with newsclips of events described by those interviewed. The interviewed are of all social levels, from leaders in several countries during that period to a variety of residents in the vicinity of Clermont-Farrand, a city near Vichy, the French capital during the occupation: two farmers who were in the Resistance, one of them sent to Buchenwald when a neighbor turned informer, two schoolmasters, a pharmacist, a hairdresser who after the war served fifteen years for collaboration, many others. No accusations are made, no moral lessons drawn. This is a historical record, with instances of courage and cowardice, heroism and disloyalty, and viewers may draw their own conclusions about responsibility and guilt and the meaning of events.

Harlan County U.S.A. (1976), a strong documentary made by Barbara Kepple over a four-year period in a coal-mining community in Harlan County, Kentucky, is concerned with a strike in 1973, but it shows the poor homes and hard daily routines of the miners and their families as well as the confrontations with spokesmen of the company, armed strikebreakers, and police. The director's sympathy is with the miners, but she gives an honest, unsensational view. She is especially successful in filming the women, individually and in groups, showing the grim, worn faces as the women carry out their own plans for opposing the common enemy. Contrasting scenes after the strike is won by the miners show the return to normal living, with closeups of relaxed or smiling faces, some of the miners singing. The picture carries implications about all communities of hardworking, impoverished people leading dangerous lives, with little defense from the thoughtless or callous decisions of employers.

Problems in Presenting Fact

A stage equivalent of the film documentary, sometimes called the theatre of fact, differs from the documentary in using professional actors, but it adheres closely to the factual material on which it is based. Instead of pictures and flashbacks, it uses only words, often the exact words spoken as testimony in a trial. In the decade after J. Robert Oppenheimer, one of the top scientists who created the atomic bomb, was tried and disgraced, mainly because he opposed the further development of atomic weapons, a German writer, Heinar Kipphardt, wrote a play based on his trial, called *In the Case of J. Robert Oppenheimer*. It was presented in many cities, especially in Europe, and won the praise of those already in agreement with its premise.

As playwrights and producers try to represent real events and real people on the stage or on the screen, they often stir up anger and controversy. Since actors can never be exactly like the people they represent, it may be more effective to change the names and consistently keep the details slightly different from actuality. Then the play is clearly a metaphor, a semblance, a work of art with carefully controlled aesthetic distance. Since the theatre (stage and film) is more immediate, more public, than the other arts, people cry out, "That's not the way it was!" when it gets too close to their own knowledge and experience. It may be easy to unite an audience in dramatizing a problem, but not easy to get them to agree on the solution. Aristophanes satirized many people of his time by name, but when he wrote a whole play about the current dictator, he made up a nickname for him. Everybody expected Aristophanes' satire to have fantastic exaggeration and not get too close to the bare facts.

All the President's Men (1976), a successful film that was not a real documentary since it used professional actors, nevertheless adhered closely to the facts in the story of two reporters who persistently sought the truth about Watergate. Real names were used, but Richard Nixon was shown only in newsreels of his public appearances. Produced less than two years after Nixon's resignation of the presidency, the film did not attempt to cover the last days in the White House and the pardon that outraged some citizens. Hence it could count on audiences in complete agreement that the illegal acts should be exposed.

The plays and films that deal with the Nazi extermination camps have a special problem. The extermination of more than six million people is too shocking ever to be forgotten. In what perspective can we think about it? How can we relate it to other human deeds—the bombing of Coventry, Dresden, Hiroshima, the close-at-hand massacre of civilians at My Lai in Vietnam? Who is responsible? In the 1960s a powerful play by Peter Weiss, *The Investigation* (1965), did not try to show the camps, but only the witnesses and survivors as they testified at trial, with selections from actual testimony. In Germany the play aroused considerable controversy, though it appeared to be a simple documentary, an example of theatre of fact.

Far more disturbing was Rolf Hochhuth's play *The Deputy* (1963). It asks why important people, the Pope for instance, did not do something to stop the wholesale killing of the Jews. Hochhuth does not use the theatre-of-fact form but the familiar form of a combination of romance and realism. As he recreated the story, the Pope, afraid of disturbing his already difficult relations with the regimes in Italy and Germany, failed his opportunity. The play brought angry denials that the Pope could have been expected to do more than he did. The same idea expressed in an editorial or a speech might have been disturbing, but it would not have had nearly as strong an impact as the play. The stage has the solid appearance of objective reality; what is said and done there seems much more than the subjective opinion of an author.

A spectrum of moral judgments about responsibility for the concentration camps was the basic material of Marcel Ophuls' *The Memory of Justice*, a powerful film documentary released in a more-than-four-hour form in 1976. Ophuls reviewed and reassessed the trials of war criminals at Nuremberg in the 1940s. Some of those accused or condemned, witnesses, judges, German civilians, and a large number of observers from Europe and America were interviewed, and the interviews were interspersed with shots of concentration camps, newsreels of the war years, and other pertinent material. Ophuls then added a comparable study of the moral problem of the Vietnamese War.

Even in a film that makes no pretense to be fact, the episodes in one of the extermination camps are disturbing. In Lina Wertmüller's *Seven Beauties* (1976) the principal character is a rather stupid, egotistical Italian show-off nicknamed Seven Beauties, who exploits his sisters and other women. After killing a man, he schemes and compromises his way from courtroom to an easy prison, then to the army, and lands in a German concentration camp. There he survives by a more desperate compromise—seducing the woman commandant. He lives to get back home, physically alive but morally dead. That the movie has a great deal of wry comedy, especially in the Italian scenes, has brought angry protests. What limits should be set for art as to pleasant and unpleasant, serious and comic, moral and immoral? Whatever the answers, it is clear that it is easier to deal with reality by keeping it at a safe aesthetic distance. Shaw called on the theatre to be a prompter of conscience. Shaw himself was always able to get his rather well-educated audience to see the moral while they were being entertained.

Film Realism after World War II

At the end of the Second World War the movies rediscovered the harsh reality of direct realism, but not in Hollywood. Hollywood made *The Best Years of Our Lives* (1946) about the men coming back from the war, telling a real story and including an actor who had had both hands shot off in action. But it turned out to be the same old slick formula film.

New Realism in Italian Films

It was the new Italian films that offered something vital. Roberto Rossellini finished *Open City* in 1945 as the Germans were leaving, presenting actual street scenes and using harsh black and white film because he could not afford better. But the sun-drenched Roman streets, the sharp shadows, the tenement rooms, and the fresh, nonprofessional

5-7 Naturalism in the movies. A suggestion of inarticulate compassion in a rough life. Zampano, circus strong man, abandons the waif who has travelled with him. Anthony Quinn and Giulietta Masina in Fellini's *La Strada (The Road).* Photo Janus Films.

performers made a very exciting, unsentimental picture of violence and terror at the end of the war. Italian audiences were not much interested in such a frank presentation of their poverty, but American audiences were fascinated by the real people, real streets, real economic problems, and real political passions. Since 1945 the Italian film has been one of the strongest influences in Western cinema. Vittorio DeSica filmed *Shoeshine* in 1946, with street urchins as actors, and when a bricklayer's face caught his fancy, a man who had never acted before became the star of *Bicycle Thief* (1949). The masterpiece of Italian realism was Federico Fellini's *La Strada* (1954), a most touching story of tramp carnival performers. A coarse wandering entertainer, Zampano, played by Anthony Quinn, picks up a young, not very bright girl, Gelsomina, sensitively played by Giulietta Masina, Fellini's wife. He buys her, in fact, from her impoverished mother. She learns to play a trumpet, to dance, and to do her part in making their living, accepting Zampano's rough treatment and infidelities. They join a troupe of carnival people, and an acrobat befriends her.

When Zampano kills the acrobat and he and Gelsomina are outcasts on the road, Zampano is unable to cope with her grief and abandons her. Obsessed with the memory of the girl, he eventually finds the village where she had wandered, only to learn that she is dead. In the last sequence he throws himself to the ground on the shore of the gray sea, overcome by grief and despair. Here, with excellent naturalistic acting and directing, are the basic elements of nineteenth-century naturalism—inarticulate characters driven and destroyed by crude natural forces, in harsh but rich-textured surroundings, invoking not our moral judgment but our compassion and objective understanding.

Film Realism in Other Countries

The British filmmakers found a new realism a decade after the Italians. Actually John Osborne's play *Look Back in Anger* of 1956, filmed in 1958, set the pace for both stage and film. Soon a new generation of writers and moviemakers were dramatizing the gritty turmoil of the slums and ghettos of the industrial cities of northern England, with provincial dialects and local color and the frustrations that the welfare state had not been able to eliminate. Shelagh Delaney's play *A Taste of Honey* (1958), filmed in 1961, is one of the best, with its picture of a desperate daughter, about to have a baby, repudiating her coarse mother and setting up housekeeping with a homosexual boy. Among the better films are *A Room at the Top* (1958), which follows the career of a poor man in his climb to position and wealth through a loveless marriage to the boss's daughter; *Saturday Night and Sunday Morning* (1960), in which a young couple make a futile attempt to break free from a world "dead from the neck up;" and *Billy Liar* (1963), which shows a young man yearning for release from a drab provincial life but unable to bring himself to leave with the free spirit Liz on the midnight train for London.

In Sweden Ingmar Bergman has created his own kind of symbolism, but many of his films reflect the grim, relentless seriousness of the naturalistic plays of that other Swedish playwright, August Strindberg. Bergman's trilogy of the early 1950s—*Through a Glass Darkly, Winter Light,* and *The Silence*—follows his characters through the winter twilight of tortured guilt and destructive emotions. Even as Bergman follows his symbolism and suggests far more strange and unexplained inner torture than we expect in realism, even as he uses such supernatural figures as the character Death in *The Seventh Seal,* still, for the most part, his method is realism. His characters respond to their environment, rich in texture, and the wintry atmosphere creates mood for the tense anguish of the characters.

India's very large film industry produces conventional romantic spectacles, but the one Indian filmmaker who has found a Western audience, Satyajit Ray, presents with great originality the simple, everyday life in the Bengal villages and the slums of Calcutta. His trilogy of the 1950s, *The World of Apu,* was greatly admired in European countries and America. A much later film, *Distant Thunder* (1975), gave a beautiful and moving treatment of the Indian famine of 1943, caused by disruption of trade in the Second World War and by the demands of armies for food. Ray's humane faith is shown in the change that takes place in the one member of the Brahmin caste in a stricken village, from arrogance to compassion and a sense of responsibility for his fellow men, even those he cannot love or respect. Ray is not interested in the social reform aspects of naturalism but rather in the changing complex feelings of a few real people in their everyday surroundings.

Belated Realism in American Movies

Realism could not get far in American cinema until there were major changes in the public attitude, changes in laws, and changes in the film business itself. Victorian prudery was very strong, and middle-class, small-town people were fearful of anything that might soil their respectability. Self-appointed guardians of public morality were sure that since the movies were the entertainment of the masses nothing should be shown that might startle a conventional American family. Under the threat of national censorship that followed a notorious Hollywood scandal in 1922, the producers had set up a "code of decency" that prohibited, among other things, scenes of passion, sexual perversion, white slavery, miscegenation, venereal disease, and childbirth. The camera could not even show a double bed in a married couple's house. Of course profane or obscene language was taboo. Not until *Gone With the Wind* in 1939 was the word "damn" heard from the American screen. There could be any amount of overt violence or oblique indication of sex, but no serious treatment of the darker aspects of human psychology.

After the Second World War, however, changes took place that paved the way for stronger realism in the movies. For one thing, the overwhelming power of the Hollywood studios was broken, partly by legal action separating production from distribution, partly by independent producers working in foreign countries and using new material. But the biggest blow to Hollywood was television. By the 1950s television had become the mass entertainment of America, and thousands of movie houses closed as the movies became a minority art. When the movies and radio in the 1920s had taken the mass audience, the legitimate theatre had lost its wide support, but as a minority art it greatly improved. It did not have to conform to the lowest common denominator of taste or the most conventional ideas of what is proper. In the same way the moviemaker had far greater freedom as a worker in a minority art. Moreover, censorship had become less stringent through a series of legal decisions, and in 1953 the Supreme Court ruled that the screen shares with the press the protection of free speech guaranteed by the first and fourteenth amendments to the Constitution. In its earlier days Hollywood had neglected or greatly modified the naturalistic plays of Eugene O'Neill, but in the 1950s and 1960s the even more shocking plays of Tennessee Williams were put on the screen without flinching from the themes of cannibalism, castration, and homosexuality.

By the mid-seventies taboos in subject matter and language had almost ceased to exist. Frank, sometimes crude, treatment of drug addiction, unconventional sexual behavior, and homosexuality was commonplace. In some films dialogue was liberally sprinkled with profane words. Nudity, which had first appeared in Off Broadway shows and was then promoted to Broadway and made notorious by *Oh! Calcutta!*, reached the screen in brief glimpses in the sixties and more freely in the seventies. Since the screen provides closeups, nudity and erotic situations were more vivid than they were on the stage. Moralists still cried out in alarm, but less loudly, and young people were delighted with the greater freedom.

Extreme violence was very fashionable in the 1970s, much of it for sheer excitement, without any attempt to suggest that it was not natural and inevitable. We remember that Aeschylus dealt with offstage violence, but showed how the chain of violence ever provoking counter violence could be broken by a concerted shift from private vengeance to public justice, a change that required religious and psychological reconditioning. He had a hopeful view that violence belonged to an early, primitive age that could be replaced by higher concepts of order. But only a few of the many extremely violent movies have had any suggestion of a more hopeful perspective beyond the moment. In *A Clockwork Orange* (1971) violent cruelty is considered a mental aberration that might be altered by psychological reconditioning. But the film shows that the reconditioning does not prevent the patient from being beaten up by his former pals. Many conservative people condoned the violent and shocking scenes of *The Godfather* (1972) and *The Exorcist* (1973), on the ground that the films made an appeal to moral or religious principles, but condemned the frank sexual scenes of *The Last Tango in Paris* (1972), though the film had a strong psychological interest, a superb sense of style, and perhaps the best acting of Marlon Brando's screen career. The Victorian heritage of a puritanical attitude toward sex persists; there is no comparable deterrent to excesses of violence.

The harsh ruthlessness of the city is one of the themes of the young director Martin Scorsese, who won praise for *Mean Streets* (1973), a movie based on the life of loafers and small-time gangsters in New York's Little Italy. He gave a more sympathetic picture of the highways of the Southwest in *Alice Doesn't Live Here Any More,* as a young widow wanders from one drab town to another, trying to support her twelve-year-old son and make a new life for herself. Scorsese's violence is harsher in *Taxi Driver* (1975), as he sends his psychotic character (well acted by Robert De Niro) through the strange night lights of city streets, encountering ugly violence and immoral behavior, until he starts on a killing spree himself, killing anyone he disapproves of. At the end he is driving a taxi again, as if nothing had happened, leaving the audience puzzled. Should they consider him a hero, or is the ending an ironic comment on indifference to the law?

In a world of wars, assassinations, lawless heads of state, business bribes, and street crimes that may or may not be punished, it is no wonder that writers and moviemakers see "reality" in harsh and bloody terms, frankly shown without evasion or cover-up.

Movie realism can be as powerful as stage realism, and with photography of actual places, it can seem even more real. By cutting in scenes of skies and trees, light and dark, the film can create powerful impressionistic moods. By going outdoors as easily as indoors, by including work, eating, play, the film can present much more of the environment than can be brought to life on the stage; the screen, though two-dimensional and often without color, seems to be the most perfect medium for presenting the real. Many people have argued that since the camera can far surpass the stage in showing reality, live theatre should give up realism and try to put on the stage only the fantastic, the artificial, the truly theatrical. Yet the film, by so easily using its textures of reality to validate fantasies, sentimental stories, conventional characters, and shopworn ideas, still caters to the idle daydreams of the masses. Only the more determined script writers, directors, and moviegoers—ardent fighters with the spirit of Zola and Ibsen—can forget easy entertainment and deal with real life.

Realism on the Television Screen

Through radio, broadcast drama grew up as a distinct form, and its relation to the audience is different from that of the movie or stage play. The viewers have not gone out for a special occasion but are sitting at home, perhaps with family or friends, expecting every week or every day, in the midst of countless commercials, the same familiar news broadcasts, variety shows, and soap operas in neat half-hour or hour programs. Such a relaxed audience did not encourage the development of serious drama. Nevertheless, the late forties and the fifties saw a remarkable development of live television drama, with new plays brought to the screen several times a week and with a new school of playwrights who explored the documentary realism and quiet intimacy of radio drama to develop a form that was especially effective for television. The miniature masterpiece of this "Golden Age of television drama" was Paddy Chayefsky's *Marty* (1954), about a worker in a butcher shop who finds relief from his loneliness in a big city by marriage to an unglamorous girl as lonely as he. In this and other plays of the period, there were a number of realistic insights—conflict between mothers and sons, frustration and anger in crowded apartments and boarding houses, conflicts between the values of the big city and the small town or old city neighborhoods. But such realistic insights were not enough to save this form of drama from the simultaneous expansion of the national economy and the television audience in the late 1950s and the 1960s. The wider, more affluent audience was not interested in little plays about little people or in the themes of frustration and the acceptance of limitations—the themes of intimate realism since Chekhov.

The most interesting achievement of realism in the sixties was the rescue hero. He was a descendant of the romantic rescue heroes of radio in the 1930s and 1940s, especially the mysterious, all-powerful, masked Lone Ranger, who appeared from nowhere to save worthy people from disaster, and John J. Anthony, a Bronx cab driver who set up a Marital Relations Institute and gave advice every Sunday evening to distressed husbands and wives. The rescue hero of the sixties—doctor, lawyer, reporter, or schoolteacher—gave mature, professional advice and undertook to face complex problems that could not easily be solved. But by 1965 public interest and advertisers' favor had veered from rescue series to the more conventionalized suspense drama, with the simpler kind of battle against international conspirators or old-fashioned bandits and cattle thieves.

In the seventies "All in the Family" was one of several series that brought social and political problems into the home in a mild way. The father of the family was laughed at for his prejudices again and again, but the emphasis was on the amusing eccentricity of his wife and that time-tried element of domestic drama, the ingenuity of wife, husband, and children in getting the better of one another or in cooperating for some good end.

But the big breakthrough for drama, old or recent, romantic or realistic, came with the advent of educational television, with some federal funding and the sponsorship of particular programs by large corporations that did not insist on interruptions for advertising. Through the Public Broadcasting Service, theatre enthusiasts were able to see dramatizations of novels or biographies, occasionally live but usually filmed or taped productions of Shakespeare's and Marlowe's plays and other classics, contemporary plays by British or American authors, as well as excellent programs of opera, ballet, and modern dance. For the first time, American television offered what had been offered in England on the famous "Third Programme" almost from the beginning. Some of the best drama on PBS originated with the British Broadcasting Company. On the regular channels, also, good dramatic offerings became more common. In spite of the persistence of much trivial entertainment, the outlook for television drama at the end of the seventies is very promising. More than the movies, it may bring us the best theatre of past and present.

Just as realism never replaced all earlier styles, so realism has not been replaced by the new developments of the twentieth century. It remains the most familiar norm, the approach expected by the general public in the theatre and on both movie and television screens. But that does not mean that realism has shown no change. Many new offshoots have appeared since it was established a century ago. In the next chapter we will look at some of the more important modifications.

6

Realism
Transformed

EPIC REALISM. BRECHT AND WEILL'S *THE THREEPENNY OPERA*. BARTER THEATRE, ABINGDON, VIRGINIA, 1976.

In the nearly one hundred years since realism began to dominate the theatre, various transformations have occurred as a result of efforts, not to abandon realism, but to find a more effective way of presenting reality. Among these transformations are selected realism, stylized realism, Oriental realism, and, most important of all, epic realism. We will examine these later in the chapter, but first we will look at certain blends of realism with other kinds of theatre that are not always the result of conscious effort but of the playwright's, director's, and actor's mixture of familiar theatrical elements.

Theatrical Blends

In the last two chapters we have considered romance and realism as separate genres, and indeed in their beginnings they reflected quite different attitudes toward life. But as time has passed each has tended to encroach on the territory of the other, until, in the late twentieth century, a new play will more often be a blend of the two than a clear example of either. Similarly realism, taken with dead seriousness by its proponents, especially Zola and other naturalists, has tended to absorb elements of comedy, both farce and high comedy.

Realism and Romance

Such romantic forms as the musical, and even opera and dance, have been influenced by realism and have been adapted to show the interaction of complex characters with grubby environments, or even the strange obsessions of the inner mind.

In *West Side Story* (1957) the musical had come a long way from the Viennese operetta of the late nineteenth century, where all was glamor and charm, with a handsome prince and a beautiful woman in disguise, with sorrow and joy, anxiety and relief, even heartrending disappoint-ment, but all very remote and picturesque. Indeed *West Side Story* stretched our definition of romance to the breaking point. It was an adaptation of the most romantic of all plots—the story of Romeo and Juliet, lovers who defy the medieval world of feuds and hatreds and give their lives to bury their parents' strife. But the treatment was very differ-ent from the conventional one. The opening was not a show number, with singing and kicking, but a scene of a gang suddenly arriving in a slum street of New York, moving tensely in dance rhythm as they looked around quickly, first in one direction, then another, for a possible enemy. The movement was patterned, exact, unmistakably dance, yet also the simplest, most direct expression of reality. That scene and others in the play could be described as realism.

We need a new term for the blend of realism and romance that had become common by the middle of the twentieth century and that defined a distinct attitude toward life. If art is a celebration of life, why not celebrate in song the less glamorous moments as well as the joyous and ecstatic? For several decades now, the American musical has done just that, using hardened city types, sardonic moods, destructive and antisocial aspects of human character. *Pal Joey* (1940) was so unsentimental and sardonic that it repelled a large part of the regular audience, though it had one of the best Rodgers and Hart scores and the young Gene Kelly as the conniving hoofer who dreams of owning a fabulous night club. It was a wry version of the American success story, showing its stupid and unsavory aspects. Still, it seemed to many people a new and exciting kind of musical, and when Columbia brought out a recording in 1952, the show was revived in New York and has found a real audience since then. *Guys and Dolls* (1950), with its tough-skinned but soft-hearted gamblers and racketeers, was a bit more sentimental; its sinners were softened and reformed in the end. Both these musicals were revived with full appreciation in New York in 1976–77, *Guys and Dolls* with an all-black cast.

In the last decade Stephen Sondheim, one of our most talented song writers, has explored the realms between realism and romance. His *Company* (1970) seemed the complete opposite of romance, with its abstract setting of pipe frames and elevators and its lonely bachelor hero watching his friends' marriages at their worst, but its wit and lively music caught the wry mood of the New York audience of 1970. In *A Little Night Music* (1973) Sondheim moved nearer the charming and sad moods of romance, but here is no brassy, romantic joy, only tenuous, delicate moods, almost as casual and impressionistic as Chekhov, much of the music sung by a chorus of three ladies no longer young. *Follies* (1971) does conjure up from the past some vigorous moments, but the characters are aging, retired performers trying wistfully to recapture a life that is gone.

Even opera has felt the impact of naturalistic determinism, though only a small group of people go to hear modern operas. Alban Berg has attracted some devoted followers through the dense, tortured music of *Wozzeck* and the more cheerful music of *Lulu*. Kurt Weill, who composed for both popular musicals and serious opera, set to music Elmer Rice's *Street Scene*, one of the strongest studies of people defeated by their environment.

In the other direction, a naturalistic play may be given a romantic, even glamorized treatment. In its situation Tennessee Williams' *The Glass Menagerie* is a relentless study of the defeat of hope and longing, and we have mentioned it as an example of the impressionistic mood of frustration of the 1930s. It shows the Wingfields, mother, son, and crippled daughter, seething and quarreling in a small apartment in St. Louis. The mother dreams of departed glory and of a rich gentleman caller who will marry her daughter. The daughter, too fragile to cope with the modern world, escapes into the world of glass animals that she collects. And the son, trapped in a dreary job and tortured by his family problem, dreams of following the example of his father and running away. Williams softens the harsh impact of naturalism by presenting the play as a memory, with an atmosphere of sentiment and candlelight, soft draperies and a gauze veil. The crippled daughter is treated with tenderness and some charm, and even the exasperating mother is treated with admiration and affection.

Realism and Comedy

A blend that combines comedy, and often romance as well, with realism—what we may call comic realism—has been far more popular than the severe forms of realism. From romance it borrows a love story and a leading man and woman who, if not great heroes, have a touch of idealism. It may have such moods of impressionism as a blending of many small frustrations with local color of a particular group or landscape, but the conflict usually reaches a definite climax of success or defeat. Thus it captures some of the excitement of melodrama. At the same time it has enough details of daily life to seem realistic, and the characters are closely related to the environment. Much of our popular light entertainment, whether for dinner theatres, community theatres, or theatres of summer resorts, may be called comic realism or comic romance. This is the easiest kind of play to act. As it is usually set in a middle-class home, a designer need only be an interior decorator to reassure the audience with the comfort of the familiar. A large part of television drama follows this standard pattern as "situation comedy," or "sitcom."

In a small theatre in the slums of Naples, Eduardo de Filippo has written and acted in plays in the Neapolitan dialect that present a comic drama of people losing their battles with family, neighbors, and the budget. In 1974 his *Saturday, Sunday, Monday* (in translation) was given a comic-realistic production in London. The setting of the first act reproduced a kitchen in exact detail, and throughout the act the English actress, as an Italian housewife, concocted a *ragu* which simmered on a real stove while the strong odor of onions and spices was wafted to the audience. The main theme, the temporary estrangement of husband and wife, is developed with a variety of amusing evasions and confrontations.

A more sophisticated example of the popular mixed genre is *Same*

Time, Next Year (1975) by Bernard Slade. It is rather daring in romanticizing adultery, showing six scenes of a couple who every year for twenty-four years meet for a weekend together. They are tempted to run away from their own families and make this a permanent marriage. Instead, they keep this relation on an ideal romantic plane, untouched by the daily strain of marriage and children. There is low comedy in the danger of being caught, and high comedy in their complex relationship and the acceptance of a kind of controlled bigamy. They must adjust to the changes of the years, and are frequently out of phase with each other, not only in their personal needs but as they are swept by the fads and fashions of the times. When she is a hippy war protestor, he is a climbing, ambitious supporter of the establishment. The year he is exploring sensitivity training and the occult, she is a very successful business executive. But love conquers all.

A far deeper combination of naturalism and comedy was presented by several Irish playwrights many years ago; at least the plays seem profoundly naturalistic and wonderfully comic to the rest of the world. The Irish, like many other minority ethnic groups, have not always been able to laugh at realistic pictures of their own traits. J. M. Synge's *The Playboy of the Western World* (1907) caused riots in Dublin and in America by seeming to make fun of the Irish. We see the play as a serious study of group hysteria as the women and girls of an Irish village idolize a wandering young man who brags of having killed his father. He is shown up as a braggart and liar when the father appears, wounded but not dead, and the most entranced young girl realizes there is a vast distance between a romantic story and a "dirty deed." In his use of the racy Irish dialect, Synge created a language both poetic and comic.

Two plays of Sean O'Casey achieve even more comic and poetic effects from the dialect of the Dublin slums and the eccentricities of the Irish character, yet both plays present devastating pictures of the human destruction caused by poverty and the guerrilla warfare of the Irish liberation. The gift of gab, the foolhardy bravado, and the skill in self-deception create a poetic eloquence that in the irony of events is very comic. At the end of *Juno and the Paycock* (1924) the drunken old Captain Boyle comes home at night with his crony to find his family and the furniture gone, and as he stumbles around the kitchen trying to find the stove and something to eat, he blames his condition on the chaos of the times: "I'm telling you . . . Joxer . . . th' whole worl's . . . in a terr . . . ible state o' . . . chassis!" The scene makes us laugh and weep at the same time.

In *The Plough and the Stars* (1926) O'Casey brings the street fighting of the Easter Rebellion of 1916 to the foreground. Superpatriots who strut in dress-up parades when the conflict is in the stage of demonstrations, keep at a safe distance when burning, sniping, and killing go on in the streets, but they continue their colorful bragging and threats. The ironic contrast between the posturing and petty quarreling and the suffering of the slum people moves the audience to both laughter and deep anguish. Both plays are cries for compassion.

In 1976 a comic-realist emerged in Texas. Preston Jones had worked for a decade, as actor, director, and playwright, in the Dallas Theatre Center, before the production of his *Texas Trilogy* at Kennedy Center in Washington and then on Broadway made him nationally known. He chooses a very narrow environment—Bradleyville, an imaginary town of 6,000 in West Texas that has an oil boom in its past and nothing in its present—and shows ordinary men and women with various dreams of escape from drab lives and with various adjustments to what fate allows them: a dead end of living. There are scenes of longing, tenderness, frustration, and resignation, of malice and petty intrigue, and there are word battles and physical violence, but the audience is invited to laugh as well as sympathize or deplore. The first play of the trilogy, *The Last Meeting of the Knights of the White Magnolia,* is a picture of a few male citizens trying to keep alive a moribund secret order founded on outdated prejudices. Comedy becomes farce as the initiation of a new member proceeds by rule and misrule. But the play turns serious when the ceremony breaks up with the collapse of Colonel Kincaid, a World War I veteran, and fighting among the other members, who finally admit that the brotherhood is adjourned for the last time.

Whether the people of West Texas laugh at the plays of Preston Jones has not been reported. It is not easy to laugh if realism brings the situation close to home. O'Casey left Ireland and found his audience in England and America. Not many minority groups are able to look on devastating defeat with hearty laughter—far better to ignore the realistic environment and let the whole play have a farcical or high comedy tone, or to present selected realism, where the individual escapes or triumphs over the environment.

Selected Realism

Before such hybrids as we have been describing appeared—in fact, shortly after the beginning of the realistic movement—many plays had made theatregoers familiar with what we may call selected realism, which results from relaxation of the harsh philosophy of naturalism and simplification of the detail in setting. Many novels and plays have presented a serious struggle with environment leading to at least partial triumph.

6–1 Selected realism. The details of a middle-class Norwegian home are simplified and organized into a design of dignity. Alla Nazimova and Harry Ellerbe in Ibsen's *Ghosts*. New York, 1935. Photo Vandamm.

Escape has not always seemed a futile dream, as it does in Chekhov's naturalistic plays. Many people have escaped from slums and small towns or from other cramping environments. Or a play may suggest that apparent defeat for the principal character is not actually a bad outcome.

In Shaw's *Man and Superman* (1903), though the tone is that of a vigorous high-comedy quarrel between a man and a woman, the theme is the same naturalistic one of an attempt to escape. Jack Turner, feeling that marriage would be the end of his intellectual independence, struggles to escape the wiles and powerful appeal of Ann Whitefield, who seems the essence of blind nature, determined to use him and destroy him just to propagate the race, with no regard for his human, intelligent purposes. Yet when he does capitulate there is no defeat. He has had a dream of a great debate that his predecessor Don Juan holds in hell, a dream that ends with Don Juan and Donna Anna leaving the comfortable world of hell to tackle the difficult job of creating a higher, more intellectual man—a superman. When Jack realizes that woman, whom he has seen as the blind force of nature, may also will the intelligent, as Donna Anna did, he no longer objects to giving in to nature by marrying.

In many realistic plays the human personality is not subordinated to the background. A few bold characters assert their will with sharp, comic acting. The stage setting does not present the full, overwhelming detail of naturalism but only enough detail for the action or for local color. If the play indicates that the characters have some control of their destiny, it is fitting that the setting reflect such artistic control as line, form, proportion, rhythm, color, and even a fair amount of symmetry—elements that would be neglected or hidden in a slice-of-life play. Designers feel much more challenge in creating in the style of selected realism (Figure 6–1).

Stylized Realism

Both naturalism, in which the individual is overwhelmed by the details of the environment, and selected realism, in which he has some control, still kept an objective view of one real place at a time. But that objective view did not suffice when the naturalistic character felt menaced by the machine age and when irrational fears burst into the conscious mind. It was not so much the immediate surroundings that were terrifying as the isolated images: rhythmic, mechanized sounds, dehumanized groups of people, fragments of many past experiences. This explosive conflict called not for selected realism but for stylized realism, which kept the central character intact but, in order to present the violence of the conflict, used abstraction and distortion to break up the environment into fantastic fragments.

Eugene O'Neill's *The Hairy Ape* (1922) is an excellent example of stylized realism. Yank, a ship's stoker, is a typical naturalistic character who makes a blind attack on his environment, ignorant of how that environment might be improved but acutely aware of the spiritual anguish of not belonging to it. He has tried to identify himself with the steel, the coal, the power and speed of his time, but he finds that the machine age needs only his muscle; he has become a dehumanized brute. When the daughter of the shipowner calls him a hairy ape, he leaves the ship in a rage, throwing himself against the rich people coming out of a church on Fifth Avenue. But they are not human. Without looking to right or left, they walk along in rows, repeating in stylized, mechanical rhythms the phrases of their inane chatter. In some productions they wear masks. The street and the people are shown not objectively but subjectively, stylized and distorted as they would appear to Yank's bewildered mind. It is only the environment that is unreal, however; Yank remains a naturalistic victim, but one who refuses to accept his fate and explodes in violence.

The expressionistic distortion in *The Hairy Ape* is only incidental, intended to show the mental state of the main character. The more extended and systematic stylization of the environment makes O'Neill's *The Emperor Jones* (1920) an expressionistic play. Yet in this play, too, the main character is a naturalistic victim in explosive conflict with the

6–2 Stylized realism and expressionism. Jones in his fantasy sees the enormous crocodile god. O'Neill's *The Emperor Jones*. Design by Donald Oenslager for Yale University production. Photo Peter A. Juley and Son.

environment. A clever black Pullman porter, Brutus Jones, exploiting the ignorant natives of an island in the Caribbean, has made himself Emperor. When his subjects become restless he tries to escape, but in the terrors of the jungle night he loses his veneer of civilization and is destroyed, not so much by the natives as by his own fears. The environment is stylized in the regular drumbeat—one of the most famous theatrical devices of early twentieth-century theatre—which starts early in the play and continues without interruption through the brief intermissions to the end. The environment, as much subjective as local, is stylized also in the phantoms that appear to Jones each time he pauses in his flight. Each hallucination goes further into his past, peeling off another level of his consciousness. First there are just vague shapes, then the crap games, fights, court trials, and chain gangs of his own past, and finally the crocodile gods of his primitive ancestors—all stylized in mechanical, terrifying rhythmic movement. By using an abstract and symbolic form,

O'Neill makes his play suggest the violence of colonial peoples, ready to turn on their exploiters and destroy them even when, as here, both exploiter and exploited are black.

Stylization is now a common tool of stage or screen. A good example is the film *Midnight Cowboy* (1969). As the Texas cowboy is baffled by the confusing appearances of New York, we see either stylized fragments of the New York scene, the bleary colors of a psychedelic party, or the fast, distorted flashbacks of his memories of Texas.

Oriental Realism

One important transformation of Western realism has resulted from contact with Oriental theatre, especially the Chinese. We have commented briefly in the Prologue on the form and conventions of the Chinese stage and their stimulating effect on theatre in the West. It was the Chinese theatre that suggested to Thornton Wilder his new approach in *Our Town* (1938). He had spent part of his boyhood in China, where his father was an American consul, and he was fascinated by the free, highly imaginative methods of the Oriental theatre. From the Chinese theatre he learned that even the important events of everyday life can be presented by actors on an open platform, reacting not to a realistic setting but to the private thoughts and personal relations of the characters. After the successful production of his play, the West began to see Oriental theatre not just as a ceremonial and playful treatment of human relations but as a fundamental way of treating reality. We will discuss Wilder's play in detail in connection with epic realism.

Still a living art, the Chinese theatre uses plays that are three hundred to seven hundred years old and traditions that were well established by the Tang dynasty, more than a thousand years ago. The stage has no front curtain, scenery, or realistic properties. A temple canopy, sometimes held up by two lacquered columns, decorates the acting area, and the back of the stage is a decorated screen or beautiful embroidered cloth that carries the imagination into romantic realms of fancy but tells nothing about the individual scenes. Both the orchestra and the property man are on stage and visible at all times. The actor, a man or a man impersonating a woman, entering by one of the conventional doorways in the back cloth, mimes the opening of sliding doors and comes down to tell the audience exactly who the character is and what he plans to do. The property man provides chairs or other properties for the performer as they are needed, making no attempt to hide his actions. The same standard chairs and tables serve for many different levels—hills, walls, river banks, platforms.

The property man sets the chairs on a table, and the performer climbs a high mountain pass. To indicate a journey by chariot, the actor crouches and trots between two flags on which wheels are painted. Using only a whip to indicate that he is riding a horse, the actor shows great skill in suggesting the essence of a person getting on or off a horse.

The few scenic effects are highly conventionalized. To indicate mountain country, small panels painted with the traditional mountain and stream pattern are brought out and leaned against a chair or table. To show an attack on a gate, attendants hold up a long pole from which hangs a painted cloth representing a section of wall with a gate, and behind it the defending general climbs on a chair and table to speak from above the wall. But such devices are subterfuge: it is the actor who creates the reality—marching, riding, shouting, brandishing a weapon, whirling, fighting furious duels with all the rage of battle but rarely coming close enough even to touch weapons with the opponent, shivering to create the illusion of a storm while a demon of winter dances and the property man shakes paper snow from a box. (See P–4.)

The characters also sing many songs, so that the drama almost seems to be an opera—indeed the Western name for the drama is "Peking Opera"—and there are formal dances and stylized movements. The orchestra reinforces the melody and rhythm of the songs and gives shape and rhythm to the action by marking each step, gesture, and movement, using numerous instruments: flutes, violins, gongs, drums, bells, cymbals, and blocks of wood. The famous Peking actor Mei Lan Fang, on his tour of America in the 1930s, demonstrated that the conventional method of the Oriental theatre can create an illusion of reality just as convincing as our theatre of realistic detail, and perhaps more compelling. Mei Lan Fang specialized in acting women's parts. Only in the twentieth century, under the influence of Western ideas, did women take over some of the female parts.

In American college theatres, Oriental plays have been successfully performed, with elaborate costumes, painted faces, and many of the Oriental conventions, in a colorful structure suggesting Chinese architecture with the formal entrance and exit doors of the Chinese stage (Figure 6-3). The actors have used English prose spoken in a slightly exalted style with a light suggestion of Oriental music as a background, especially for the more poetic passages, and much percussion for entrances and movements. Two Chinese plays have been widely popular. *The Circle of Chalk* is the Oriental version of the story of the wisdom of Solomon. To determine which of the claimants is the mother of the child, the Emperor uses the test of the circle of chalk. The child is placed within it, and the women are told that only the mother can remove him. Actually the Emperor

6-3 A colorful imitation of the Chinese stage, with the property man at one side and the orchestra at the other. *The Circle of Chalk*. University of Iowa production, directed by Harold Crain, designed by A. S. Gillette, and costumed by Berneice Prisk.

knows that the true mother will not hurt her child's arm by jerking him away from the other woman; therefore he correctly declares that the woman who removes him is not the child's mother. There is more conventional romance in *Lady Precious Stream*, which made a great impression in both London and New York in the 1930s in an adaptation by S. I. Hsiung. The young heroine chooses to marry the gardener, and, when he goes away, waits faithfully in poverty, despite the machinations of her wicked brother-in-law. But when her husband returns, pursued by the loving Princess of the Western Regions, she makes him play some high-comedy games before she will take him back, and the Princess has to agree to be only a second wife. In the English adaptation, the Princess wears Russian costume and has helped make the gardener her king but has not yet married him, and she agrees to remain his friend and to respect the position of the little wife.

More and more, the Western theatre in the twentieth century has moved toward the freedom and imagination of the Oriental theatre. Authors write monologues and direct addresses to the audience. Scenery is changed, often in full light, before the eyes of the audience; the use of masks, symbolic properties, and fragments of settings is acceptable to the theatregoer. Time and space can be made completely flexible. In Friedrich

Dürrenmatt's *The Visit* (1958) the events of many days are telescoped into a few scenes, and the train, town councils, and crowd scenes are suggested by the actors as freely as in an Oriental play. Imaginary darkness, suggested by the actors in full lighting, was startling in the storm scenes of Peter Brook's production of *King Lear* (1962), but in Peter Shaffer's *Black Comedy* (1965) the audience could easily suppose the visible actors to be in a room totally dark from a blown-out fuse. Even animals can now be presented on the stage in an Oriental fashion. In the musical *Camelot*, the serious drama *Becket*, and the epic drama *Indians* (1969), some of the leading characters came prancing on, wearing the frames of hobbyhorses around their waists.

Although Japanese theatre has not exerted as strong an influence on Western drama as the Chinese, it too has fascinated some playwrights, composers, and dancers. The Irish poet William Butler Yeats attempted some dance dramas in the spirit of the mystical Noh drama of Japan, but the more colorful and sensational Kabuki stage has been of greater interest to most Westerners. The most conspicuous example of the Japanese influence on the American stage is the musical *Pacific Overtures* (1975). For this colorful piece Stephen Sondheim turned to the Japanese Kabuki theatre for his principal effects. Japan had been used as a setting for a musical by

6-4 Theatre of make-believe in the West. Actors are costumed as lion and oxen, and stylized units of scenery serve to indicate the city of Rome. Shaw's *Androcles and the Lion*. New York, 1946. Photo Vandamm.

6–5 Symbolic painting of a sacred pine tree on background. Oriental thrust stage for actor, chorus, and musicians. Japanese Noh theatre on the estate of a feudal lord. Drawn by Bobbie Okerbloom.

6–6 Scenic spectacle combined with make-believe for the popular Japanese theatre. Eighteenth-century Japanese Kabuki theatre. Drawn by Bobbie Okerbloom.

Gilbert and Sullivan in *The Mikado* and for an opera by Puccini in *Madama Butterfly*. But Sondheim's borrowing was in a more realistic spirit. The story deals with the opening up of Japan to Western influence after more than two centuries of isolation, through the exploratory visit of Commodore Perry. Sondheim not only blended into his songs some suggestions of Japanese music but used a Japanese orchestra, with musicians sitting crosslegged at the side of the stage, and presented many episodes with the conventions of the Kabuki stage. One number was the famous Kabuki Lion Dance, performed by Commodore Perry in appropriate costume. All Japanese characters were portrayed by Japanese-Americans or actors recruited from Tokyo. But the Japanese touches were after all rather superficial, and the final number was danced by a chorus of Americanized Japanese in Western dress with the exuberant style of any new Broadway musical.

Epic Realism

The most important transformation of realism is epic realism. It differs so greatly from the naturalistic theatre of 1880 to 1920 that many people consider it one of the revolts against realism. Like stylized realism and expressionism, it breaks the world into separate fragments, but unlike them, it pieces all the fragments together into one meaningful picture of the real world. It does not break from realism into dreams and fantasies, though it may simplify the scenic elements even to the point of abstraction in order to show the wide sweep of an institution or an idea. The word epic comes from Aristotle, who made a sharp distinction between the dramatic form, which ideally presents one concentrated action in a limited time and space, and the epic form, which, like Homer's long narrative poems, the *Iliad* and the *Odyssey*, involves many people and covers many episodes in many times and places. Aristotle did not think that the theatre could handle the epic type of action, but twentieth-century theatre has done just that many times.

Like the theatre of fact, epic realism is a form of documentary, but it has its own special methods. Where naturalism might show one realistic scene of people waiting in a breadline, an epic treatment of the economic problem might show briefly the farmer, the banker, the miller, the wheat failure in Siberia, the operation of the stock market, and a congressional hearing—all part of the picture of scarcity, high prices, and hunger. Epic realism is frankly didactic; that is, the idea or theme is all-important. Hence the characters and what they do are part of a demonstration—typical examples to illustrate some abstract idea.

The Book of Christopher Columbus by the French poet Paul Claudel is a good example of the epic method. Though written earlier, it was produced after the Second World War by Jean-Louis Barrault and proved effective with both French and American audiences. The play is a judgment, a hearing with an expositor who calls the forlorn, old Columbus out of a lowly inn in Valladolid to come onto the forestage and watch as another actor, playing Columbus, presents the story. The techniques employed include moving pictures, symbolic images, vague shadows projected on a screen, ballads, and narratives, and dialogue that both occurs within the event and describes its significance from a later time. The play reviews Columbus' long career, showing his departure from his home in Genoa, his appeal to the King of Spain, the mutiny of his sailors, the curses of the gods of the New World, and finally an apotheosis as Queen Isabella leads him toward the gates of glory. It is like a trial, with accusation and defense spoken directly to the audience, then illustrated by the dramatic scenes and made theatrical through music, movement, mobile scenery, and projections.

American Epic Theatre in the Thirties

In the depression decade of the 1930s, such large problems as public health, housing, wages, and farm income seemed more important than stories about individuals, and America developed its own form of epic theatre. Sidney Howard's *Yellow Jack,* produced in 1934, was a landmark. It set on the stage a series of episodes in the long fight to control yellow fever, from laboratories in London and West Africa to tents in Cuba, where soldiers died from fever or served as guinea pigs for the long experiments. Clifford Odets' *Waiting for Lefty* (1935) interrupts the strike meeting of a taxi drivers' union to cut in on the forestage short scenes of the desperate home lives of five drivers, while the whole circle of union members is dimly visible in the background—a reminder that individual frustration could be relieved only by union action. For the theatre documentary called the Living Newspaper, New Deal journalists joined with theatre workers to present reports on national problems. The first Living Newspaper, *Triple-A Plowed Under,* dramatized the farm problem, with angry farmers, city customers, and government officials contending and asking questions. There was more human appeal in a later issue called *One-Third of a Nation,* a Living Newspaper about housing. In a large setting of a four-story tenement, a fire and a family tragedy led a little man, Mr. Buttonkooper, to ask police, politicians, and inspectors how conditions had gotten so bad, why property owners did so little to improve them, and what might be done by government-supported rehousing. Many demonstration scenes were brought onto the forestage. One of the most vivid showed the history of the city in miniature, as land dealers set up a little plot of grass, with street signs a few feet apart, and sold off one lot after another to the crowds of immigrants who arrived and sat close together on the stage, each filling his plot of land.

More important than such plays in shaping the ultimate form of epic theatre have been two plays of Thornton Wilder: *Our Town* of 1938 and *The Skin of Our Teeth* of 1942. These are not always called epic because, instead of social, economic, and political problems, the subjects of earlier epic plays, they deal with historical and mythical events and philosophical, religious, and metaphysical ideas. In *Our Town* Wilder wanted to present an idealized picture of growing up, getting married, and dying in an American town before the complexities of the large city had changed the meaning of family and town, and, by showing the pain of loss in time, to prove the value and beauty of each moment in time. Wilder did not agree with the naturalist's view of everyday life as restricted, petty, and degraded. He showed that the homely daily relations with parents, partners, and children take on a glow of beauty and importance if looked at in a wide perspective of time and place.

Wilder found the conventions of the Chinese stage perfectly suited to his purpose. He planned *Our Town* to be produced with no front curtain, no scenery, no romantic lighting, and no properties beyond a few chairs, a couple of ladders, and some garden trellises pushed out at one point "for those who think they have to have scenery." He used a Stage Manager as demonstrator, combining the Chinese property man with a Prologue-Expositor, letting him comment directly to the audience and bring on scenes or interrupt them, himself playing small roles—the clerk at the soda fountain and the preacher at the wedding, for instance. The Stage Manager brings in testimony by a historian and a geologist to add the dimension of the past—the time of the settlement by European immigrants, the earlier time of Indian tribes, and the time of the stone formation of millions of years ago.

The first act shows the daily life of the town, from the preparations for breakfast and the arrival of the newsboy and milkman to the return from choir practice in the moonlight and the settling down for the night. In the second act, the daily kitchen and breakfast activity is concentrated on getting ready for the wedding of Emily and George, but before the wedding scene itself there is a flashback to a drugstore scene showing the first time the couple knew that they were made for each other. In the third act, the dead Emily arrives in the cemetery, where, in chairs set in rows to represent graves, the other dead sit and speak. Emily realizes that she can revisit the living and decides to look at her own twelfth birthday. A few

6-7 Abstract realism. Death and eternity are suggested by simple theatrical means. The living characters stand with umbrellas around Emily's grave, while she joins the rows of the sitting dead. Wilder's *Our Town*. New York, 1938. Photo Vandamm.

feet in front of the sitting dead, she watches her mother start the day, until the pain of seeing her youthful self in the light of later time becomes too strong and she gladly returns to take her place on the hilltop. The act ends with the dead quietly talking about the stars and the millions of years it takes their light to reach the earth.

The Skin of Our Teeth may be considered an even better example of epic realism; it covers an even wider range of time, juxtaposing first the ice age, then the flood, and then any modern war, with present time in New Jersey. Besides being a modern family, the main characters are also Adam and Eve and Cain. The play dramatizes the perennial need to pick up some threads of civilization and start over again after a catastrophe. The epic method includes the use of an expositor speaking over a loud-speaker, slides, allegorical figures, myths and parables, and a parade of actors quoting passages from Plato, Spinoza, and the Book of Genesis.

The Epic Realism of Bertolt Brecht

Most discussion of epic theatre is concerned with the plays and theories of Bertolt Brecht. Brecht's techniques are no longer novel, but he is still appreciated for his characters and—ironically, since he was forever preaching against illusion or too much sympathy—for his poetry, and for the anguished plight of his main figures.

Brecht started writing in the chaotic, disillusioned Germany of the 1920s, when in both politics and the arts old ideas were being questioned and new forms were being tried. During the First World War he had been a medical orderly helping to patch wounded men up quickly so that they could go back into the trenches and be shot at again. After the war he saw in Germany the lines of unemployed, the abortive attempts of labor groups to gain control, the terrible inflation that wiped out all savings, the corruption, venality, and exploitation in the cities. He enjoyed the satiric songs of the cabaret and the rowdy give-and-take of the sports arena. He saw Max Reinhardt's productions of *The Circle of Chalk* in the Chinese style and the eighteenth-century comedy *A Servant of Two Masters* in the improvised-platform style of a *commedia dell' arte* troupe. The Dadaists in France were setting an example for all Europe in contempt for established order.

Brecht's most sensational success came in 1928 with *The Three-Penny Opera*, a vivid musical satire based on John Gay's *The Beggar's Opera*, which had been the sensation of London in the 1720s and had had a spectacular revival there in the 1920s. Brecht created his own grotesque picture of the world of beggars, thieves, and corrupt officials, of love, exploitation, and betrayal, with many bitter comments on human depravity and with forebodings of destruction. Yet the bitterness is lightened by irony and song. The young composer Kurt Weill, creating his own German version of American popular music, wrote songs for it that are still sung. The play has been popular with university drama groups and has had several professional revivals, one in the Beaumont Theatre of Lincoln Center in 1976. (See pages 150–51.)

Whereas this early play showed a cynical, demonic individual, Macheath, or "Mack the Knife," triumphing in a ruthless world, *Mother Courage and Her Children* (1941), like most of Brecht's later plays, shows a more sympathetic character trying to survive in a world that outrages all sense of what is human. Dragging her peddler's wagon across central Europe through the Thirty Years' War in the seventeenth century, Mother Courage loses her sons to the corruption of war and sees her daughter scarred, maimed, and finally shot for trying to save victims of war. The many songs, instead of giving charm to the piece, increase the ironic sense of the futility of war.

Two of Brecht's later plays that have been widely produced in America take the form of parables, and both borrow in method from the Chinese theatre. In *The Good Woman of Setzuan* (1943), a kind-hearted girl, set up in a shop by three roaming gods, finds that her kind heart has no place in the world of business. To save herself from complete ruin, she disguises herself as a male cousin so that she can deal ruthlessly with her kinsmen and her trading associates. But she finds no way to reconcile the two ways of life. The gods only smile and tell her to go on being good, leaving the audience to conclude that perhaps they themselves should change the world of starving dependents and ruthless trade and not ask

6–8
Complex multiple setting for epic theatre, using rough textures, like junk sculpture, for a "confrontation" style. The gods descend in a rickety elevator in Brecht's *The Good Woman of Setzuan*. University of Texas production, directed by Francis Hodge and designed by John Rothgeb.

one young woman to try to lift the universe. The other parable, *The Caucasian Chalk Circle* (1948), gives an entirely new ending to the old Chinese play. Another tender-hearted girl, running away from the palace during a revolution, rescues the young prince abandoned by the heartless mother. Although the child repeatedly causes her trouble, she loves him and takes care of him. Later the mother, needing her child to claim large estates, demands him from the girl. But a picturesque judge, the village rogue Azdak, sets up the old test of the circle of chalk. When each claimant takes an arm of the child to pull him out of the circle, the real mother easily wins, because the one who really loves him refuses to risk injuring him in the struggle. The judge gives the child to the loving foster mother, repudiating old ideas of legitimacy and showing that people and things belong where they can be best cared for, "the children to the motherly, the carts to the good drivers."

Much of Brecht's theory was developed in negative form as an attack on the established conventions of the realistic stage. He despised the conventional audience looking for emotional thrills and identifying with helpless heroes. Such an audience, he felt, did not think or judge, but only drifted in pity and empathy. The play showed them man as a known entity, his fate settled and finished. Their emotions were stirred, then exhausted, and at the end they were reconciled to their imperfect world. But Brecht wanted to wake up his audience, to make them think, compare, question, and see the implication of the play for their own world and not just lose themselves in the psychological problems of the leisure class. Hence he theorized a great deal about breaking the illusion, about devices of interruption, about keeping the emotions in check. He wanted on the stage the objectivity of a lecture by a scientist, with important demonstrations, to be watched thoughtfully. He did not want his actors to lose themselves in complete identification with the characters. Brecht felt that the actor could indicate a character and his social implication far better by standing at a distance.

Brecht's term for this objectivity, *alienation,* has caused much confusion; many people suppose that he wanted to give only a cold, dull lecture. He invented the term when actors thought that talking directly toward the audience or changing scenery before the audience would break the illusion. Brecht, confident that the theatre would be better without that kind of illusion, was perfectly willing to break it. Today, when we so easily accept the methods of epic theatre, we realize that an actor can create a new kind of illusion, even with the interruptions and the fast epic pace. Certainly the central characters of Brecht, when they are well played, create a high degree of sympathy and identification. It is not cold acting but the interruption by the narrator or by the contrasting scenes that sets the characters at a greater aesthetic distance, in *Our Town* as well as in Brecht's plays.

What emerges in a Brecht play is a heightened sense of the individual struggling heroically in a chaotic world. In the back of his mind, Brecht looked to a Marxist revolution and the coming of communism, but his plays do not celebrate any communist order; they show the failure of a corrupt bourgeois world to maintain humane values. Many of Brecht's characters have no individual motivation at all; they are merely symptoms of a fragmented society. Hence the portrait of the central character is drawn by presenting a number of confrontations with the fragments of the society—symbolic characters, who are often more functional than individual, and facts, statistics, and localities. No one fragment is all-determining; there is no need for a full, enclosing, naturalistic setting. Yet each fragment must be convincing, with the right feel, smell, texture, and dialect. The audience itself has to put all the fragments together and, while concerned over the plight of the individual, ask how a better social order can be built. Thus epic drama, with its insistence on fact, belongs to the main tradition of realism. The goal in epic theatre is the better understanding of the actual world, with the hope of improving it.

6–9 Epic realism. Titles, projections, voices. Abstract, cut-down setting that, with slight changes, serves many separate episodes (see also photos at left). An indictment of the Nazis, written before World War II. Brecht's *The Private Life of the Master Race*. Texas Tech University production, directed by Clifford Ashby, designed by Joe Skorepa, and costumed by Larry Randolph.

Epic Plays of the Sixties and Seventies

In the 1960s and 1970s epic techniques were used for a wide variety of subjects. In *The Royal Hunt of the Sun*, which we have already discussed as an example of modern tragedy, a chorus of soldiers mime the climb of the army up the Andes and the attack on the Indians. Instead of the standard theatre curtain, the first act is ended by a group of howling Indians who pull down from the high golden medallion of the throne a blood-stained cloth that billows out over the stage and marks the end of a great massacre—a vivid adaptation of the Chinese convention of movable symbolic scenic elements. Even the vast epic sweep of Napoleon's invasion of Russia was suggested in a stage adaptation of Tolstoy's long novel *War and Peace* by actors moving miniature figures on a large map mounted on a sloping table. As in a movie, the scenes of the particular characters on the forestage alternated with a demonstration on the map of the progress of the war.

The epic form was used successfully by Arthur Kopit in *Indians* (1969), a very serious study of the misunderstandings between the white man and the Indian. The hero is Buffalo Bill, prancing on his hobbyhorse, friend of the Indians, friend of the President, creator of the popular image of the sharpshooting scout of the West. In his Wild West show he presents Indians, real and fake, to white audiences all over the world, but he gradually breaks through the mask he has created to realize what he, and all white people, had done to the confused Indians, and he tries hard to help correct the injustices. Serious scenes of a congressional delegation trying to understand the Indians are interwoven with buffalo-hunting scenes, buffalo dances, Indian dances of self-torture, and scenes from Buffalo Bill's Wild West Show, some completely fake and one of an actual

6–10 History, fantasy, realism, symbolism, and dance combine with Oriental freedom in Kopit's *Indians*, an epic drama about race relations. Below, a model for the set, designed by Oliver Smith. At right, Stacy Keach as Buffalo Bill, making a show of the Wild West. New York, 1969. Photos Martha Swope.

chief who is required to reenact at each performance his final, tragic appeal for help for his dying people before their surrender to the white soldiers. The play opens and closes with a scene of glass museum cases showing wax figures of Buffalo Bill and the Indians, and at intervals in the play prehistoric masked gods of the plains are brought on. If the stage cannot, like a film, show a cineramic battle and the massacre of thousands, it can show a powerful dance-mime of a dozen Indians spreading a great sheet of snow, on which they lie down to be frozen in their final anguish. The stage can use realistic scenery when it needs to, but by using only symbols and fragmentary scenes, it can give more of the meaning of a large subject than a film can. (See Figure 6–10.)

Curiously, the film version of *Indians*, called *Buffalo Bill and the Indians* (1976), made by Robert Altman with Paul Newman as Buffalo Bill, has far less scope than the play. Altman gives much less attention to the central theme of Buffalo Bill's horrified awakening to what he and others have done to the Indians than to an old theme, the contrast between reality and show business, and to Buffalo Bill's worry about his ladies and his wig.

The Persistence of Realism and Naturalism

In spite of the ways in which realism has been modified in this century, the basic impulses persist, and naturalistic playwriting, setting, and acting are still vital. In fact there was a strong resurgence of realism in the 1950s and 1960s in England. We have noted this resurgence in film, and it was no less strong on the stage. It brought in new material, especially about life in the industrial cities and in such groups as North Country and Jewish families—material that seemed fresh and robust to a London audience used to genteel plays about the upper classes. The movement started suddenly in 1956 with the electric response to John Osborne's first play, *Look Back in Anger*. Jimmy Porter, the main character, is caught in an environment he hates, but he is not inarticulate. He spits back with a fiery anger that gave a name to a generation in Britain: the Angry Young Men. The welfare state is a boring fact that leaves him still frustrated. The old establishment is still intact, and he is still outside the regular social order. Jimmy is not fighting for any social cause; his problem is spiritual, as shown in his changing relationship with his wife, Alison. He torments her and drives her out, and he can accept her only when she too is humiliated and crushed by intense suffering. Though Osborne's play does not have the wide scope of Sean O'Casey's or Eugene O'Neill's plays, its depth of suffering, its cry for compassion, its vividness of speech almost put it in the class of their best naturalistic plays.

With *A Taste of Honey* by Shelagh Delaney and a number of other strong realistic plays and films, the force of the Angry Young Men was spent. New playwrights with very different interests appeared, but realism was not dead. The young English playwright David Storey had several successes in the 1970s with what seems like the most casual everyday action on the stage. In *The Contractor* (1970), a group of workmen arrive, put up a canvas pavilion for a family celebration, then take it down afterwards and leave. In *The Changing Room* (1971), a football team of working men who play on weekends for extra money arrive in the locker room, change to their playing clothes, then after the tough game change back to street clothes and go home. When one of them is injured, the bravado of casual companionship weakens for a moment, and we get a glimpse of human concern—but only a glimpse. The shell of isolation returns. *The Farm* (1976) had much the same manner, showing a country family in their daily life but giving only vague clues to their deeper feelings or motives.

Realism has persisted no less strongly on the American stage. Arthur Miller made his first success in 1947 with a typical, Ibsen-like naturalistic play, *All My Sons*. After two decades of exploring several other forms—epic theatre, period tragedy, stylized monodrama, and even a modern Western for the movies—Miller returned twenty years later to the simplest form of naturalistic drama. *The Price*, with one setting and four characters, is as tight a well-made play as any of Ibsen's, with the brothers reexamining in great detail their relation to their dead father and to each other, trying to come to some understanding of how their past and their environment have shaped them and what price they have had to pay for the choices they unconsciously made years before.

The American playwright David Rabe, after having two antiwar plays produced—*The Basic Training of Pavlo Hummel* (1971), very free in form, and *Sticks and Bones* (1971), partly nonrealistic—wrote *Streamers,* which was produced at Lincoln Center in 1976. The setting, though not behind a proscenium frame, showed the essential details of the barracks room of three American Army trainees, two white men and a black. The three men have established an agreeable relationship, but a disgruntled friend of the black man intrudes, disrupting this army home, and violence finally results. The inner lives of the four men are partly revealed through conversation, as in any realistic play. When *The Basic Training of Pavlo Hummel* was revived on Broadway in 1977, with Al Pacino, it was acceptable to regular theatregoers on realistic terms, in spite of the free treatment of time, life, and death.

The Shadow Box by Michael Cristofer, the 1977 Pulitzer Prize play, which uses several techniques of the newer theatre forms, is still basically an example of realism. A simple cut-down structure of several levels in front of a forest of trees indicates fragments of cottages in a hospital grounds. At the beginning and end, the characters speak directly to the audience. The playwright is obviously a man of the theatre of the 1970s, but his characters and their difficulty in facing reality are very much in the tradition of naturalism.

The three occupants of the cottages—a very old woman and two middle-aged men—are terminally ill and must face death. Like the naturalistic characters of Gorki and O'Neill, they are helpless victims of natural forces, protesting in vain. At the end the victims are braver than their relatives. As in *A Taste of Honey,* one of the sufferers finds help in an unconventional person, a homosexual boy. The central values of naturalism are here: compassion, endurance, and an ambivalent view of illusion, which may be necessary for some but is possible only by a complete denial of reality.

It seemed likely early in this century that realism would drive out all "artificial," "conventional" forms of the theatre, or that expressionism or symbolism or some other *ism* would drive realism off the stage, to remain only in the documentary film. But neither displacement has occurred. Realism has been a strand in most of the newer forms, and realism itself, even in the extreme form of naturalism, will probably last as long as journalism, sociology, and social service keep a large part of our attention. To show people in relation to their own environment is to "show it the way it is."

7

The Theatre
of Disruption

Disruption and conflict have existed ever since two tribes came close enough to realize how much they differed in customs and ever since children first wanted to do things their parents had not done. Comedy, as we have seen, deals with limited anarchy, with controlled chaos, and makes laughter out of surprise and incongruity. In very early times, the spirit of holiday took over the five days of disorder at the new year, when the surrounding waters of chaos flowed back into the floating island of creation. The five-day break in the 360-day circle of the year was the time for all to revel, to defy normal rules, and to exchange places in the social hierarchy. When the festival days were over, normal ways were resumed. But in a century of interminable wars, economic depressions, and general uncertainty and fear, when times of peace bring only confusion, disruption is more than an annual lighthearted festival. In Hindu mythology the four-armed dancing god Shiva had one hand to destroy the world and one hand to create it all over again. Early Christians looked for a speedy Second Coming when the world would be destroyed by fire, never to be needed again, but most people in the Western world have held the hope that education and ethics could always restore order.

Over the ages art has been primarily concerned with order, with tracing the possible paths through areas of apparent disorder. But many twentieth-century artists are so dubious of the old paths and so aware of recent upheavals in the landscape that they are more inclined to prepare the traveler for a rough journey than to trace new paths out of the disorder. Yet there are new paths and some fragmentary maps pointing toward possible reconstruction of order.

Plays about disruption, understandably enough, are not easy to classify, but theatre people have been able to discuss most of them under five or six key headings. For the works of the first part of the twentieth century, *symbolism* and *dream* and *expressionism* are the important terms. For drama of the 1940s and 1950s, *existentialism* and *the theatre of the absurd* are the key terms.

Symbolism and the Inner Drama

At the very time when naturalism was getting under way in the nineteenth century, a number of poets were setting themselves against the scientific, rational view. They felt that objective, materialistic art ignored important aspects of the mind and spirit. Such poets as Arthur Rimbaud and Stéphane Mallarmé rejected both nature and reason; instead, they attempted to evoke the eternal beyond the visible by creating suggestive symbols. Like the painters, they were fascinated by symbols of human-ity's alienation—masks and harlequin tramps and clowns. They cultivated free association of words and images, inducing abnormal states of mind—hallucinations and even hysteria and madness—through the use of drugs and alcohol and through frantic sensuality. To them, love was only a demonic force linked with death.

The symbolist poets had a considerable influence on the theatre. Ibsen used much symbolism in his later work, even in plays that seemed realistic—the wild duck in the play of that name, the white horses seen before a death in *Rosmersholm,* the tower that was a fatal challenge in *The Master Builder.* The symbols suggested irrational forces driving men and women, sometimes to fulfillment but more often to destruction. But the chief importance of symbols was as images of the mind in the dream plays and expressionistic plays.

Strindberg's Exploration of the Mind

The first great explorer of the new inner geography was August Strindberg. Even Strindberg's great naturalistic plays of the 1880s, such as *Miss Julie* and *The Father,* were far from the objective studies of heredity and environment that Zola, the great champion of naturalism, had called for. *The Father,* in particular, is a turgid study of destructive hate between husband and wife, a torment no one knew better than Strindberg, whose three tempestuous marriages had led quickly to angry separation and divorce. For some years after the breakup of his second marriage, Strind-berg was on the verge of insanity and put himself into a private hospital for the insane. He wrote several autobiographical novels analyzing his torment and developing his mystical idea that God sends pain to men and lures them with attractive but hateful women in order to purify them. But a more important result of those "inferno" years was a new dramaturgy, a series of plays using many details of his own private life but setting them on the stage with revolutionary techniques. To express man's inner suffer-ing and guilt, he invented phantoms and dream images that could appear out of nowhere, dissolve, and change. O'Neill called him "the precursor of all modernity in our present theatre," and he remains one of the great figures of the age.

Two of Strindberg's plays in particular have influenced the later theatre of disruption: *The Ghost Sonata* (1907) and *The Dream Play* (1902). In *The Dream Play,* the daughter of the god Indra sets out to discover whether human life is as bad as human beings say. After each episode she concludes that "human beings are to be pitied." She encounters four variants of the dreamer—the lover who waits in vain for his love, the

7–1 Surrealism. Both setting and characters suggest the fantasy and transformations of dreams. Cocteau's *Orphée*. Yale University production, directed by Frank M. Spencer, designed by John Koenig, costumed by Sarah Emily Brown and Frank M. Spencer, and lighted by Charles Elson.

lawyer whose hands are black from contact with the crimes of his clients, the ugly quarantine master who impounds contaminated people, and the poet whose agonized cry for mercy she reads for the heavens to hear. Many strange phantoms appear both singly and in choral groups—monsters, officials, ballet dancers and singers coming from the opera house, the misshapen clients of the lawyer, starving workmen watching the rich pass in the street, and sailors frightened in a storm singing "Christ have mercy." As Strindberg planned it, the transformations were made by scenic changes, the opening and closing of backdrops, while the same actors quickly changed costumes for their next appearance. Later producers saw that phantoms of the mind could be transformed without going offstage, by suggestive indications of costume change. Such a flexible dynamic choral group has become one of the most important theatrical devices of the twentieth century.

Pirandello's Exploration of the Mind

The other great germinal figure in the exploration of the mind was Luigi Pirandello. As steeped in pain as Strindberg, he created a more metaphysical terror in his plays. Perhaps all living is acting before a mirror, he seems to say, a mirror that distorts or gives several different reflections. Must each person keep on acting, since the only reality is in the fleeting reflection? Where writers of high comedy find zest and entertainment in the idea of life as acting a role, Pirandello found only pain. He spent years looking after his insane wife, finding solace neither at home nor in the outside world.

Several of Pirandello's plays made a worldwide impression, and they were probably more influential than Strindberg's dream plays in causing a profound change in the treatment of reality. Some of them are realistic enough on the surface. A group of gossiping neighbors in *Right You Are— If You Think You Are* (1917) are determined to learn the truth about the little wife whose husband and mother give quite different accounts of who she is. But the wife herself cannot tell them, and the neighbors find that their intrusion has only increased the pain of people who are trying to sustain the difficult relationships of a family. The husband in *As You Desire Me* (1930) is confident that the cabaret singer he has found is the wife he had lost in the war, but she herself is not so sure.

Two other plays of Pirandello have had even stronger influence. When modern characters appear in the medieval court in *Henry IV* (1922), we learn that servants and relatives of a nobleman have for years kept up the pretense of living in another period because, as the result of an accident while masquerading as the German Emperor Henry IV, the nobleman thinks he really is Henry IV. When the relatives, accompanied by a psychiatrist, stage a shocking surprise in the hope of curing him, he confesses that he is sane but has chosen to remain Henry IV rather than be subjected to the illusive uncertainties of his own life. He chose to live in the past because history, like art, is settled and fixed. But in a fit of anger he kills a cynical friend, and he realizes that he must forever remain Henry IV, though now his attendants know he is acting. In *Six Characters in Search of an Author* (1921), six people interrupt a rehearsal in a theatre, insisting that the director write a play about them. They show him painful scenes of their story, disagreeing violently over the real relations between the father, mother, stepdaughter, and rejected son. The suicide of the younger son provides a sudden interruption both of the unfinished story of the characters and of the contention between the director and real actors and the real-unreal characters, now never to be fixed in art and never to agree on what their reality was or is. (See Figure 7-2.)

The image of acting has proved an even more fruitful metaphor of humanity's uncertain condition than Strindberg's dream images. And Pirandello went further than Strindberg: he implied that there is no systematic reality in the world—that it is not merely a question of a dream as a disarrangement of reality in the twilight zones of the mind, but that the world of thought, undependable and multiple as it may be, is prior to, and basic to, any knowledge of the "facts" of reality.

7–2 Photographer's impression of a Pirandello play. The characters are caught in the shifting planes of reality. Pirandello's *Six Characters in Search of an Author*. University of Texas production, directed by Francis Hodge, designed by John Rothgeb, costumed by Lucy Barton, and lighted by Neil Whiting.

Expressionism

Strindberg's and Pirandello's disturbing explorations of the mind and of the nature of reality were soon followed by the more positively disruptive movement known as *expressionism*. Where realism and naturalism were sharp rebellions against the cheerful sentimentality of Victorian life, the new theatre forms, beginning with expressionism, have been rebellions against realism. Realism seemed too dull and quiet, with its muted colors, understated dialogue, restrained acting, and commonplace surroundings. Where naturalism showed a helpless victim determined, or even overwhelmed, by the environment, expressionism showed an angry little man spitting back at a machine-made, fragmented world. Expressionism reveled in sounds, colors, rhythms, and movement, all presented directly to the audience—a style labeled *presentationalism*, as distinct from the *representationalism* of the realistic style.

Expressionism in drama was in keeping with what was happening in the other arts at the end of the First World War. Painters were smearing raw colors on their canvases, using cubistic angles and planes, paying little attention to the appearance of reality. Musicians were breaking away from the muted moods of impressionism, the controlled discords of Debussy and Ravel, to explore the multitonalities, atonalities, and twelve-tone scales, the interruptions, sharp contrasts, complex rhythms, and violent climaxes of postimpressionism. Isadora Duncan and other dancers had broken from the ritualized steps of the ballet to open the way for a freer use of body movement in dance. Why should the theatre disregard the excitement of vivid colors, strange shapes, loud sounds, strong climaxes, and machine rhythms, at once fascinating and terrifying?

The spirit of revolt rejected the bourgeois-imperialistic dominance in Europe. Even during the war, in 1917, a group of disillusioned artists in Zurich, led by Tristan Tzara, started the Dada movement, which deliberately destroyed patterns and made nonsense of the conventional. It was a negative, partly satiric impulse, but it discovered possibilities of excite-

7–3 Expressionism in the movies. Setting, costumes, and movement are treated as seen in the nightmare of a distorted mind. *The Cabinet of Dr. Caligari*, 1919. Directed by Robert Wiene. Photo Museum of Modern Art.

ment as well as of shock in the juxtaposition of incongruous fragments. Its fur-lined teacups and pasted collages of scraps and objects suggested new ways of using texture even as they defied conventional thinking. If the war was the result of bourgeois conventionality, the Dadaists said, then let's destroy the whole tradition—in fact, all tradition, political, cultural, and artistic. Dramatize the insanity of a military-commercial machine age. Explode firecrackers. Paint mustaches on pretty nudes and conventional madonnas. Destroy the institutions and habits that have enslaved and misled mankind. Open the way for a new world, socialist or communist or utopian. By destroying false ideals that had commercialized, mechanized, and militarized bourgeois society, they hoped to create the spiritual brotherhood of man.

It was out of this postwar spirit of revolt of the 1920s that expressionism was born. Some people have spoken of all revolt against realism as expressionism, but now the word is used primarily for a particular movement that took place mostly in Germany and the United States. One aspect of this movement, which followed the experiments of Strindberg, was a revolt against the objective view of the world in order to show the inner mind, especially in its tortured and distorted states. A second aspect was a reaction to the mechanization and dehumanization of mankind. Thus the dream and the machine were the two poles of postwar expressionism.

The Techniques of Expressionism

In this time of artistic ferment, almost everything that could be called "experimental" was tried on the stage. Some attempts were silly and ineffective, yet a number of important techniques were invented or adapted from older forms. We can classify these techniques into four groups: first, techniques for dramatizing the inner life; second, the use of sounds, movements, and color to build to a climax; third, the use of stylized (that is, rhythmic and sustained) voice and movement patterns to suggest the unreality of a dream or the monotony of a machine; and fourth, generalized, as opposed to individualized, characterization.

The simplest way to dramatize the subjective was to revive the soliloquy and the aside, letting the character put into words his private thoughts, or his "stream of consciousness," an important technique in the modern novel. For soliloquies the spotlight became very useful, allowing one character to speak his thoughts while the background and other characters sank into shadow. The opening scene of Elmer Rice's *The Adding Machine* (1922) is a long stream-of-consciousness monologue by Mrs. Zero as she is going to bed; she reveals the resentment she feels at the empty life she has led in twenty-five years of marriage to the little

7-4 Expressionism. The leaning bars of the courtroom windows suggest the terror of the inner mind as the little man, Mr. Zero, is tried for murder. Rice's *The Adding Machine*. New York, 1922. Photo Vandamm.

bookkeeper Mr. Zero. In the second scene, the conversation at the office between Zero and his assistant is interspersed with asides telling their hidden thoughts. The most famous use of asides is in O'Neill's nine-act psychological drama, *Strange Interlude* (1928), a fairly realistic play in which the action is suspended and the dialogue interrupted repeatedly as one character at a time utters thoughts he would not speak aloud. In *Kennedy's Children* (1975), by Robert Patrick, there is no direct action but only five separate stream-of-consciousness soliloquies in one bar-lounge. Five young people who do not know one another and do not hear one another, alternate their dramatic statements of what it had meant to have the hope and idealism that President Kennedy had inspired, and then to experience the traumatic letdown in the years following his assassination.

A dream fantasy that actually shows the inner thought is more powerful than words. *Beggar on Horseback* (1924), an expressionistic comedy by George S. Kaufman and Marc Connelly, begins with a realistic scene as the poor composer Neil decides that he should marry the rich girl who has just visited him rather than his poor sweetheart. In a dream fantasy he sees the rich girl's family, grotesquely exaggerated. Her mother wears a rocking chair; her father, a business telephone; and her little brother, who is a baseball fiend, an enormous yellow tie and bat.

The second technique of expressionism is the building of a climax by means other than speech. Something more powerful than the soliloquy of a single actor is needed to show an inner crisis, especially since audiences have come to expect very restrained acting. The Greeks, Shakespeare, and Racine wrote long speeches with slow, rhetorical crescendos, expecting the actor to use a wide range of voice and movement. But a machine-age theatre has other resources. When Rice's Mr. Zero is fired, to be replaced by an adding machine, a crescendo of feeling builds to a climax in which Mr. Zero stabs his boss. First the soft music of a distant merry-go-round is heard, and slowly the part of the floor with the desk and stool starts to revolve. As the boss goes on with his impersonal spiel—"Sorry to lose an employee who's been with me for so many years. . . . I'm sorry—no business—business—business—business"—the platform revolves faster and faster, and the sound rises to a tremendous climax.

Stylization, the third technique of expressionism, is a deliberate break with realism. Stylization in stage design immediately indicates unreality by omitting some details and distorting others. Since the emphasis in expressionistic plays is on the insane or abnormal state of the modern world, the distortion is a direct expression of the subjective. Walls lean, posts curve, roofs hang without support, the right angles of normal life become acute angles and sharp points. Objects menace with hands, eyes, pointing fingers. In Georg Kaiser's *From Morn to Midnight*, written in 1912, a tree takes on the appearance of a skeleton. Scenery, usually so static a background, moves before the eyes, falling, leaning in, swinging around, taking an active part in creating the nightmare.

Intensified rhythm is the most conspicuous aspect of expressionistic stylization. The rhythm of a realistic play is always subordinated to the atmosphere of the place, but in the dehumanized megalopolis of the expressionist, rhythm becomes insistent, often dominant. It is usually based on endless repetition of the same movement and sound, such as the monotonous flow of an assembly line or the passage of shiny new automobiles down a highway.

The fourth technique of expressionism is the generalization of character. The central character must represent Everyman, almost as in a medieval morality play. Whether he is the stupid eternal slave Mr. Zero, Yank the Hairy Ape, or just The Young Man or The Poet, he is the dream figure for audience identification, the truth-seeker. That generalized personality moves in a phantom world of even more impersonal characters. We take our name for these machine men from a play of 1921 by Karel Čapek called *R. U. R.* (Rossum's Universal Robots), in which the few human beings still trying to be human contend with mobs of mechanized robots. The Cashier—the hero of *From Morn to Midnight* who steals money and abandons his dull family so that he can try all the vices that money can buy—finds at the races a chorus of identical attendants, and then, at a cabaret, nameless guests and nameless girls in masks. The Salvation Army Lass leads him to a Salvation Army hall, where nameless penitents make their confessions against a chorus of derisive scoffers. One group of actors, of course, with quick changes of costume, serves for all the nameless mobs in such a play, because they are all part of the same dehumanized nightmare of modern life.

The rapid decline of expressionism—it lasted as a movement only from about 1910 to 1925—was due partly to its weaknesses: it was too hysterical and rhapsodic, and its lack of real characters made it too mechanical. But the swift loss of interest in it was due even more, perhaps, to a changing attitude toward the machine and modern life. Where the old heavy machines were noisy and required the monotonous motions of many workers, the later machines are quieter and more nearly automatic. Most people have learned to use the machine as an inconspicuous servant in the background of their lives. The nightmare has lost most of its terror.

The Influence of Expressionism

Although expressionism as a widespread movement is past, it has left traces in realistic plays. One moment in *Death of a Salesman* reminds us that terror of a noisy machine can still be felt. Willy needs human consideration, but the young boss does not listen to him. Instead, he is fascinated by a new mechanical gadget, a tape recorder, on which he has just recorded his young son's recital of the capitals of all the states. When Willy has finally been fired and is left alone, he beats his fists on the desk, accidentally turning on the recorder with its mechanical repetition of a meaningless list. There is a naturalistic explanation of this machine, but the inhuman noise and its terrifying effect on Willy are a vivid moment of expressionism. The flashback scenes in the film *Midnight Cowboy* are a brilliant expressionistic means of showing the hero's present tension. His confrontation with the religious fanatic, for instance, is cut in with the terrifying stylized memory of his boyhood baptism.

A similar moment of obsessive terror makes the inner life of Blanche Du Bois clear to the audience in *A Streetcar Named Desire*. Any new moment of panic makes her relive in memory her young husband's suicide. The audience hears dance music growing louder and louder, and then the pistol shot. Yet no one thinks of *Streetcar* as anything but a completely realistic play. Both the realistic theatre and the film have so completely absorbed the incidental expressionistic technique of presenting a subjective experience that no one takes special notice. A dream character like Uncle Ben moves in and out of *Death of a Salesman,* visible to some characters and invisible to others, without disturbing the sense of reality. It is not even necessary to give him artificial or dreamlike rhythms and movements.

Expressionism is a frequent element in plays of the free new forms of the sixties and seventies. Peter Shaffer's *Equus* (1973) consists largely of a series of flashbacks as the psychiatrist goes deeper and deeper into the boy Alan's disturbed personality. The other characters act as a sustaining chorus in some of these probings. Exorcism of the consuming obsession with Equus, the horse-god, is effected by a re-creation of the ritual of the boy's night rides with his god. The mechanical means used to suggest these rides is a platform revolving at increasing speed, the boy in the center mounted on a man with a horse mask. The eerie background sound, which suggests a mingling of the human, animal, and mechanical, is another expressionistic means to intensify the terrifying exhilaration of the boy's experience. In David Rabe's *Sticks and Bones,* the Vietnamese girl the returned American soldier had abandoned moves about his family home, visible to the soldier and the audience, though not to his parents and brother.

Existentialism in the Theatre

Existentialism, the philosophy that came to dominate much of the thinking of the 1940s and 1950s, especially the thinking of the playwrights, grew out of the disillusionment that followed the Second World War. Thoughtful men and women, despairing of the traditional values formerly found in nature, science, politics, and history, turned inward in the hope of rediscovering a genuine identity, an authentic life of the self. The sense of disruption was far greater than that felt after the First World War. Not only was there a more drastic break with the past, with old buildings destroyed, old institutions discredited, and old patterns of life broken, but now a radically new element had appeared—the atomic bomb. The holocaust at Hiroshima in 1945 seemed to put an end to all that had gone before. If the result of three centuries of science was to be the annihilation of every living thing on the globe, what was to be gained by studying science? Even if destruction could be avoided, the new age of political and economic power that would follow the release of nuclear energy would be so radically different that all traditional values would seem irrelevant.

A Philosophy of Disillusionment

Many people were disillusioned with political action. The methods of liberalism seemed too slow, its piecemeal gains inadequate. In 1917 the Russians had turned to communism, and in the twenties and thirties the Italians and Germans had turned to fascism and nazism, but it soon became clear that none of these regimes would permit individuality. Yet even in France, England, and America, where liberal institutions survived, the individual felt lost in the masses, a nameless object in a crowd. The impersonality of the city and the constant stream of commercial advertising and political propaganda, a stream that increased with the spread of television after 1946, deprived people of a sense of authenic life; all their experiences were secondhand.

In this depressing spiritual climate, existentialism became the support of many intellectuals. Its great appeal was its rediscovery of the self, an entity with an authentic inner life, a complete being free to choose, free to create values, whether or not the universe supports them. By facing death and nothingness, the individual finds the courage to be; by accepting his isolation and loneliness, he finds strength in his freedom. His anguish and uncertainty are a mark of the authenticity of his experience. Just as his death will be his own and not a statistical abstraction, his choice is his own and he creates himself in making it.

After a century of scientific objectivity, of exact measurement, of facts and statistics, the existentialists were ready for the opposite extreme of subjectivity. If scientists insisted on defining reality, nature, and history as independent of human values, then there was no reason to pay any attention to science or history. Many existentialists wrote as though science and history did not exist, and ignored nature as though they had never been outdoors in their lives.

The existentialist mood appeared first in France, where it was especially pertinent during the long, traumatic experience of the German occupation. From 1940 to 1944 each moment seemed one of critical decision—whether and to what extent to collaborate, or whether to say no and face the consequences. Character seemed purely a matter of individual decision, not the result of social forces or natural environment. As thinkers developed the point of view, they discovered that a similar philosophy had been outlined a hundred years earlier by the Danish religious philosopher Søren Kierkegaard, who emphasized a person's isolation and uncertainty and the anguish of making choices "in fear and trembling."

Some Existentialist Playwrights

The existentialist movement after the Second World War was developed most of all in the plays, novels, and essays of two Frenchmen, Albert Camus and Jean-Paul Sartre. Camus' novels made a much stronger impression than his plays, though *Caligula* (1945) interested many people because of its startling hero, who follows the logic of his idea of absolute freedom to the point of killing his friends. Camus' essay *The Myth of Sisyphus* (1942) is one of the classics of existentialism. Sartre's plays were concerned with many problems of guilt and responsibility, from the short *No Exit*, written during the war, to the study of a German's sense of guilt over Hitler, *The Condemned of Altona* (1959). Perhaps more important than his plays are two essays published at the end of the war: *Existentialism Is a Humanism*, probably the most widely read definition of existentialism, and *Forgers of Myths*, which made a radical redefinition of theatre, repudiating the tenets of naturalism. To Sartre, individual differences of human beings, the qualities due to heredity and environment, were unimportant. A person or a character in a play achieved identity only as he made a decision. Though he was responsible only for his own choice, he knew that other individuals might make his choice their own. At least he could say no. A large number of plays since the war have been designed to say no.

As if to illustrate what Sartre was thinking, Jean Anouilh in 1944 wrote his own version of Sophocles' *Antigone* and actually got permission for a Paris production from the German occupation authorities. It is a political play in which a girl defies a dictator, but Anouilh presented both sides of the dilemma in a way that made his play acceptable even to the Nazis. Sophocles' Antigone believes that the laws of the gods are more important than the commands of men; the chorus and the prophet Tiresias support her, and finally Creon, the dictator, admits that he was wrong and she was right. Anouilh, on the other hand, completely isolates his Antigone, allowing her no support outside herself. She has no real belief in God, and she finds no validity for her sacrifice in external facts. Still, by saying no to Creon's world she creates a value for herself. At the end, her weak sister Ismene makes the same decision. Choice is contagious; other individuals may be influenced by example.

Anouilh changed the character of Creon even more than that of Antigone from Sophocles' conception. In the Greek play, he is a tragic figure whose pride is humbled, but the modern Creon remains set in his cold, impersonal view to the very end. He compares the state to a storm-tossed ship that he has taken over because somebody has to issue orders. The mob must be led, and anyone who disobeys orders must be shot. He cannot believe that Antigone, or any human being, would go against the

7–5 Existentialism. Isolated individuals in a meaningless abstract structure. A flexible room, or "black box," arranged with a thrust stage in one corner and audience on several levels. Anouilh's *Antigone*, University of Texas production, directed by James Moll and designed by John Rothgeb.

herd instinct. "*No* is one of your man-made words. Can you imagine a world in which trees say *no* to the sap? In which beasts say *no* to hunger or to propagation?" But existentialism, as Sarte pointed out, is a humanism. An individual decision raises man above the animals. (See Figure 7–5.)

The Theatre of the Absurd

Even Sartre derived a strong sense of commitment from his existentialism and worked with the Communists and other groups as he approved of their immediate aims, but the theatre of the absurd, the avant-garde theatre of the 1950s and 1960s, discovered no values worthy of commitment. The absurdists even celebrated the breakdown of language and communication and deliberately baffled the audience. If confusion and chaos are the human condition, then the form of the play itself must make use of interruption, discontinuity, incongruity, and senseless logic and repetition. Eugène Ionesco called his first play, *The Bald Soprano* (1950), an "antiplay." Some absurdists went so far as to write no play at all but to arrange a set of directions for both actors and audience in a "happening."

7–6
An American play of the absurd. The constructivist setting of different levels is decorated as junk sculpture. Schochen's *The Tiger Rag.* University of Illinois production, directed by Barnard Hewitt, designed by George McKinney, and costumed by Genevieve Richardson.

While existentialists like Anouilh, Sartre, and Camus wrote carefully constructed plays that drew the conclusion that the world has no dependable order, the absurdists expressed disorder in the very form of their writing.

It is significant that three of the most important absurdist playwrights are exiles by choice, living in Paris and writing in a language other than their native tongue—Samuel Beckett, an Irishman, Eugène Ionesco, a Roumanian, and Arthur Adamov, an Armenian-Russian. A fourth, the Frenchman Jean Genêt, feels that he is set apart from humanity as a criminal and pervert and glories in his defiance of what is lawful and normal. These men have chosen to emphasize the sense of alienation, which Camus described in a much-quoted paragraph in *The Myth of Sisyphus:*

> . . . in a universe that is suddenly deprived of illusions and light, man feels a stranger. His is an irremediable exile, because he is deprived of memories of a lost homeland as much as he lacks the hope of a promised land to come. This divorce between man and his life, the actor and his setting, truly constitutes the feeling of Absurdity.

The breakdown of conventional language—the use of empty phrases that not only prevent communication but also destroy the sense of identity—was the subject of Ionesco's *The Bald Soprano.* He got the idea from the numerous meaningless phrases in an English phrase book written for foreigners. During a social evening, the Smiths and the Martins courteously and charmingly repeat statements that are not only inane but also contradictory. The Smiths exhaust all the processes of logic in debating whether a ring of the doorbell always or never means there is someone there. The Martins reach the amazing conclusion that since they arrived in the same compartment of the same train and live in the same room, they must, by coincidence, be husband and wife. But after a theatrical climax, the Martins take the place of the Smiths and start the evening over again. While the expressionist hero contended with a depersonalized, nameless crowd, in search of his own identity, here all is inanity. The characters have no hunger, no conscious desires, no identity. They are interchangeable, and everything ends where it started.

In America infantile regression is made amusing in two of Edward Albee's absurdist plays, in which Mommie and Daddy are lost in baby talk, and the rejected, senile grandmother has to find her own death. In *The Sandbox* she finds a kind angel of death; in *The American Dream,* she finds an emasculated muscle man, an empty dream of vitality.

Things, objects that give meaning and rich texture in naturalistic plays, become in absurdist plays of the 1950s and 1960s the grotesque symbols of mankind's emptiness or even terror. In *The Caretaker,* by the English playwright Harold Pinter, piles of junk fill the rooms of the two brothers, who first show kindness to the down-and-out tramp, letting him feel a new security in the promise of becoming caretaker, then turn on him and eject him from his junk-pile paradise. In Ionesco's *The Chairs,* chairs are frantically brought in to fill a large room as an old couple welcome a world of invisible guests to hear the old man's great message. When everyone is there, including the emperor, the old couple, after introducing the orator who is to deliver the old man's message, jump out the windows into the sea. The orator can do nothing but mutter.

In his longer plays, Ionesco has used a typical "little man," called by the common French name Bérenger, as a sympathetic if ineffectual symbol of modern man facing a baffling universe. *The Killer* is a horror story. Bérenger cannot stop the mysterious killer, though he appeals to him with all possible defenses of human values, and he finally submits to his own death. In *Rhinoceros* Bérenger defies the crowd, not entirely convinced as everybody in his town, even his sweetheart Daisy, turns into a rhinoceros. At least Ionesco's little man makes an attempt to stop the reversion to the barbaric.

Role-playing

The compulsion to act a role, a role that becomes more real than reality, has been the theme of Jean Genêt, whose play-acting scenes conjure up more grotesque images than Pirandello ever created. Genêt follows some of the principles set forth by the French dramatic theorist Antonin Artaud in his influential work *The Theatre and Its Double*, which advocates the theatre's return to the intensity of primitive rituals, of cruelty, incantation, and dream. His plays, in various ways, act out rites, whether the social rites of maids pretending to be their mistress in *The Maids* or the ritual violation and murder of a white woman in *The Blacks*. All Genêt's plays include observers watching a performance, recognizing with mixed feelings the Freudian images of their own suppressed desires.

The brothel in which Genêt's *The Balcony* is set is more than an ordinary brothel; it furnishes not only mirrors but costumes, settings, and actors so that the clients may act out their secret desires—to be a bishop hearing the lurid confessions of a young woman, a judge ordering a half-naked executioner to whip a beautiful girl, or a triumphant general riding a horse, played by an almost nude girl wearing a tail. Outside, a revolution is taking place in the town; the chief of police eventually puts it down by presenting the madam as the new queen and getting the clients to act as a real bishop, judge, and general. The chief gets his fulfillment, the achievement of an image, when finally a client comes to the brothel who wants to play the chief of police. Everything returns to normal, and the madam gets ready for the next clients. The indecent rites of role-playing go on in both the brothel and the real world. As in Pirandello's *Henry IV*, the play-acting becomes more real than the reality outside (Figure 7–7).

Play-acting as a brave pretense in the face of postwar despair was the theme of John Osborne's *The Entertainer* (1957). The run-down music-hall performer—a vivid role for Laurence Olivier on both stage and screen—was a symbol of postwar England. He is facing bankruptcy and failure, but he refuses to give up his music-hall routines and move to Canada. Osborne makes brilliant use of the banality of the popular tradition of stage songs to express the cheap emptiness of modern life. Archie Rice, the entertainer, treats his father, wife, and daughter with bitter harshness, cynically planning to take a mistress, snarling at his own lack of human feeling. As with many people in the modern world, his values are exhausted. He remembers with envy the real feeling of a Negro blues singer he heard once, and when his son is killed in Africa—an event with symbolic overtones—he finds true depth of feeling in singing the same song. When the play was adapted in the seventies for a movie starring Jack Lemmon and given a setting in California, it lost its overtones of the decay of England but developed the similar American theme of the banality of

7–7
Theatre of illusion. Identity is achieved by play-acting in a brothel. One of the clients plays the role of a general with a girl as his horse. Genêt's *The Balcony.*
New York off-Broadway production, 1960. Photo Martha Swope.

popular success in the entertainment field. That has been the theme of two vivid American musicals. The Broadway musical *Chicago* (1974) satirizes the cheap life of journalists and nightclub entertainers, and Robert Altman's movie *Nashville* (1975) shows in epic sweep the frantic competition for empty popular success in the commercial recording and broadcasting of popular country music.

Desolation and Despair

Samuel Beckett seemed haunted by images of confinement and loss of freedom. In *Waiting for Godot* (1952) two tramps are unable to leave the desolate rim of the universe. In *Endgame* the two main characters are shut up in an underground dungeon, one confined to a wheelchair, and a legless old couple reside in two ashcans. The woman in *Happy Days* is buried up to her waist, and later up to her neck. In another play called simply *Play*, the characters are enclosed to their chins in urns.

Beckett's *Waiting for Godot* is the masterpiece of the theatre of the absurd; of all the plays it is the most perfect in its form, the most complete in its desolation, the most comic in its anguish. Two lonely tramps are waiting for Godot, who sends word every day that he will not meet them

7-8
Theatre of the absurd. The past
is discarded as meaningless. The
old parents in their ashcans try to
kiss and console each other. Beckett's
Endgame. Texas Tech University
production, directed by Julie
Schuerger, designed by Gail Wofford
and make-up by Perry Langenstein.
Photo Jane Aker.

today but surely tomorrow. The place where they wait is a desolate road, empty save for a stick of a tree not sturdy enough to hang oneself on. But the tramps are also theatrical clowns, using comic routines of vaudeville days, putting on and off their hats, boots, shirts, coats, and ties, arguing, interrupting, telling anecdotes, munching carrots and turnips, paying mock deference to each other, stumbling and falling, alternating groans with sudden squeals or grimaces. Even the most painful moments are exploded into laughter by the clownish antics.

To the existentialists, freedom is a challenge; to a few people, like William Saroyan, freedom is a delight. But to Beckett's tramps, freedom is hell. They have no inner resources, no friends, no memories, and no orientation in place or time; they do not know where they were last night or indeed if it is the Saturday they were told, they think, to wait for Godot. If the audience wonders why they do not join the activities of the world, the answer appears in the arrival in each act of Pozzo, a fat, active master driving his slave, Lucky, by a rope around his neck—a hideous but comic image of all masters and slaves, all employers and employees.

The play has a remarkably strict form, expressive of its meaning. The form of each act is a series of moments that start with an assertion, a plan, a hope, and quickly dissipate it. Discontinuity is both the theme and the form, deflation the theme and the comic method. The repetition in the second act of the first-act pattern, with a slight development, has a classic perfection that is like mathematics, logic, or music.

Waiting for Godot does not point to any of the known sources of values, yet it is a passionate cry for some new faith, and in that sense it is a very religious play. The problem is certainly metaphysical. No economic improvement, no psychological adjustment, no doctor's pill, but only a new definition of mankind, a new relation to the universe, will serve these forlorn creatures. In its exploration of the last possibility of emptiness, the play may be considered a turning point. Anyone with such passionate need for the spiritual plane will either renew old definitions of God or find new ones.

Intrusion and Menace

The most popular writer in English to follow the absurdists is Harold Pinter, though on the surface his plays seem well-made, realistic plays about ordinary people. Pinter's characters, like those of Ionesco, are caught up in obsessive talk, issuing cascades of cliches, volleys of irrelevant chatter, or rapid-fire, terse phrases punctuating the pauses—Pinter's famous pauses, which may hide a terrifying silence. Pinter's is not an empty universe, but one full of undefined menace. It is a world of insiders versus outsiders, stirring one of our most primitive fears, the fear of an invader breaking into our home and driving us out. The threat is made all the more terrifying by the ambiguity of the relationship. Often the insider invites the intruder in, welcomes him and finds they have much in common. Host and stranger may have had some uncertain contact in the half-forgotten past. In *The Caretaker*, a lonely tramp, while asserting his independence, wants badly to find a secure home, but the insiders drive him out. In *No Man's Land*, the lonely tramp is an older, cultivated poet who never made it, and his host is a rich literary epicure, guarded by two attendants. In a sustained, bristling battle the adventurer-tramp is defeated. To make sure that their host never seeks such an encounter again, the two attendants put him through a ritual committing him to forego any change, any existentialist uncertainty. He is now in No Man's Land, "which never moves, which never changes, which never grows older, but which remains forever, icy and silent." Like Pirandello's Emperor Henry IV, he is fixed forever.

The simplest melodrama of undefined menace is *The Birthday Party*. Stanley thinks he has found a secure place in a boarding house in an obscure spot, but, as in the terrifying stories of Franz Kafka, two strange bullies arrive from some strange organization, terrify him until he is speechless, and take him away. The simpleminded landlady does not even notice. The most delicate anguish is in *Old Times,* as a husband and wife are visited by a woman who had been the wife's roommate, and perhaps lover, years ago. The three try to reconstruct from their vague memories just what their relations used to be, in order to know what they feel about one another now. There are no Ibsen-like bombshells of "now the past must be told," but as delicate an exploration of the nuances of feeling and memory as in the novels of Marcel Proust.

Dominance and its frightening loss is an important theme in many of Pinter's plays. In the radio play *A Slight Ache,* the smug, secure husband is the one who invites in the stranger who had stood for days just outside the gate, selling matches. In challenging the stranger, the husband shows his own insecurity and finally breaks down completely. The wife embraces the stranger, handing the husband the tray of matches—the two have changed roles. In *The Homecoming* a man who returns home with his wife watches spellbound and helpless as his aggressive brothers and father take over his wife for their own sexual purposes and propose to set her up as a commercial prostitute on the side (Figure 7–9).

7–9
Comedy of menance. A wife looks with
mixed feelings toward her hapless husband
as his brother and father are taking
her over. Pinter's *The Homecoming.*
Photo Joseph Abeles.

The barrage of vivid language in many different styles is Pinter's highest achievement. Sometimes, for example, he creates a kind of dramatic poetry by using phrases and cliches that half hide and half reveal the insecurities and terrors of the inner mind. Here is the husband in *A Slight Ache*, about to lose his wife and his own sanity:

> I understand you met my wife. Charming woman don't you think? Plenty of grit there, too. Stood by me through thick and thin, that woman, in season, out of season. . . . Let me advise you. Get a good woman to stick by you. Never mind what the world says. Keep at it. Keep your shoulder to the wheel. It pays dividends.

In *Landscape* and *Silence,* two short plays that are Pinter's most poetic pieces, we see two or three characters, mentally detached from one another, sitting quietly most of the time, evoking in their private consciousness beautiful moments of the past. Natural images and subtle feelings of wonder, joy, and love recur, as in poetry, and the bits of speech and the pauses create a beautiful rhythmic pattern. Since *No Man's Land* followed these lyric plays, it cannot be said that Pinter underwent a complete change, but at least he has shown himself capable of a gentler treatment of people and life experience. *Landscape* ends with this speech by the one female character, which is a poem in itself.

> He lay above me and looked down at me. He supported my shoulder.
> *Pause*
> So tender his touch on my neck. So softly his kiss on my cheek.
> *Pause*
> My hand on his rib.
> *Pause*
> So sweetly the sand over me. Tiny the sand on my skin.
> *Pause*
> So silent the sky in my eyes. Gently the sound of the tide.
> *Pause*
> Oh my true love I said.

Promise of Reconstruction

Antidotes to the gloom and menace of some absurd drama have come from several sources, even from absurdist dramatists themselves. They reassure us that human beings are not necessarily helpless in the grip of natural forces but have the power of the creative mind to sustain and rescue them.

The primacy of the creative power of the mind is shown in *Rosencrantz and Guildenstern Are Dead* (1967) by Tom Stoppard, a brilliant young English playwright. Most of the play is an absurdist drama about the two nonentities who are called to the Court of Elsinore to solve the mystery of Hamlet's strange behavior but who wander helplessly, finding out only that they are to be sent to England to be killed without explanation or reason. In their inability to find any purpose in the directions they are given, they are very much like the two tramps of *Waiting for Godot*. But this play is not merely another absurdist play. In the first place, their Elsinore is not quite the empty universe of the Beckett play. There seems to be something going on within the court, though they are left at the edge, unable to understand. Most indicative of a new age that has gone beyond the drama of the absurd is the presence in the play of the Players. The Players know they are facing the same death as Rosencrantz and Guildenstern, but they are creative artists, not miserable victims of that elementary knowledge. They have learned all there is to know about death by acting it in its multitudinous forms. As creative artists they also know about life, and hence they are free. They know who they are and what they have to do with their lives.

American existentialists have never been quite so despairing as the Europeans. The world Americans picture, even in their loneliest anguish, is not so completely empty as that of Beckett's tramps. Somewhere, they believe, religion, history, and human purpose are to be found, even if we have to create new definitions and hunt out new paths. There are memories of leaders of the past and of mythical and literary figures to cheer us in our desolate night. The heroes of our poetry, novels, and popular myths are as much a part of our past as the actual people of history.

One such mythical figure is Kilroy, the popular image of the wandering American soldier. In Tennessee Williams' surrealist and absurdist fantasy, *Camino Real* (1953), Kilroy staggers out of the desert into a walled Latin American village where various fugitives, historical and fictional, are trying to escape. He is beaten, made to put on a clown's nose and a clown costume, cheated by a Gypsy's daughter, and dissected by an anatomy teacher while two laughing street cleaners with a white can wait for his body. Camille, with Casanova's help, tries to get on the one unscheduled plane, and the elegant dandy from the novels of Proust is beaten to death. No image is spared of seediness, deception, exhaustion, and cruelty. Yet these echoes of the past are reminders of the triumphs of the human spirit. The legendary Camille, the courtesan who made the mistake of falling in love, and Casanova, now King of the Cuckolds, find companionship and solace in each other. Lord Byron departs to sail back to Athens, to contemplate the Acropolis with its reminders of an earlier dream of purity and freedom. At the end, Kilroy and Don Quixote go out the high gate to cross the terra incognita toward the mountains. It is not a futile life-lie but an indomitable courage we see in the hearts of Williams' characters. The walled town is not the whole universe but a temporary prison, from which people may escape if they have imagination and faith.

It is faith that supports the characters of William Saroyan, a subjective faith that is stronger than objective "truth." They know the "truth" but are searching for something better. Saroyan is as devoted to the subconscious and the dream as any surrealist, and he starts with a human condition as lonely as any the absurdists have portrayed. But since he reaches exactly opposite conclusions, he is dismissed by many critics as sentimental. When his characters realize and accept loneliness and the primacy of faith over facts, they discover both the love of God and kinship with all other lonely creatures. In *The Time of Your Life* (1939), when Joe assures the truck driver and the streetwalker that he believes in their dream of themselves, they have strength to be what they dream and to love each other. Saroyan's immigrants and rural characters, bringing dialect and a touch of color to the bars, public libraries, or forsaken buildings where they gather, find friendship and a racy variety in American cities. A Saroyan hero, unafraid of the machine, challenges a super-pinball machine and finally wins. Every character in Saroyan has some ability—singing, dancing, reciting, yarn-spinning, or merely believing— a picture that is much too cheerful and lively for some theatregoers. Saroyan accepts a world of contradictions, of life and death, inhale and exhale, comedy and tragedy. Where the existentialists chose Kierkegaard and Kafka as their models, Saroyan resurrected from the same past the energetic affirmation of Walt Whitman and the witty zest in dialectic of Shaw. A man is free to choose.

Charles Gordone's *No Place to Be Somebody* (1969), the first play by a black author to win the Pulitzer Prize, presents a cross section of lonely humanity looking for friendship and hope at a public bar as in *The Time of Your Life*. But Gordone's picture is more desolate than Saroyan's; the dreams meet sudden defeat, the gangsters are ruthless and deadly, and the relations between whites and blacks are in the end bitter. Yet even as he reflects the urban violence of the 1960s and 1970s, Gordone shows affection for the outcasts who for a moment find common ground in the public streets and bars of America.

The most characteristic American existentialist play is *J. B.*, the Pulitzer Prize play of 1958–59, by Archibald MacLeish. It is the modern version of the Book of Job, in which Job becomes J. B., a successful American businessman faced with the destruction of his children one by one, through war, accident, and crime. In the last act his wife leaves him after an atomic bomb explosion, and he is alone, in pain as desolate in his baffling universe as any European existentialist hero. The active functions of God and Satan in the Bible are represented by two broken-down circus

7-10 Wilder's *The Skin of Our Teeth* produced as a theatrical fantasy in the tradition of American musicals. In a New Jersey living room suggested by bright-colored fragments of walls, a mammoth and a dinosaur are family pets. Eastern Illinois University production, directed by E. G. Gabbard, designed by John E. Bielenberg, and costumed by James Koertge. Photo Bertram.

actors who put on masks as they speak the words of the Bible. Mr. Zuss, impressed by the might and majesty of the universe, tells J. B. he must accept his pain out of fear of God. Nickles tells him he will never accept such a cruel universe, but will spit it back in God's face. Sarah, J. B.'s wife, does come back, and in the end, when J. B. gives up any expectation of finding justice, he realizes that in his lonely choice of love he has found a new relationship to the deity.

There is one American play, now more than three decades old, that forecasts both the absurdist drama of the 1950s and 1960s and the wider historical view that seems possible in the seventies. In its understanding of both disruption and survival after disruption, Thornton Wilder's *The Skin of Our Teeth* (1942) seems one of the most important of all modern plays. It recognizes the constant danger of disruption yet shows that people with creative minds can pick up the fragments of the past and start civilization over again. The disaster of the first act, the Ice Age, is entirely external; it is out of human control, and all one can do is build fires and try to preserve a few accomplishments or aids in starting over again. The flood of the second act is not so external. Now people have earned their destruction by living for the moment, falling from their earlier dedication; Mr. Antrobus, relaxing at a convention, is about to abandon his wife and children for another woman. Faced with emergency, he rediscovers his dedication to the human family and herds them and the animal representatives into the Ark waiting at the end of the pier. The third disaster, war, is entirely the responsibility of human beings. Mr. Antrobus faces the surviving enemy, his own son Henry (who is also Cain), and soon the two are at each other's throats. The son resents authority, and the father has been so sure of the importance of past achievements that he has not bothered to consider the son's own thoughts and choices.

But even in moments of the play that have the most serious implications, absurdity reduces the tension. At the end of the first act, as the ice gets closer, the family takes in refugees: Homer, the blind singer; Moses, the judge; a doctor; and the Muse sisters, who all sing around the fire. As Mr. Antrobus is teaching Henry the multiplication table, the lights dim, and Mrs. Antrobus starts reading to Gladys from the Bible—"In the beginning God created the heavens and the earth. . . ." When tears come into the eyes of the audience, the absurd interrupts; the ushers start breaking up chairs and the maid, Sabina, says to the audience, "Will you please start handing up your chairs? We'll need everything for this fire. Save the human race." At the end of the play, after the fight between father and son has been settled and mankind is ready to start over, a parade of actors, representing the hours and the planets passing over the sky, speak passages from the great prophets and philosophers—Spinoza, Plato, Aristotle—and that same beautiful passage from Genesis. At the line "And the Lord said let there be light and there was light," the stage lights go out. When they come on, Sabina is starting the play again.

There is acute awareness that the thread of contact with past values is fragile but also that a person is free at every moment to choose values and create a new world. Like Mr. Antrobus, we can start over again, and unlike Beckett's tramps, we have a vision to guide us. (See Figure 7–10.)

The ferment in the theatre in the fifties and early sixties led to an extraordinary liberation of the theatre in the late sixties and the seventies. That achievement is the subject of the next chapter.

8

A Liberated Theatre

TOTAL THEATRE. POPULAR AND
HISTORICAL IMAGES IN A SATIRIC
FANTASY BASED ON THE IRONIC
MONOLOGUES OF THE NIGHTCLUB
COMEDIAN LENNY BRUCE. JULIAN
BARRY AND TOM O'HORGAN'S *LENNY*.
NEW YORK, 1971. DESIGNED BY ROBIN
WAGNER AND COSTUMED BY RANDY
BARCELLO. PHOTO MARTHA SWOPE.

It has been the task of the decade of the seventies to pick up the pieces after the confrontations of the two previous decades, confrontations that reached a climax of anarchic rebellion in 1968. That year was marked by a rock festival at Woodstock, New York, that gathered several hundred thousand young people to celebrate their music and their life style and, more ominously, by riots in Paris and Chicago and protests and demonstrations on some American college campuses that almost disrupted teaching completely. Champions of youth liberation led the pack, but also in the procession were workers for black liberation, women's liberation, gay liberation, Indian liberation, and others. At the end of the seventies we look back, trying to understand why the surge of anarchical feeling among young people was so much stronger than in earlier rebellions, what has happened in the theatre in the wake of some of these liberations, and which of the new developments now seem excessive and which seem valid and useful for a more conservative period.

The Youth Rebellion

At first the youth movement seemed just another gathering of refugees who had rejected the aggressive competition and sterile respectability of the bourgeois cities. In the nineteenth century many youths from all over Europe and from America settled in the low-cost "Bohemian" section of Paris to paint, write, make love, and talk about art and life. They became legendary, and their joys and sorrows are celebrated in the popular opera *La Bohème*. In the 1920s many young people spent a few carefree years on the Left Bank in Paris or in New York's Greenwich Village before going back to moneymaking and respectability in their home towns. Following the San Francisco pattern after the Second World War, many young people all over the world developed a subculture of enclaves and communes with their own costume style and explored heightened states of consciousness through popular music, sexual freedom, drugs, and occult practices. The Beatles, with their long hair, their new rock music, their vision of fresh, youthful enjoyment, set a fashion for revolt around the world.

The angry reaction of conventional older people to so harmless a symbol as a fashion in hair helped to convince the young that there was a generation gap, with people over thirty hopelessly devoted to materialism, police power, and war. If short hair was a symbol of conformity, materialism, and repression, then long hair became a symbol of rebellion, joy, sexual freedom, peace, and brotherhood.

The psychology of the youth rebellion is made clearer by the comparison that anthropologist Victor Turner makes with the initiation ceremo-

8-1 Seizing the freedom of Oriental conventions, an individual character emerges from the choral group of singers and dancers. *Hair*. New York, 1967. Directed by Tom O'Horgan. Photo Martha Swope.

nies of several traditional cultures in central Africa. In the middle part of the initiation, after the youths have broken from the daily patterns of society and before they are reborn and reintegrated as responsible adults with set roles in society—in that unstructured time, they feel the joy of freedom and a mystic sense of unity with one another, with all mankind, indeed with the universe. Turner calls this sense of cosmic identity "humanitas." We recognize it in the strong group loyalty of rebellious youth in the 1950s and 1960s. Initiation also often involved some humiliation or self-abnegating gesture, as, for instance, the putting on of the clothes of humble people. The initiates felt in tune with the heart of meaning, in an altered state of consciousness. It was like a return to some primeval age before the differentiation of classes, or even of the sexes. Similarly, the hippy style, almost a uniform, borrowed the jeans of workmen, the ragged scraps of tramps and clowns, and the beads and headbands of the Indians. For flower power, bright-colored patches of gingham were added.

This joy in group solidarity, this *humanitas*, is clearly developed in the musical *Hair* of 1967, performed as an "American tribal love-rock musical" by a cast of about twenty-five. Only a few characters emerged with names. One young man was expelled from school and another was drafted. The tribe celebrated the burning of a draft card (which turned out to be a library card), the glory of long hair, the defiance of rules and restraint, and the use of marijuana. The songs and dances wove together images of Hindu love gods, black and white companionship, love-ins, hopes of peace and freedom, draft boards, the war in Vietnam, the Civil War, the Indian wars, Shakespearean actors, Buddhist monks, and Catholic nuns. With an orchestra on one side of the bare stage, actors bringing on suggestive props and symbols as needed, and actors in the group stepping in and out of roles, *Hair* used the happy, imaginative flexibility of the Oriental theatre and the mobility of epic realism to celebrate group joy and the hopes of rebellious youth (Figure 8–1).

Black Liberation

The Black Liberation movement also reached its extreme in the late sixties. The more aggressive blacks took a militant turn, declaring that whites and blacks could never get along together, that Black Consciousness must recognize implacable hostility and work for complete separation. Some dreamed of a black state carved out of the nation. Some tried to "return" to Africa, but without much success. Others joined radical groups that hoped to destroy Western society and were confirmed in their hatred when police deliberately shot down Black Panthers in their home. A few blacks converted to Judaism and many more to Islam, hoping to find in the Third World a base for self-respect and identity that seemed impossible to attain under what appeared to them a hypocritical, racist Christianity.

Le Roi Jones set the pattern in Black Theatre, with such plays as *The Toilet* (1964), *Dutchman* (1964), and *The Slave Ship* (1967). *Dutchman* dramatizes vividly the encounter of a black man with a white girl in a subway. She starts a flirtation and denounces him when he responds. He expresses his anger, and when he starts to leave the train she stabs him. Another black man enters the subway as the play ends, and we know that the conflict will be repeated. The action of the play is symbolic of an antagonistic relationship of white and black that cannot be altered. We are not surprised that this playwright abandoned his Anglo-Welsh name Jones and his French name Le Roi and took the African name Imamu Amiri Baraka.

When Martin Luther King was killed on April 4, 1968, many blacks who had been opposed to extremism and violence turned militant. As one black enthusiast wrote, "Dr. Martin Luther King was the last prince of nonviolence. He was a symbol of nonviolence, the epitome of nonviolence. Nonviolence is a dead philosophy, and it was not the black people that killed it." Now the Black Arts movement must be identified with the

Black Power movement, and Black Power demanded a new, militant aesthetic. One leader wrote, "The Western aesthetic has run its course: it is impossible to construct anything within its decaying structure. . . . Implicit in the Black Arts movement is the idea that Black people, however dispersed, constitute a nation within the belly of white America. . . . It is on this idea that the concept of Black Power is predicated."

The plays of such black authors as Langston Hughes and James Weldon Johnson were denounced as catering to the point of view of the whites. Even Lorraine Hansberry's play *A Raisin in the Sun* (1959) was scorned as showing blacks trying to adjust to white values, eager to reassure whites that blacks could be good neighbors. Those who adopted the principles of Black Power did not want to be good neighbors. Especially despised was the fine black actor Sidney Poitier, whose roles in Hollywood showed how painless social integration could be for a charming, well-educated, well-dressed black, and of course the blacks who were radical in their point of view had no patience with the bourgeois, well-to-do blacks who enjoyed the high comedy *Purlie Victorious* and the musical *Purlie*, plays we described in Chapter 3. Militants got pleasure out of the film *Superfly*, reveling in the angry violence of a black man who defies the law and makes it rich.

By 1964 a Black Theatre Directory listed thirty-seven groups in the United States, nine in Los Angeles and one, the Free Southern Theatre, in New Orleans, that aimed at all-black or mostly black companies, to play whenever possible for black audiences. Most of them used plays by American black playwrights, with a few by South African or Nigerian writers. Ed Bullins wrote naturalistic plays, exploring, like the European naturalists of the beginning of this century, the desperate lives in city slums, with thieves, junkies, nightclub entertainers, lesbians, prostitutes, and drunkards. The problems of more stable black families are presented compassionately, without bitterness, in *Ceremonies in Dark Old Men* (1969) by Lonne Elder III and *The River Niger* (1972) by Joseph A. Walker, which had successful runs in New York. Elder has been one of the leading figures in the Negro Ensemble Company, founded in 1968 with help from the Ford Foundation. It is one of the best training and production companies in New York, and many of its productions at St. Mark's Playhouse have been transferred to Broadway. (See Figure 8–2.)

Two plays of Athol Fugard, a white man now tolerated, now jailed, in South Africa, have had some of the best acting New York has seen in the last decade. *The Island* (1975), set in an isolated prison, traces the changing hopes and despairs of two black political prisoners. Fugard's *Boesman and Lena* (1970), beautifully played in New York by James Earl Jones and Ruby Dee, gave an unforgettable picture of a lonely South African man and woman of mixed race, hounded by police, torturing each other in their desperation and need for pity and affection, bravely enacting a kind of comedy.

Claudine, an excellent black movie of 1974, with appeal for both black and white audiences, was made by John Berry, the white director of *Boesman and Lena.* It is a story with romantic, realistic, and comic elements about a Harlem widow with six children, her affair with a sporty garbage man (James Earl Jones), her relations with a welfare agency, and her problems with a rebellious son and a teenage daughter who becomes pregnant. The plot is not very original, but the film has been praised both for technical excellence and for the fresh portrayal of Harlem life, with sympathetic treatment of character and natural acting. A large number of black films, most of them of poor quality, have been made for black movie houses ever since the 1920s, but better financial resources and the training now available for all film technicians, actors, and directors promise great improvement.

Two films prepared especially for television have presented the black experience in historical perspective: *The Autobiography of Miss Jane Pittman* in 1974 and Alex Haley's *Roots* in 1977. Through the supposed reminiscences of a woman 110 years old, *Miss Jane Pittman* gave the racial experience from the Emancipation Proclamation to 1962—an experience of many perils and some joys. The impersonation by Cicely Tyson was all

8-2 Realistic study of a lively, affectionate family in Harlem. Joseph A. Walker's *The River Niger.* The Negro Ensemble Company. New York, 1972. Directed by Douglas Turner Ward. Photo Bert Andrews.

but perfect, and when, in the big moment of her life, Miss Pittman tottered up the steps of a Louisiana courthouse to drink from a fountain reserved for whites, freedom at last became real not only for her but for the viewers.

For his book *Roots,* Haley had delved into the history of his family and visited the country of his free ancestors in Africa, and the twelve-hour broadcast in one week of eight episodes about the family's bitter trials as slaves and their release to freedom and new trials became the epitome of the American experience of an entire race.

Some Avant-Garde Groups

Closely related to the movements of liberation was the phenomenon of small groups of enthusiastic young actors who, under the leadership of an imaginative director, were willing to forego possible success in the commercial theatre in order to experiment with new kinds of plays and new techniques of production, especially new relationships of actors and audience.

Tom O'Horgan, before he directed *Hair* for Broadway, had been involved with the lively experiments of Ellen Stewart's Café La Mama and had taken a small company of young American actors through Europe, exploring group acting of the most acrobatic and ecstatic kind.

Joseph Chaikin developed the Open Theatre, where *America Hurrah* (1966), a group of three one-act plays by Jean-Claude van Itallie, found a wide public. The first two plays were of the expressionistic type familiar

8–3
Grotesque image of mutual destruction. Two oversized cardboard puppet figures with actors inside destroy each other by removing strips of cardboard. Van Itallie's *America Hurrah.* New York, 1966. Photo © 1971 Fred W. McDarrah.

8-4
A modern version of Euripides' *The Bacchae* in terms of primitive ritual. Presented in an "environment" created in an abandoned garage (the Performing Garage), with actors and audience in one room. The Performance Group's production of *Dionysus in 69.* New York, 1968–69. Directed by Richard Schechner. Photo Fred Eberstadt.

in the twenties and thirties. The third play was a novel work in which the action was presented by two larger-than-life mannequins who tore apart a motel room and then stripped limbs and pieces of cardboard off each other (Figure 8–3).

The Performance Group was started in 1968 by Richard Schechner with a few students from New York University. The group played in a garage reconstructed into an "environmental theatre," that is, one in which there is no formal stage, space is arranged to fit each particular play, and the audience sits and stands around or among the actors so that it becomes part of the action. Schechner wanted to integrate the actor, the art, and the spectator into one event that created the immediacy of primitive ritual. The most important presentation of the Performance

Group was *Dionysus in 69* (1968–69), loosely based on Euripides' *The Bacchae*, a play dealing with the power of the Greek god Dionysus, patron of revelry, sex, freedom, ecstasy, and frenzy. The formal text was interwoven with "actuals," consisting of the actors' personal associations, their interaction with the audience, and contemporary rituals such as Yoga meditation. Some members of the audience were encouraged to remove their clothing and participate.

The Living Theatre

Of the avant-garde groups the Living Theatre was the most controversial and the most persistent in its attack on the established social order. From 1951 until 1963, Julian Beck and his wife, Judith Malina, kept the Living Theatre together in New York, producing a wide range of plays, from poetic drama and classic tragedy to partly improvised pieces dealing with drug addiction and other contemporary subjects, challenging their actors to work constantly on new techniques. The Beck group's fresh approach and defiance of convention won it an ardent following.

Closed down in New York in 1963, the Living Theatre found a responsive audience in Europe. But when their engagement at the Avignon festival of 1968 ended in conflict with the police, they and all their following were ordered to leave town. Back in America in the glow of their defiance of the European establishment, the company produced a sensational effect with performances at Yale, the Brooklyn Academy of Music, and in several other cities. Some people were annoyed that the suffering, crying, cooing, caressing actors came into direct contact with the audience. Others were outraged at the long scenes of the writhing, almost naked, scrawny bodies in a drama that seemed never to get anywhere. But nothing in theatre had so fully excited the rebellious spirit of youth. In addition, the style of performance seemed the most advanced an American audience had seen. Not only did the actors move among the audience, but the audience were invited to take off their clothes and join in on the stage. There were powerful choral scenes where body movement and inarticulate sounds—grunts, groans, screams, wails—counted more than words.

Paradise Now, perhaps the most characteristic production, began with thirty-seven long-haired, near-naked actors coming down the aisle, saying to each member of the audience, "We are not allowed to travel without a passport"; "I do not know how to stop war"; "I do not have the right to take off my clothes"; "One cannot live without money." Suddenly the audience was aware of the policemen at the doors and joined in the chant, voicing their sympathy with all rebels against authority. Here was pop mysticism with the hypnotic power of ancient rituals, with images of sex, savagery, and salvation.

More spectacular was the Living Theatre production of *Frankenstein*. A quiet moment of Yoga meditation led to a wild run of actors through the audience, trying to escape pursuers but captured and dragged back to the stage and killed in various ways. By their resurrected bodies the group formed a laboratory for the creation of the monster, then formed his huge body. Then in the head of this creature, in nine separate cells, the actors illustrated different aspects of the ego that must be transformed from hostility into love before mankind can be free of its prison. But the performance created more hostility than love; there were fights in the audience, and many people angrily stormed out.

The Becks returned to Europe with their company in 1970, but the group soon broke up. Some radical members were not satisfied with the nonviolent revolt of the Becks, and the Becks themselves, who had operated on a shoestring for twenty years, were exhausted by the financial problems.

Grotowski's "Poor Theatre"

Where the Living Theatre saw modern men and women in their relation to a corrupt society, the "poor theatre" of Jerzy Grotowski set out to study religious crises of the inner self. The actors of his Polish Laboratory Theatre dedicated themselves to concentrated work in a small group for a very small, selected audience. Subsidized by the Polish government, Grotowski worked in a small Polish city and produced not in regular theatres but in small rooms, where he could bring forty to a hundred people into an intimate relationship to the play—for each play, a different relationship. They watched the torture and martyrdom in *The Constant Prince* as if looking down from the wall of a hospital operating room or a cockpit; they watched the hallucinations in *Kordian* as fellow inmates between the beds of an insane asylum—close but with no direct contact.

The visit of the Polish Laboratory Theatre in America in the fall of 1969, though only a very few people saw the performances, produced more discussion than any other theatrical event in many years. Here were subjects that seemed extremely pertinent to the spiritual crises of our day—actors performing a classic Polish play about the high points of civilization while they were constructing a gas chamber out of rusty pipe. Here was an intensity of expression in voice and body that could come only from years of work with techniques quite different from Stanislavsky naturalism. Here was group action as intense and rhythmic as a primitive ritual dance. Here were words used as incantatory sounds—or were they

8–5
"Poor theatre." Jerzy Grotowski's Polish Laboratory Theatre enacts the great myths while building an extermination chamber of rusty pipes in Wyspianski's *Akropolis*. London, 1968. Photo Douglas H. Jeffery.

words? We are told that long passages were unintelligible to Polish audiences.(See Figure 8–5.)

On the production side, the "poor theatre" was equally startling. Having decided early on that it would be ridiculous for the theatre to compete with film and television in effects, Grotowski eliminated everything that the actors could not handle or create themselves. There were no classic texts, no settings or lighting effects, no musical accompaniment, and simple costumes, some of coarse cloth, some near nudity. The poor theatre was theatre stripped to the two essentials: actors and spectators.

Grotowski's was a religious theatre, and his plays often showed a saintlike figure surrounded by a chorus of only slightly differentiated characters—a Christian prince who brings a blessing to the common people who torture and devour him but finally glorify him, or a Christlike village simpleton who provokes the villagers into crucifying him. Yet Grotowski could not view the old myths without bitter awareness of the gas chambers of the modern world. That awareness gave a mocking tone and contorted tensions to acting that was already extremely acrobatic and tense.

If Grotowski had continued in the theatre, would he have gone beyond his Hiroshima complex, his mocking tone, his obsession with the eating of saints? By the mid-seventies, while his company still occasionally performed, he had left the theatre to conduct sessions of sensitivity exploration in the wooded hills around his castle.

Experimental Groups in the Seventies

Like comets, the Living Theatre and the Poor Theatre quickly captured attention, created great excitement, and as quickly faded away. Several other experimental groups, just as dedicated, still survive. Some of the actors in these groups have to work at other jobs during the week and can perform only on weekends. Some groups can make enough money to devote full time to experimenting and performing, at least for a short season each year. One booking agency for these numerous small companies is called A Bunch of Experimental Theatres, Inc.

Quite modest but very dedicated is the Mabou Mines company, founded in 1970 and now sponsored by Joseph Papp in a small room of the Public Theatre. In the visual version of Samuel Beckett's radio play *Cascando* in the 1976–77 season, the company achieved remarkable concentration as each actor followed one line of simple everyday business, often in counterpoint to, rather than in support or illustration of, the words. But *Dressed Like an Egg* (1977), designed and directed by JoAnne Akalaitis, was more effective. Taking brief, unconnected passages from the works of the French writer Colette, the actors, three women and two men, created a composite image of early twentieth-century Paris and the men and women Colette loved. In narrating and describing, more than acting, animating personal properties as much as speaking, the company achieved in small compass the visual excitement of the painter's art and the poetic feeling and dramatic intensity of theatre (Figure 8–6).

In his Ontological-Hysteric Theatre, Richard Foreman has created startling plays, if they can be called plays, from his ontological concern with the nature of reality. They usually have long, arresting titles and are often in two or more parts, presented at different times, as *Book of Splendors: Part Two (Book of Levers): Action at a Distance*. His main character in all the plays, Rhoda, played by the same actress, Kate Manheim, finds that reality is not dependable at all. Both people and things may move away suddenly, or tilt over at odd angles, or answer you, or speak your thoughts for you over the loudspeaker. As one image follows rapidly after the other, each one contradicts the last. Everything baffles Rhoda,

8–6

Theatre of Images, without plot or sustained character. The styles, moods, and qualities of the Paris of Colette are evoked by sounds and phrases and a moving series of visual elements. *Dressed Like an Egg*. Mabou Mines Company. New York, 1977. Directed and designed by JoAnne Akalaitis. Photo Richard Landry.

8–7

A series of images, actors, and sounds, in changing relationships, creates a logic of its own. Foreman's *Rhoda in Potatoland*. Ontological-Hysteric Theatre. New York, 1976. Photo Babette Mangolte © 1976.

but she goes doggedly on. When she is most puzzled, she takes off her clothes as though looking for something. In 1976, as *Rhoda in Potatoland*, she was more surprised than Alice in Wonderland. It is a strange but haunting world that Foreman creates (Figure 8–7).

The productions in his small theatre, a fourth-floor room in a building on lower Broadway, were so successful that Foreman was asked to direct Brecht's *Threepenny Opera* and Strindberg's *The Dream Play* for the Beaumont Theatre in Lincoln Center. Although Brecht's musical in the original German production had been a riotous parody of opera, Foreman's production was very serious, with much less of the parody and laughter that have made his own productions popular.

The master of parody is Charles Ludlam, who is playwright, director, and principal actor in the Ridiculous Theatrical Company. A writer for the Ridiculous once said, "We have passed beyond the absurd. Our position is absolutely preposterous." Ludlam's plays have been described as "sprawling, fantastic epics couched in a kaleidoscope of styles ranging from Jacobean tragedy through Grand Guignol to Marx Brothers knockabout farce." Parody, especially in the campy style of female impersona-

8–8 Romantic acting exaggerated and burlesqued. *Bluebeard*. Written and directed by Charles Ludlam. Presented by Ridiculous Theatrical Company. New York, 1971. Photo Max Waldman © 1971.

tors, is a large element in the plays, as some titles suggest: *Gorilla Queen, Bluebeard, Big Hotel, Stage Blood.* But the material, drawn from popular entertainment stars, from literature and drama of East and West and from contemporary life, is a wild comic mixture. Beginning in a spirit of rebellion, using a loose, unstructured form of drama, Ludlam has moved toward the traditional form of the well-made play, but some plays are still written partly in rehearsal, members of the company suggesting dialogue and plot changes. (See Figure 8–8.)

The two leaders who have done the most to foster dedicated experimental groups and encourage new playwrights have been Ellen Stewart and Joseph Papp. At her Café La Mama, Stewart started production of new off-beat plays in the 1960s and encouraged the formation of new groups. Later she and her actors renovated an old building and created the La Mama Annex. We have described in Chapter 1 a production there of a trilogy of Greek plays. Several times she has taken groups of performers to Europe, arousing a great deal of interest in American experimental theatre.

Joseph Papp has cut an even wider swath in sponsoring small groups and producing new plays. He has not maintained one group but has been the director or producer or guiding spirit for many companies in several locations since he began in 1954 to present free Shakespeare in an East Side church. In 1962 he was largely responsible for the building, with some private funds and some from New York City, of the Delacorte Theatre, an outdoor amphitheatre in Central Park, seating more than 2,000, and he made "Shakespeare in the Park" a popular success. In 1967 the old Astor Library building was transformed into the Public Theatre, with five auditoriums (later seven) suited to different kinds of productions. It opened with *Hair,* and it has continued, in spite of financial difficulties, to offer a varied, sometimes controversial, and usually exciting program, providing a hearing for new playwrights and experimental plays. Many of the productions have gone on to Broadway, among them *Hair* and the extremely popular *A Chorus Line.* When Papp was put in charge of the large Beaumont Theatre of Lincoln Center, the conservative uptown clientele was startled at the language of some of the new plays but equally at the unusual production in 1977 of Chekhov's *The Cherry Orchard,* with young Andrei Serban, director of the La Mama Greek trilogy, as director and the lovely Irene Worth as Madame Ranevsky. Papp's overall operation is known as the New York Shakespeare Festival, and in 1977, with a budget of several million dollars, the organization had seven offspring running at the same time, two at Lincoln Center, two in Broadway theatres, and three in the Public Theatre. No one in New York has done more in recent years to promote interesting theatre in a variety of styles. Nevertheless, at the end of the 1976–77 season, Papp resigned his position at Lincoln Center, finding it too difficult for even his considerable abilities.

Some Results of the Liberation

In the course of the experiments of the avant-garde groups, a number of new patterns and relationships have been established and are accepted even by conservative producers and directors. What liberation means for the training of actors will be discussed fully in Chapter 10. The influence on the theatre at large of new, freer dance forms will be discussed later in this chapter. Here let us consider changes in performance place that bring the actors closer to the audience, as well as liberation in language, plot, and character development, and new uses of the choral group.

Place into Space

Modern lighting equipment and new concepts of stage space have made the painted stage picture behind a proscenium frame seem outmoded. It is so easy to close a scene by dimming out the lights and bringing them up on the next scene, or to change the scenery in sight of the audience, that often the front curtain is not used at all. Even in the proscenium theatre the actors are brought forward in closer contact with the audience.

We have gone far toward liberating the performance from the theatre building, proving that many other places will serve as well: warehouses, garages, abandoned railroad stations, barns, terraces, entrance steps. Indeed many religious plays are better performed in churches. Most theatre groups, from professional resident companies to college departments of dramatic arts, like a small room for "experimental" plays—one that can easily be rearranged to try different relationships between the audience and the playing spaces. For a revival of the musical version of *Candide* in 1974, a Broadway theatre was gutted and several platforms and long runways were built for the performers. The result was an environmental theatre, with many separate sections of bleachers for segments of the audience. In most scenes there was no attempt at stage setting, but a few scenic effects were used successfully. In one episode, with a small suggestion of sails hanging from above, the actors on several platforms, facing the same way, showed by their swaying that they were on one large ship. As the Chinese have shown, actors can sometimes suggest with their bodies what for centuries the West has used scenery to do (Figure 8–9).

8-9 Environmental theatre. Action on a runway, audience on benches and bleachers all around. Bernstein's *Candide*. Broadway Theatre, New York, 1974. Directed by Harold Prince, designed and costumed by Eugene Lee and Franne Lee, and lighted by Tharon Musser.

Actors and Audience

The traditional relationship between audience and playing space has been broken in the last two decades, in the hope of increasing audience response and participation. While Brecht, wanting the audience to make a cool decision about the problem presented, would interrupt his emotional scenes by songs, projections, or direct talk to the audience, other directors, especially those with political concern, have hoped to unite the audience into a public meeting of protest with ardent response that might issue in action. In 1968-69, as we have seen, both the Living Theatre and the Performance Group went to the extreme of inviting the audience onto the stage. When there were specific tasks to do, as piling up bodies after a plague, that worked well. But in the productions of both groups, the invitation to remove clothing and take part in love celebrations led to embarrassment and hostile confrontations. Though Grotowski brought actor and spectator within inches of each other and often used several playing places surrounded by spectators, never did he let the actors make a direct contact. The tension between actor and spectator is so strong that only a privileged character such as a clown or master of ceremonies can break it without serious disturbance, and he only in a very controlled situation.

The most successful audience response has been achieved by black musicals. *Don't Bother Me—I Can't Cope* (1973) stirred the mostly black audience by a strong expression of black pride and self-confidence. The several actor-singers had the audience responding in rhythm, swaying, clapping, and holding hands. Even more of the "soul" of black gospel preaching was achieved in *Your Arms Too Short to Box with God* (1977), a "service-worship" using the betrayal of Judas, the Crucifixion, and the Resurrection from the Book of Matthew. As at an old-fashioned camp meeting, the theatre congregation shouted its "Amen . . . yes, Lord" to punctuate the ecstatic chanted verses of the actor-preacher. Perhaps the proved power of the American church tradition is a better basis for the performer-audience relationship than the theory of a "primitive" African, Balinese, or Mexican ritual of magic.

Language—the Word

The theatre has been further liberated from the dominance of the literary text. Theatre is much more than "putting on a play." As early as 1905, Gordon Craig called on directors and designers to create a play out of movement, space, line, color, and rhythm, declaring that the dancer was more important as the father of theatre than the poet. The playwright had dominated too long; let the actor and director improvise words as they rehearse the action. In its way, naturalism had already subordinated the word to the actor's body language, leaving the word scarcely more func-tion than a grunt. As we have seen, the creative spirits of the 1960s rebellion, even when they started with a script, let the actors improvise much of the dialogue. Chaikin used his playwrights to give a final form after the main action and many of the words had been established by improvisation.

Once the immersion of the actor in the written dialogue is broken, many combinations of acting with lyric and narrative discourse are possi-ble. In Story Theatre a memorized narrative is illustrated by the group, or several characters in turn may take up the story. Story Theatre invites a rich use of mime and dance. There are several forms of Readers Theatre, some austere, keeping the performers, dressed in neat modern clothing, sitting on chairs or stools or standing at reading desks, some more theatrical as one or several actors, for particular episodes, step out from the reading stations and engage in memorized dialogue. It is easy to flow back and forth from reading to impersonation and acting. Dylan Thomas' radio play *Under Milkwood*, with its several dozen characters, has been staged in many ways, from the use of stools and books in hand to changing hats and skirts and jackets from a table on stage, and even with some passages sung and danced. Hal Holbrook made a brilliant evening of the comments and stories of Mark Twain, and Emlyn Williams with the sketches and stories of Charles Dickens. The short monologues of Edgar Lee Masters' *Spoon River Anthology* have been staged in several ways, usually with five or six actors, with slight changes of costume, sometimes with some sketches sung and danced.

An excellent Broadway production in very simple form was *For Colored Girls Who Have Considered Suicide When the Rainbow is Enuf*, based on the poetic monologues of Ntozake Shange. Seven young women in long simple gowns, each of a different color, on a stage bare except for one eight-foot rose, presented the experience of a dozen or so black women

8–10 Interpreters theatre. A combination of lyric and narrative, performed by four couples who, in various combinations, suggest appropriate characterization for each song. A sketch of Coward's face is projected on the setting. A revue of Coward's songs called *Mad About the Boy*. Eastern Illinois University production, directed by Donna Shehorn, designed by J. Sain, and costumed by Sue Saltmarsh.

growing up and facing adult problems in a big city. The play ran through the whole season of 1976–77. (See color plate.)

Plot and Character

Even more amazing than release from a binding text has been the theatre liberation from plot and character. For centuries action and conflict have been central to most definitions of drama, and individual characterization has been considered one of the highest dramatic values. Yet many of the more daring productions of the sixties and seventies have been almost devoid of story or character development. We have noticed that the impressionistic plays of naturalism, especially the plays of Chekhov, seemed to have no action because the characters made no decisions but let things happen to them. Wilder's *Our Town* was novel in having no antagonist and no conflict, though the playwright gave a strong propulsion forward to the wedding and to Emily's visit from the land of the dead. But in the last two decades many plays have had no plot at all, only a loosely woven web of action; they have also had characters that are only slightly individualized. The absurdists were not much interested in characterization, and, as we have seen, Pinter's characters usually remain enigmatic, their motives unexplained. In many experimental plays, characterization in depth, a goal the realists strove for, does not exist.

Extreme examples of dramatic entertainment that is plotless but absorbing are the "operas" created by Gertrude Stein and Virgil Thomson in the thirties and forties and the even stranger "operas" of Robert Wilson in the seventies. They present carefully planned sequences of movement, colors, and forms, controlled by rhythm and often music; they are without plot, character development, and sometimes without impersonation or dialogue. On first acquaintance such pieces seem total nonsense, but for those who are open to new experience they can be fascinating.

Gertrude Stein became famous overnight for her simple but cryptic statement "rose is a rose is a rose." In the 1920s, long before Artaud called for a performance with words used not for their meaning but for their incantatory power, Miss Stein wrote stories and plays using hypnotic repetitions. Her first collaboration with Virgil Thomson was *Four Saints in Three Acts*, produced in Hartford and New York in 1933 with an all-black company of singers and dancers.

More stunning was the later Stein-Thomson opera, *The Mother of Us All*, produced several times just after the Second World War and given a brilliant production at the Santa Fe Opera for the bicentennial celebration in 1976. The subject matter is Susan B. Anthony's struggle for the rights of women. More like an oratorio than an opera, more like a political rally or a

8-11 A patriotic celebration of Susan B. Anthony and the campaign for votes for women. Stein and Thomson's opera *The Mother of Us All*. Santa Fe Opera Company for the Bicentennial, 1976. Designed and costumed by Robert Indiana. Photo Ken Howard.

Fourth of July celebration than a play, this theatrical piece has its big moments in a wedding and in the apotheosis of the statue of Susan B. as admirers gather around it wanting her help and strength for other political causes. Among the Women's Rights workers move John Adams, Daniel Webster, Ulysses S. Grant, and others—all swept along in the celebration of love and laws. Here is a sample passage:

Susan B. . . . [men] are afraid, afraid, afraid, they are afraid, they are afraid . . . . and so they have written in the name male into the United States constitution, because they are afraid of black men because they are afraid of women, because they are afraid afraid. Men are afraid.

Anne. But Susan B. you fight and you are not afraid.

Susan B. I fight and I am not afraid, I fight but I am not afraid.

Anne. And you will win.

Susan B. Win what, win what.

Anne. Win the vote for women.

Susan B. Yes some day some day the women will vote and by that time.

Anne. By that time oh wonderful time.

Susan B. By that time it will do them no good because having the vote they will become like men, they will be afraid, . . . oh I know it, but I will fight for the right, for the right to vote for them even though they become like men, become afraid like men, become like men.

Like Gertrude Stein's work, Robert Wilson's productions startle us by achieving serenity and happiness in an age of disillusionment and pervasive anxiety. Wilson first gained attention in 1971 with *Deafman Glance,* built around the fantasies of a deaf boy he befriended, who joined the group to play himself. Not a word was spoken, and Wilson's theatre was sometimes called the theatre of silence, but from the first there were vivid sounds—owls screeching, animals howling. Objects, large and small, puppet figures, and people floated through the air or glided across the stage. Marie Antoinette and George Washington in white wigs moved in front of a row of black apes who were eating apples. One setting showed the Last Supper in front of a primitive hut and an Egyptian pyramid. Nearly all the movement was extremely slow, hypnotizing but puzzling. A performer would stand like a statue an endless time; another might take a half hour to cross the stage.

When in 1972 Wilson was invited by the Shah of Iran to present a production at the ancient ruins of Persepolis, he spent months in France preparing *KA Mountain and GUARDenia Terrace* and presented in France a six-hour sampling or *Overture,* part of which started at six in the evening and part at six in the morning. At Persepolis the complete performance lasted 168 hours, given without stop for a symbolic seven days and nights of creation. A typical scene of international religious imagery was a cardboard facsimile of New York City on a snow-capped mountain summit bursting into flame and replaced by the Lamb of God under a Chinese pagoda. In 1973 at the Brooklyn Academy of Music, Wilson presented a twelve-hour opera called *The Life and Times of Joseph Stalin.* More modest was the three-hour *A Letter to Queen Victoria,* produced at the Spoleto (Italy) festival in the summer of 1975 and in the fall in both Europe and New York. It made use of words not as dialogue but as a verbal element in expressionistic and satiric scenes—for instance, a scene of dancers dressed in the style of the 1920s sitting at cafe tables, wildly gesticulating and reciting "chatter-chatter" as one by one the couples are picked off by a sniper.

Einstein on the Beach was a much more ambitious project, costing nearly a million dollars to produce for the 1976 Avignon summer festival and for more than twenty performances in western Europe, before playing for two sold-out performances at the Metropolitan Opera in New York. It was a collaboration with the American composer Philip Glass, who, like Wilson, creates slow, sustained moods through the hypnotic effect of countless repetitions of short themes, with gradual transitions and changes of tone. In this opera we can see more clearly what Wilson has been trying to do. He has used as dramatic material a number of personalities who have had a strong effect on the moods and texture of the modern world: Freud, Queen Victoria, Stalin, now Einstein.

Einstein on the Beach is a meditation on the impact of science and mathematical abstraction on the modern world. *On the Beach* is the title of a novel and movie about a small group of survivors of an atomic war who at the end are expecting their own destruction. Einstein himself was a gentle man who played the violin and liked boats and trains, yet it was his calculations that made possible space ships and the atomic bomb.

The main performers are dressed like Einstein. The opera begins with a single Einstein in the pit in front of the stage playing the violin, an image that is reverberated throughout the stage space—one Einstein figure appearing like a mad scientist, one comic like Charlie Chaplin, one demonic like Hitler. Another Einstein draws mathematical figures and equations on an invisible blackboard, and his gestures are echoed by dancers. To suggest the square, the dancers move briskly on straight lines that turn sharp right angles; for triangles they move on diagonal lines; for circles they whirl like dervishes, as clocks and compasses float through the

8–12 Modern science and mathematics on trial. The judges, looking like Einstein, arrive in a spaceship. Dancers turn in figures based on the circle. Wilson's *Einstein on the Beach*. Directed by Robert Wilson, composed by Philip Glass, and choreographed by Andy de Groat. Photo Babette Mangolte © 1976.

air and a dark disc eclipses a round moon, until finally a crowd below watches a solitary figure high on a building still solving mathematical riddles.

With elaborate equipment for movement, lighting, and sound, a train moves in and out, a space ship moves into place, objects and people float through the air, like dreams of beautiful images—many recognizable from well-known paintings. A trial scene suggests that modern science is on trial, but there is no accusation. Pain and evil are indicated, and the dreaded atomic holocaust, but the sustained intensity and the slow motion of the performance create an awesome spell, a new state of consciousness that is religious and mystic, beyond morals and indignation.

In the movies, montage effects of moving objects, floating symbolic images, or variations on a theme can be presented so easily that they make only a slight impression. In the physical presence of real bodies and objects in the theatre the effect is far stronger. Will this become a new genre of theatre, or will it be absorbed into the main stream, as expressionism and many other experiments have been absorbed?

The Choral Group and Multiple Role-Playing

With the loss of plot and characterization has come an increasing emphasis on the choral group and multiple role-playing. In *Hair* the choral group was central to the action. When particular stories and characters were needed, different members of the group stepped forward and spoke lines. An actress might play a man's role and an actor a woman's. At some performances a black actress briefly played Abraham Lincoln and kicked the white servant blacking Lincoln's boots. (See Figure 8–1.)

In the Open Theatre production of *The Serpent,* a choral group carried the play. The group formed a long writhing serpent, and different actors stepped out of the mass to enact Adam and Eve, Cain and Abel, and the assassinations of President Kennedy and Martin Luther King, letting the rest of the group respond like a Greek chorus of witnesses.

There was economy of audience attention as well as economy in production in the plan of *A Chorus Line*. As particular actors were asked to speak of their personal lives, they stepped forward, the whole group remaining on stage. Thus some actors were given a touch of individuality as well as group roles to fill as anxious job candidates, then as joyful winners and game losers, and finally as triumphant performers. The hope of the applicants gave the group a romantic glow not found in the more impersonal groups of *Hair* and *The Serpent*.

The convention of an enclosing action is a well-known device to make a bridge between the audience and the actors' role-playing. Early in the

8–13
Carnival clowns in masks and makeup arrive
to put on a play about a young medieval
king. Hirson and Schwartz' *Pippin.* New York,
1972. Directed and choreographed by Bob
Fosse, designed by Tony Walton, costumed by
Patricia Zipprodt, and lighted by Jules
Fisher. Photo Martha Swope.

century Harley Granville-Barker gave a bright style and high spirits to
Shakespeare's *Twelfth Night* by beginning with the arrival of a traveling
troupe of comedians who set up their platform and took their bright-
colored hangings and costumes from a trunk. Much of the color and joy of
the musical *Pippin,* which had a long run in the seventies, was due to the
device of having a troupe of clowns perform the play with masks and
bright makeup. For the setting, a magician pulled a silk handkerchief out
of the floor, and it flew up into the air and became a decorative picture
drapery. The energy and gaiety of the clowns permeated the play (Figure
8–13).

An abandoned circus tent is the metaphor and setting for MacLeish's
J. B., as a popcorn-vendor and a balloon-vendor play an enclosing and
guiding action for a play about a modern Job. There is multiple role-
playing. The vendors make their own comments but use masks to speak
the words of God and Satan from the Bible. The four different pairs of
messengers who bring Job news of the violent deaths of his four children
at different times are played by the same pair of actors.

In the musical *Man of La Mancha,* an even more effective enclosing
action as a bridge between audience and actors' role-playing is supplied
by the choral group: rough prisoners who act out the story of Don Quixote

8–14
Mechanized spectacle of pop religion.
Jesus Christ Superstar. New York,
1971. Directed by Tom O'Horgan.
Photo Joseph Abeles.

under the direction of the author Cervantes, who has been thrown among
them. The slut Aldonza and others emerge from the choral group as
individualized characters, and Aldonza really enacts another role as she is
transformed by the Don's conviction that she is beautiful and pure.

This device of the impersonal choral group from which actors step out
to take roles is the basis of the two religious musicals *Godspell* and *Jesus
Christ Superstar,* which have been more popular with youth in the seventies than *Hair* was in the late sixties. These plays express less rebellious
attitudes and yet have much of the joy of group *humanitas. Godspell* set up
a group of young people wearing casual subculture costumes in a play-
ground with a wire fence that could be climbed to give a variety of levels.
Actors stepped out of the group to play roles in the episodes of the life of
Christ and his parables from the Gospel of St. Matthew. *Jesus Christ
Superstar,* having started as a popular recording of several connected rock
gospel songs, was expanded to a full opera with no spoken dialogue. It can
be presented very simply, but for the Broadway production Tom
O'Horgan made it an elaborate spectacle, with machinery that raised
actors and scenery into the air and carried actors floating down from
heaven. The film made from the musical started with a busload of American hippy young people setting up a playing structure of metal pipes in

the desert mountains of the Holy Land. Older churchgoers scarcely recognize the psychology or the theology of Christ or Mary Magdalen or Judas in this mode of pop culture (Figure 8–14).

Dance in Contemporary Theatre

Perhaps the most significant development in contemporary theatre is the increasing importance of dance in production and in the training of actors. As performance is freed from the tyranny of the text of the play, movement becomes all-important and approaches dance. The actor is now expected to work in a number of styles, some of them far from quiet naturalism, many of them close to dance. At the same time the two great traditions of dance, ballet and modern dance, have moved close together and both have come close to the theatre. Now an actor or a choreographer-director may move back and forth among the three.

Modernization of Ballet

The modernization of the ballet began in Paris in 1909 when the impresario Sergei Diaghilev, with a group of Russian dancers, began to produce a variety of short ballets. He and his choreographers loosened the classic techniques in order to give each ballet a distinct style. Many of the best modern painters—Bakst, Rouault, and the young Picasso among them—made designs for him, and many of the best modern composers—Debussy, Ravel, the young Stravinsky, and others—wrote music for him. More than any other man of his time, Diaghilev brought into the theatre the creative forces of twentieth-century literature, art, and music.

Ballet came slowly to America. Even as late as 1940 it was an exotic importation from Europe; no one would have predicted that by the 1960s America would be a world center for ballet. Yet there are now schools all over the country, and ballet has taken several new directions that seem particularly American. The American Ballet Theatre, founded in 1939 and subsidized for years by the millionairess Lucia Chase, continued the eclectic, international trends of Diaghilev's Ballet Russe, using national folk idioms and theatrical characters. Antony Tudor devised some striking psychological ballets for the American Ballet Theatre, and Agnes de Mille widened the style of the company to include the masculine vigor of the American West in *Rodeo*.

Most surprising has been the development of an American classicism in the ballet, the achievement of George Balanchine and the New York City Ballet. Starting with a school in 1933 and a ballet company in 1946,

8-15 American movement in ballet. *Rodeo*. American Ballet Theatre. Choreographed by Agnes De Mille. Photo Martha Swope.

8-16 Patriotic pop ballet. *Union Jack*. New York City Ballet. Choreographed by George Balanchine. Photo Martha Swope.

Balanchine has created one of the top ballet companies in the world, with its own home in Lincoln Center. Where other choreographers had turned against the classic tradition to extend the old techniques, Balanchine returned to the strict classic form. He has made less use of story, pantomime, and gesture than is found in the more romantic ballets, depending more on the abstract form of music than on the narrative form of literature. Where the simpler romantic ballets presented a fairy story of a dreamer trying to capture the dream, the newer ballets, even in their charm, show the surrealist nightmares, anxieties, and fears of the twentieth century.

Antony Tudor and Jerome Robbins have gone much further than Balanchine in creating psychological and surrealist ballets, with images of alienation, dread, fear, and flight, of neurotic Greek legends, of strange gardens haunted by memories, missed opportunities, and frustrations, of Freudian shapes, masks, and monsters, of dark journeys and phantom corridors—just the subjects that fascinate modern dancers.

New Relationship of Ballet and Modern Dance

Relaxation of the strong opposition between ballet and modern dance had begun by the 1950s, as dancers with different training met together in musical comedy and responded to the same interest in Oriental and primitive dances. A few dancers from each camp surreptitiously studied some of the techniques of the other camp. In the sixties an American, Glen Tetley, trained in both ballet and modern dance, became director of the Stuttgart Ballet and in a short time made it one of the best in Europe. In 1976 Murray Louis, a distinguished performer of modern dance, choreographed a ballet, *Cleopatra,* for the Royal Danish Ballet. It has seemed possible to mix the two kinds of dance.

The closer relationship was celebrated in 1975 when Margot Fonteyn, the English ballerina, and Rudolf Nureyev danced in *Lucifer,* a new dance drama by Martha Graham. In the same year Mikhail Baryshnikov danced with the American Ballet Theatre in Twyla Tharp's *Push Comes to Shove.* Both Nureyev and the much younger Baryshnikov had been top dancers in Russia and defected to the West because they saw no chance in Russia for experiment in dance. Established in this country, they wanted to try American modern techniques. Margot Fonteyn called the crossover a wedding celebration. (See Figures 8–17, 8–18, and 8–19.)

In the meantime, theatre had been moving closer to musical comedy, opera, and dance. As actors were brought nearer the audience and freed from illusionistic scenery and properties, they could be more rhetorical, lyric, assertive in body movement. When they formed a choral group, they became less individualized. In comparisons of acting with dancing, it has

8–17
Early modern dance with abstract
sculpture. A single dream image set
against a small choral group. Martha
Graham's *Legend of Judith*. Designed
by Dani Karavan. Photo Martha
Swope.

8–18
Dance drama with individual characters,
strong story, and elaborate setting for
action on two levels. Martha Graham's
Scarlet Letter, with Nureyev as Dimmesdale.
New York, 1975. Designed by Marisol and
costumed by Halston. Photo Martha Swope.

8–19
Baryshnikov in the carefree, impudent, cocky style of Twyla Tharp's *Push Comes to Shove*. American Ballet Theatre. New York, 1975.
Photo Martha Swope.

often been said that the realistic actor presents a specific character with a name and address, while the dancer presents an emotion or intention. Music, which is even more abstract, gives only the basic patterns of all emotions, the shape of all experience: progress, development, opposition, interruption, suspense, statement and response, venture and return, change and continuity, tension and repose, climax and resolution. As the elements of dance and music become increasingly important in "new" theatre, the actor feels the need of formal training in voice and movement.

With ballet performers, Jerome Robbins explored jazz dance, musical comedy dance, and, with the help of Japanese actors and musicians, the sustained, slow power of the Japanese Noh, bringing the dance world and the theatre into closer relation. The Joffrey Ballet of New York, by absorbing some of the modern dance techniques of Holland and Germany and responding to the twentieth-century interest in multi-media lighting and projection, approached the modern theatre from another direction.

Meanwhile American modern dance has made its progress toward a theatrical synthesis. While the first decades of modern dance were almost as austere as the "poor theatre" of Grotowski, the sixties and seventies found the Martha Graham company using a sizable orchestra, elaborate costumes, and spectacular settings.

The Avant-Garde Dance

Modern dance, like the theatre, had a rebellious avant garde in the fifties and sixties. Alwin Nikolais exploited elements of the theatre, especially costumes and properties. His performers seemed grotesque animated forms as they moved about encased in geometrical shapes, flexible cords, wrappings, and balloons. But at other times Nikolais let the human element emerge in exciting movements and groupings, with stunning costumes and settings and dynamic lighting. Or he used actors' bodies as screens for patterned projections, setting the human form and its patterned costume against changing shapes of light images. Most theatrical of all was the Nikolais sound track on tape, made up of actual sounds combined with electronic sounds that had never been heard before. Murray Louis, a pupil and collaborator of Nikolais, has created, as a synthesis of many influences, his own group with his own distinctive style.

Some avant-garde dancers carried the reaction against romantic emotions and neat compositions much further. They showed the natural impulse of all theatre people to wake up an audience that had become accustomed to a set of conventions and was therefore passive. Why not let the performer dance among the seats, or suddenly look at the audience and imitate their reactions? Put many things on the stage and let the audience choose what it wants to watch. Bring back spontaneity for performers and audience. Set a dozen musicians playing anything they want to play, mix in a few radios, electronic sounds or very loud speakers, and a siren or two. Develop a "dance by chance," leaving some movements to the whim of the performers, or let dice or cards determine the next move. Or give the audience moments of rest with nothing whatever to see.

The leader of this dance theatre of the absurd, this antidance, was Merce Cunningham, who had danced for years with Martha Graham. With the avant-garde musician John Cage, and later with the experimental artist and sculptor Robert Rauschenberg, he presented programs designed to shock the conservative, amaze the young, and perhaps now and then point out a step beyond nihilism. He used emptiness not for Zen harmony and peace but for the shock of discontinuity, with the impudent effrontery, for instance, of having a dancer stand still for several minutes and then make one jump. The wonderful leaps Cunningham had done with Graham's company were now used for violent kinetic contrasts, as he began by suggesting what dancing he could do, then interrupted himself and threw away the expectation he had created.

Other dancers have learned to use some of the discontinuity of the antidance movement without giving up all traditional order. Paul Taylor, who has created some of the most impressive new dances of the late sixties and the seventies, uses some startling absurdities as minor elements of comedy. *Orbs,* for example, delineates in its first movement a large idea of sun, moon, planets, and open space that gives a bold perspective for the more mundane human and satiric later movements. In his new way Taylor even achieves an old-fashioned charm and dignity.

Recent Dance Blends

The old and the new, the serious and the humorous, the classic and the popular, blend in the work of the black dancer and choreographer Alvin Ailey. He belongs partly in the tradition of modern dance, for he studied with Martha Graham, Charles Weidman, and Hanya Holm, but, in choreographing for the Alvin Ailey City Center Dance Theatre, he also uses ballet and jazz steps—in fact, whatever suits his wide range. His early work, designed to express through dance the black experience and pride in that experience, reached a climax in 1960 with *Revelations,* a composition set to traditional Negro music, with singing. It remains a favorite in his repertory. More recently Ailey has created striking works set to the music of the black orchestra leader Duke Ellington. One of these, *The Mooche,* has an elaborate setting and costumes to create a nightclub atmosphere. In one movement, men and women perform a jazz routine, counterbalanced by six women following behind them with precise ballet steps.

Although Ailey's company does not promote stars, Judith Jamison, who has been in the company since the mid-sixties, has become the popular favorite. She is tall for a dancer, with a majestic build, great intensity, and remarkable versatility. She can be funny or tragic, humble or proud, earthy or elegant. In the dance called *Cry,* created for her by Ailey, she becomes the proud African ancestress as, with a few sweeps of her arms, hands, and her whole body, she wraps a long cloth around her head and strides about the stage. Later, as she stretches up her long arms and slowly circles her head, she expresses the anguish of women who mourn their men, lost to drugs, prison, and death. In *Revelations* she skims on stage wearing a long ruffled dress, holding up an immense white parasol, all elegance and command; in another scene she becomes someone's affable aunt in a church congregation as she bustles on stage in a Sunday-go-to-meeting hat. In one of Ailey's compositions to Ellington's music, she appears in an elegant, black-satin pants suit, dancing *Pas de Duke* with Mikhail Baryshnikov, the Russian star of the American Ballet

Theatre (Figure 8–20). One critic has said that her most impressive skill is to keep a human dimension while projecting superhuman power and radiance.

Ailey's company has a world-wide reputation, for it has traveled extensively under the sponsorship of the State Department. Ailey keeps a "Repertory Workshop" as a touring company. He has choreographed for the Metropolitan Opera, and he includes in his repertory dances set not only to Negro spirituals, blues songs, and folk music but to works of most of the important modern composers.

The most striking new dance figure in the seventies has been the comic choreographer Twyla Tharp, who aroused such audience enthusiasm that by 1976 she was in demand all over the Western world. She dances with her own small group, but also choreographs for a number of ballet companies. Some of her best work has been for the Joffrey Ballet. She is more interested in individuals than in the group. Often her characters, each one different, wander on or burst on stage as though completely surprised to find anyone else there. Like Charlie Chaplin, her characters

8–20 Dancers from two traditions come together. Baryshnikov from Russian ballet and Judith Jamison from Alvin Ailey's company dance Ailey's *Pas de Duke* to music composed by Duke Ellington. Photo Martha Swope.

meet the fragmented, disjointed world with a cocky defiance or a flippant shrug. They may do the opposite of what is expected: a woman does what a man is expected to do, or a dominating woman easily handles two men. Her dancers wear casual sports clothes and usually sports shoes, and dance to a wide range of popular music. She uses movements from ballet, modern dance, tap, ballroom dancing, and sports. We are not surprised that she was a prize-winning baton twirler or that she choreographs for ice shows. After the dream magic of the ballet and the anguish expressed in much modern dance, it is a joy to see brave flippancy and a robust sense of humor (Figure 8–19).

Recovery of the Past

In the last quarter of the twentieth century we can see, within and beyond the various forms of liberation we have been describing, a powerful fascination with the past. This fascination leads to two quite different historical views, one charged with emotion, concentrating on a narrow interpretation of the past, the other more rational, leading to a wider perspective. Both move beyond the despair of the existentialists and absurdists of the fifties and beyond the anger of the rebels of the sixties. Both views are dynamic and creative, compelling new orientation in time and space through new definitions of history and science. Both require that the individual be seen as part of a dynamic society, a surging mass of interaction.

Ritual and History

One historical view finds meaning in regression to an earlier age. Applied to the theatre, it inspires a search for primitive ritual, in the hope of giving actors and audience a revolutionary experience, a drastic purging, a shock therapy so extreme, so cruel, that it would stir up the violent forces in the unconscious and release the vitality of our primitive ancestors. The other historical view, which compels the search for a wider perspective, is less exciting and more difficult than the search for a theatre of ritual but perhaps more rewarding in the long run. The more difficult search has been aided by developments in scientific thinking. The existentialists, in their retreat to the subjective and personal, rejected both science and history as part of the objective, mechanical, statistical realm outside of human values and of art. Now science is recognized as being subjective as well as objective, and the gap between science and art no longer seems so wide.

During the first half of the twentieth century, as scientists became less sure of the objectivity of their speculations, they gradually changed their definitions of reality. Heisenberg's "principle of uncertainty" and the contradictions between the quantum and the wave theories of light forced scientists to bring the observer back into the equation. They now use not only mathematics but models to clarify and communicate their ideas, and more than one model may be needed, according to which aspects the observer wants to communicate. The recognition that the creative mind, working in models, metaphors, and symbols, has many valid ways of dealing with reality leads to the recognition of the power of the arts to create a sense of reality in time and space, that "memory of a homeland" of which the existentialists felt deprived and so had no hope for the future. When an individual loses his memory he is subject to intense anxiety, wondering how he got where he is and what he is to do next; so is a nation lost without a sense of the past.

The seventies have seen a marked growth in respect for the arts, witness the increasing support by government and big business, and the arts have contributed more and more to our sense of the past. In the seventies it became clear that architects and city planners were taking a new attitude toward the past. Architects have always been interested in surviving monuments, but in the first half of the twentieth century they made less use of the past in their creative work than any other artists and rivaled one another in "renewing" old cities with "modern" architecture. But the economic crunch of the seventies and the stimulus of the Bicentennial, among other influences, made them see not only the economic but the emotional advantage of adapting old buildings for present use. Cleaned up and repaired, old buildings give people a sense of continuity with the past. Classical music, ballet, and opera, like historical museums, transport us into the feelings and styles of another time. But the theatre, more than the other arts, right before our eyes brings the past to life in the present.

The narrow historical view, of regression to a primitive past, has had a strong influence in the theatre. The idea of a ritual theatre has probably been the most stimulating model for theatre workers in the twentieth century, as we have seen in the study of experimental groups. It suggests and justifies the wildest intensity in dance, song, and nonverbal sound, the strongest emotions of terror, pain, and ecstasy. It is the perfect model for audience participation: under the leadership of a witch doctor or actor-priest, the whole tribe does the performance. It gives everyone a sense of taking part in the basic rhythms of nature. It implies a religious or metaphysical purpose: to propitiate and coerce the gods. It claims to explain the origin of theatre, indeed of all the arts. It justifies the liberation of a frank, healthy joy in sex from the suppressions and evasions of the Victorians. It admits, as the Victorians never would, the ambiguous, fiendish joy in killing and destruction. It seems to extend our knowledge of history back thousands and thousands of years. It offers a psychology of art in its invocations, exorcisms, ritual killings, ritual eatings, matings, processions, and celebrations—joy as fertility rites.

The idea of the influence and survival of primitive ritual under the gloss of civilization was first fully expressed in Sir James Frazer's *The Golden Bough,* the first volume of which appeared in 1890. Frazer considered that for millions of years the defining act of the human condition was the annual spring ritual of killing the vegetation spirit and resurrecting him in a wild celebration of fertility—blood and sex—and that civilized behavior was a superficial overlay of such practices. Frazer was a kind of Peeping Tom, living properly in Victorian England while being certain from his reading and research in tribal ways that an altar was *really* a chopping block for a human sacrifice, his wife's Easter bonnet *really* a fertility symbol, and a football game *really* a contest to decide which clan of the village would keep the severed head of the sacrificed victim.

The idea of a ritual theatre thus became a view of history: history as composed of two periods, the primitive and the civilized, the civilized being a brief time of scarcely over three or four thousand years, as against the hundreds of thousands, perhaps millions, of years when "primitive" people presumably lived a uniform, unchanging life. Since the primitive produced the basic, unconscious patterns of human nature, those patterns are equally present in everyone and can be brought to the surface by the incantatory rhythms of primitive rites.

But this short view of history, recognizing only two periods, is a very questionable theory. The worship of fertility gods is not universal, and human sacrifice as a ceremonial has been rare. There is no trace of it in Egypt or Greece, though Frazer thought the myths of the killing of Osiris and Dionysus proved that both countries had once had actual killing and had later substituted symbolic death. The theory of evolution from the actual to the symbolic and dramatic is based on no real evidence. The opposite theory, that the wild spring rites of magic, with ritual killing, were a degeneration from religious symbolism, could be just as well supported. Drama may be as old as ritual. What we learn about prehistory does not support the idea of primitive thinking as quite different from modern religious and scientific thinking. Recent decipherment of bones and pebbles marked as calendars, dating back twenty or thirty thousand years, shows a complex conscious control of days and seasons—scientific thinking. Further, a rational view of history—the broader view—sees modern mankind as a product not of two periods but of many gradual changes over many years.

Artaud's Vision

The great prophet of ritual theatre was the Frenchman Antonin Artaud. His essays, gathered and published in 1938, were to set the new directions for the theatre after the Second World War. A sick man himself, he called for a new theatre as drastic therapy for the sick soul of the modern world. Between headaches and opium, between breakdowns and years in an asylum, Artaud wrote essays that have caused more reverberation in theatre circles than any statement of theory since Gordon Craig's *On the Art of the Theatre* of 1911. After writing poetry and working on surrealist films, Artaud turned to the theatre and tried acting, directing, and playwriting without much response, and not until 1931 did he find his vision. That was a pivotal year for the impact of the Orient on Western theatre. In 1931 Mei Lan Fang, the traditional Chinese actor, performed in New York and Europe, and both Brecht and Thornton Wilder published several short plays with Chinese conventions. In that year Artaud saw the dancers of the Balinese theatre in Paris. With no need to understand the language, he found that the sounds, gestures, and action transcended reality and put both performers and audience in direct contact with the unconscious, with the dark, mystic powers of the soul. The ritualistic Balinese art made the popular entertainment of Paris boulevard theatres seem trivial. The modern Western world seemed to Artaud outworn, false, and barren, and that theatre seemed dead which merely repeated the standard "masterpieces." He dreamed of a new theatre for the West that would be an overwhelming experience, stirring up in both actor and audience the vitality of the primitive soul. Such a transformation might require a holocaust. The theatre would become a theatre of cruelty, with every impulse carried to the utmost extreme. Such a relentless theatre would be like a plague, draining the abscesses of a sick world.

> The theatre [Artaud wrote in *The Theatre and Its Double*] like the plague is a crisis which is resolved by death or cure, and the plague is a superior disease because it is a total crisis after which nothing remains except death or extreme purification. . . . the action of theatre, like that of plague, is beneficial, for, impelling men to see themselves as they are, it causes the mask to fall, reveals the lie, the slackness, baseness, and hypocrisy of our world.

For Artaud, a necessary part of the cure was to abandon theatre buildings in favor of a large room with the audience in the center and the action in the corners, to disregard the play and the playwright and use words for their mood or percussive impact. He wanted to confront the modern lie with the truth and vitality of a primitive magic ritual.

Unlike the story of Adam's expulsion from Eden, this view of the fall of mankind is not of the loss of innocence but of the loss of vitality through the trivial rounds of modern life. Artaud saw the regaining of this lost vitality as cruel, relentless, but necessary. He wrote:

> We can now say that all true freedom is dark, and infallibly identified with sexual freedom which is also dark . . . and that is why all the great Myths are dark, so that one cannot imagine, save in an atmosphere of carnage, torture, and bloodshed, all the significant Fables which recount to the multitudes the first sexual division and the first carnage of essences that appeared in creation.

Peter Brook's Experiments

The English director Peter Brook, strongly influenced by Artaud and even more restless, has had far greater ability to carry out his dreams and experiments. His wilder experiments of the 1960s and 1970s, however, followed two decades of work in the establishment, especially in directing Shakespeare.

Like Artaud, Brook was fascinated by the idea of ritual drama, and like Artaud he accepted the theory that human nature, shaped by eons of primitive ritual, was basically violent and cruel. Throughout his career he has repeatedly come back to the idea of regression to the bloody and violent primitive state. His brilliant movie *The Lord of the Flies* (1963), based on the popular novel of William Golding, showed a group of nicely trained British schoolboys, shipwrecked without any adults on a tropical island, shedding the veneer of civilization, reverting to aggression and violence, and creating a primitive religion out of their superstitious fear.

Brook's work was less convincing when he tacked on a ritual fertility celebration at the end of Seneca's *Oedipus,* produced in London at the Old Vic in 1968. After Jocasta impaled herself on a long sword that seemed to penetrate her womb, a band of revelers with golden boughs brought on and unveiled a tall gilded image of a phallus. They pranced around it and out into the audience singing "Yes, We Have No Bananas." This exhibition did not transform the audience to anything but embarrassment and giggles. One remarkable aspect of the production, however, was the use of sound. Several actors stationed about the auditorium delivered lines with strange effects of drowning or choking, attempting to adapt what they had heard in recordings of primitive ritualistic speech.

In a single decade, Brook directed three plays of Shakespeare with radically new interpretations. In *King Lear* of 1962, he followed the ideas of Jan Kott, who, in *Shakespeare Our Contemporary,* contended that Shakespeare saw life as absurd and desolate. Brook presented a savage society in a gray, desolate landscape. The entire play, even the heath scenes, where the mad old king and his companions usually stumble about in semidarkness, was presented in full light as though in the spotlight of a police investigation. In a production of *The Tempest* in 1968 Brook took wild liberties with the text, cutting radically, repeating many phrases or echoing them with other voices, as in expressionism. He also added striking scenes to bring out the violence he imagined behind the gentle plot: a scene of the birth of the evil Caliban from his monster-mother Sycorax, whom Shakespeare does not include in his cast, then an orgy of bestiality as Caliban imagines taking over the world. *The Tempest* was produced in The Roundhouse in London, an old railroad shed formerly used for storing or turning trains. Brook followed Artaud's suggestion of putting actors and audience in an open, unshaped environment. The platforms and scaffolding were similar to the environment built in a New York garage for the *Dionysus in 69* of the Performance Group.

Much the most successful of Brook's experiments with Shakespeare was *A Midsummer Night's Dream* of 1970, which played not only in Stratford and London but in New York and as far west as Los Angeles. There was no tampering with the text, but the concept of the production was highly original. Instead of the moon-drenched magic forest of traditional productions, the brightly lighted setting suggested a gymnasium with white padded walls. Oberon and Titania, King and Queen of Fairies, and the mischievous Puck swung on trapezes or ropes, sometimes spinning silver plates on sticks. The fairies and even the two young human couples were acrobats, running, leaping, tumbling, climbing. Costumes were simple gymnasium clothes or circus garments, with strong-colored silks and satins only for the wedding. Too harsh and too bawdy to be very charming, the play was good robust fun. And all the poetry was there, clearly and beautifully spoken by the well-trained British actors. (See Figures 8–21 and 8–22.

Brook has repeatedly gathered a group of actors and directors to work together for months exploring acting and its relation to the audience and searching for deeper meanings of theatre; and the study group has several times led into new experiments in production. For his most ambitious experiment, a tremendous outdoor performance in Iran, he was able to gather an international company in Paris for several months. Invited by the Shah of Iran for the summer festival of 1971, he created a production to be given on the mountain ledges and before the rock tombs above the ruins of the ancient palace at Persepolis. To get the full ritual effect of

8-21

Titania makes love to the ass's head.
Classical ballet style. Melissa Hayden in the
ballet *A Midsummer Night's Dream*.
New York City Ballet. Photo Martha Swope.

8-22

Titania makes love to the ass's head. A very
unconventional production of *A Midsummer
Night's Dream*—one with acrobatic actors.
Royal Shakespeare Company. Directed by
Peter Brook. Photo Retna.

speech that Artaud seemed to demand, Brook decided to use a totally new language. With the collaboration of the actors, Ted Hughes, a poet and friend of Brook, built a language he called "Orghast," and that became the name of the play. For sacred moments the company used Avesta, the ancient sacred language of the Zoroastrian religion.

The story, combining myths from Greece, Spain, Persia, Africa, and Japan, dealt with the theft of a great ball of fire, the torture of Prometheus for stealing it, and the ambiguous effect of light on a captive prince so unaccustomed to light that he reverts to primitive violence when he is free—a situation borrowed from Calderon's *Life Is a Dream.* The narrative then shifted to a Japanese tyrant-samurai who woke to find he had ceremonially killed his wife and child and was denounced by a vengeful woman and pitied by one who could offer no real help. An African offered a small light of wisdom, but the ball of fire had brought both wisdom and suffering, light and blindness. The full meaning of this loosely woven tale is far from clear, but, as ever, Brook is haunted by images of reversion to the primitive.

The next year, 1972, found Brook again experimenting with actors and audience, trying out his group in the performance of simple stories in African villages, still searching for some primitive idiom of sounds and meanings that might transcend differences of language and race. From the African experience he produced a new play for the West called *The Ik,* about a real African tribe that had reverted to the simplest antisocial violence when dislodged from its community traditions and patterns.

In his brilliant book of theory, *The Empty Space* (1968), Brook expresses his disgust with "the deadly theatre," his term for the commercial and conventional theatre. "Rough theatre" he can approve as the lusty entertainment of common people. But his real approval is for "holy theatre," which he identifies with ritual and "the invisible." In the last chapter he comments eloquently on the terrible power inherent in the theatre and the abuse of that power, and on the need to recognize that the theatre is never permanent but always changing.

A Theatre of Complexity

Complexity is the most baffling problem of the twentieth century. It would be easy if the world were all black or all white, all communist or all capitalist, all conventional or all unconventional. Some romantics have hoped for a world-wide uniformity; it was the goal of some promoters of the League of Nations after the First World War and of some promoters of the United Nations after the Second World War. But no one is ready for uniformity. The prospect of a standardized "man or woman of the establishment" has been so terrifying that many a young person, in grave moral earnestness, has set out to destroy society. But comedy has always shown that society is not an organized conspiracy but an unpredictable and therefore flexible complex of human relationships, and that a certain amount of anarchy is desirable.

In this chapter we have seen complexity in the work of experimental groups and of individuals, and it is fitting that, as we approach the end of our inquiry into what has happened to theatre in the last two decades, we should give another look at that complexity. We will do it by examining three very different plays that have made a strong impression on theatre-goers: Peter Shaffer's *Equus,* Tom Stoppard's *Travesties,* and Peter Weiss's *Marat/Sade.* Each of the plays makes some use of ritual patterns but points in its own way to the wider view of history. (See Figures 8–23, 8–24, and 8–25.)

The most popular serious play of the 1970s has been *Equus* by Peter Shaffer, whose *The Royal Hunt of the Sun* we discussed in Chapter 2 as modern tragedy. *Equus* captivated audiences chiefly by its sympathetic picture of the disturbed boy Alan and by its imaginative staging. But although these are the most obvious interests of the play, it also has implications about mythic and spiritual values for modern men and women and about possible misdirection in the search for those values.

The story is a case history, which the psychiatrist Dysart unravels. Alan, a sensitive boy whose mother has fed his imagination with Biblical stories and tales of noble horses, creates for himself a horse-god Equus, and performs a nightly ritual of prayer to a picture of the head of a horse that stares at him from his bedroom wall. When he gets work as a stable boy, the horses are manifestations of his god, and he often takes one secretly at night for an orgiastic ride in open country, which he calls the Field of Ha Ha, and then kneels in ecstasy before the horse. When a girl enters the stable at night with him and they take off their clothing, he cannot make love to her because he knows that his jealous god is watching. In a frenzy of desire and fear, he blinds the horses. For the psychiatrist Dysart, he gradually recreates the episodes in his past that led to this shocking act. By full realization and confession, he will be cured. Meantime, however, Dysart has become entangled in his own problems and shaken in his professional confidence. His marriage has given him neither sexual satisfaction nor congenial companionship, and he has sought spiritual solace by trips to Greece, where he immerses himself in the mythic past. He has found the modern world barren of spiritual values, and he envies the boy who has found some god, even though worship has led to

8-23 New form from old conventions. An expressionistic flashback, slightly stylized in
rhythm, on an accelerating turning platform. Dream figures of horses played by
actors in masks. The disturbed boy has an ecstatic ride on his horse-god. Shaffer's
Equus. National Theatre Company, London. Directed by John Dexter. Photo Van
Williams.

disaster. In curing the boy he will return him to a normal world he despises. He says:

> I'll set him on a mini-scooter and send him puttering off into the Normal world. . . . I'll take away his Field of Ha Ha, and give him Normal places for his ecstasy—multi-lane highways driven through the guts of cities. . . . He'll trot on his metal pony tamely through the concrete evening. . . . Passion, you see, can be destroyed by a doctor. It cannot be created. You won't gallop any more, Alan. . . . You will, however, be without pain. . . .

Shaffer's play is, in part, a modern tragedy, the world in chaos and human beings lost, without a god, without passion. Dysart says at the end: "There is now, in my mouth, this sharp chain. And it never comes out."

In a very real sense, *Equus* is a view of history. The boy's reversion to primitive ritual is no answer to his problem. The psychiatrist, in longing to identify with mythic Greece, reaches a dead end. How is the desire for a link with the past and with the cosmos to be gratified in the godless world of the present? As drama has often done, the play presents a problem, without a solution. It seems to say that we seek and do not find, but it does not say that we can never find.

Tom Stoppard's *Travesties* (1975) seems at first view just an extravagant spoof that offers a chance for a tour de force of acting. In some respects it is like Stoppard's earlier play *Jumpers* (1972), in which the acrobatic antics of an earnest amateur group of gymnasts is half the fun (and not pointless fun either). But *Travesties* suggests an interesting view of history. The device that ties the past to the present is a seedy-looking Englishman of advanced years, bragging with a twinkle in his eye of how well he knew three famous men who were in Zurich at the same time in 1917, when he was working in the British consulate during the First World War. This tips us off to expect a fantasy, but within the comic point of view it probably is a truthful picture of the times, when Switzerland was a quiet enclave surrounded by a warring world. The three famous men were Lenin, the exiled communist who was shortly to lead the Russian Revolution, Tristan Tzara, the founder of Dadaism, a nihilistic cult of nonsense, and James Joyce, who in his novels was playing a complex game with words, conventional phrases, snatches of ballads, and ancient myths.

When Stoppard read that Joyce and an English consul had sued each other after presenting a performance of Oscar Wilde's *The Importance of Being Earnest,* he had the idea for a comedy placing the three famous men in contrast with the two charming heroines of the play, Cecily and Gwendolen, whom he borrowed and set working in Zurich as librarian and secretary. Much of the dialogue is taken from Wilde's play, though usually put into a quite different context. Of the three irrational responses to a world in an agony of war, we are not sure which is the craziest. Tzara writes poems by drawing from a hat scraps cut from newspapers and putting them together at random; Joyce sings ballads, puts on Wilde's play and then sues his partner, and works out verbal ingenuities for his novels; Lenin makes even less sense as he delivers speeches in praise of freedom of speech—so long, of course, as it does not contradict the party line. For comic wisdom, a fourth man, Oscar Wilde, represented by his play, wins hands-down, and we leave the theatre, sure that what 1917 needed was less Lenin and more Wilde.

The third play, and much the strongest, if not the most appealing, gives a startling view of the complexity of the social order. In 1965 Peter

8–24 Comedy, war, and words. A reconstruction of history. Stoppard's *Travesties*. Royal Shakespeare Company production, 1974. Directed by Peter Wood and designed and costumed by Carl Toms. Photo Sophie Baker.

8-25 Stirred by the violence of political revolution, inmates in an insane asylum—the play's choral group—threaten the audience. Weiss's *Marat/Sade*, University of Arkansas production, directed by Thomas R. Jones, designed and lighted by Richard Harrill, and costumed by Patricia Romanov.

Weiss, a German living in Sweden, sent Peter Brook a play about the French Revolution with the amazing title *The Persecution and Assassination of Jean-Paul Marat as Performed by the Inmates of the Asylum of Charenton under the Direction of the Marquis de Sade*, and Brook gave it one of his most brilliant productions. *Marat/Sade* looks back from 1808 to the climax of the Revolution fifteen years before, which led to a Reign of Terror and eventually to the rule of Napoleon. The setting is the bathhouse in an insane asylum, where the inmates have been herded by attendant nurses and male keepers to enact a play written by the notorious inmate the Marquis de Sade. The Director of the asylum and his wife and daughter have been invited to see the performance, and they sit apart, their elegant dress and manner in sharp contrast to the nondescript garments and crude behavior of the inmates.

The play is about the murder of Marat, a leader of the Revolution, by Charlotte Corday. The inmate playing Marat is seated in a tub of water, for Marat spent much time submerged in water because of a skin disease, and he was murdered in his bath. The main action is interrupted many times: when Marat and de Sade argue about the Revolution, when the Director protests against seditious statements, when a herald and other commentators make ambiguous remarks about the Revolution, when a group of brightly dressed singers chant ironical songs. Music and movement give variety and intensity to the complex picture of revolution. And central to the performance by madmen, with the implication of the madness of all mankind, is the presentation, now serious, now ironical, of an episode in history. Marat is an idealist, who defends revolutionary violence by arguing that it is a necessary prelude to a reign of peace and harmony; the skeptical de Sade believes that there will always be violence because human beings are moved by self-interest and greed and love bloodshed. The Director believes that perfection has been reached in Napoleon's rule. This startling new examination of history, with its implications of human madness and depravity, does not encourage optimism about the future, but it does suggest that we may be able to deal intelligently with the future only by facing the worst in the past.

Complexity of viewpoints is matched by complexity in staging, with the use of every theatrical device thought up in the modern age. The stage has been made an "environment," with stark walls, several levels, gratings, and bars. There is a choral group, the inmates who are putting on a play; multiple layers of role-playing; expressionistic and ritual sounds and rhythms; enclosing action and a play-within-a-play; several levels of commentators and observers; slogans and announcements; interwoven movement of inmates, keepers, spectators, commentators, singers. The ritual element is strong. The several attempts at the murder of Marat before the final blow proceed as in the repetitive stages of a ritual. Free or rhymed verse is used effectively for every conceivable form of discourse, from oration, public proclamation, and debate to songs and angry chants. The irregularity of the verse, with rapid shifts from free verse to epigrammatic rhymed couplets, emphasizes the irony that pervades the play and gives the effect of hectic excitement and knowing madness that Weiss desires. An insane patient chants:

> I've helped commit a million murders
> The earth is spread
> The earth is spread thick
> with squashed human guts

A herald ironically lectures the revolutionaries:

> Work for and trust the powerful few
> what's best for them is best for you

The revolutionaries in their turn cry:

> We want our rights and we don't care how
> We want our Revolution NOW

Marat/Sade is a remarkable play, a landmark in recent theatre history.

For all the improvisation used by experimental directors, we still rely on playwrights to give us strong plays, well constructed and well written. Yet the playwright's work is only one element in the theatre. Stage architects and designers are constantly trying new forms of space. Especially in the past two decades, experiments by directors, actors, dancers, and poets have promised to transform our theatre even more than experiments by professional playwrights. Hence we will examine, in the next three chapters, the art of the director, the actor, and the designer.

9

Planning the Production

IN ADDITION TO CREATING MOOD AND
ATMOSPHERE, THE STAGE SET DEFINES
THE PATHS OF MOVEMENT FOR THE
ACTORS. BERLIOZ' *LES TROYENS*.
METROPOLITAN OPERA PRODUCTION,
NEW YORK, 1973. DESIGNED BY PETER
WEXLER. PHOTO © BETH BERGMAN.

The theatre is a synthesis of all the arts, and yet it is a complete art in itself. A play is a composition not merely of story in words (and sometimes there is neither story nor words) but of color, line, space, and light, moving in rhythmic order toward a definite goal. The audience sees primarily the actors, but the actors are only part of a large team of workers bringing many different skills to the theatre. Hence, in both stage and film production, the director is the central artist, often better known than either playwright or actors. Whether he is using an old play or one in the process of being rewritten by the playwright, or even if he is creating something new out of movement and sound without a playwright, he has to plan carefully to coordinate the work of his complex organization. There must be a central plan, a basic, agreed-on idea of what kind of play all the workers want to create, and very careful supervision and coordination during the preparation of the play.

The director became important a century ago as the repertory and stock companies, which were actor-oriented, began to give way to long-run, carefully prepared productions. T. W. Robertson in the 1860s was both playwright and director, subordinating his actors to the overall mood of his plays and insisting that every detail of setting, properties, and costumes be right for each particular play. In the 1870s and 1880s Europe was impressed by the traveling productions of a minor German prince, the Duke of Saxe-Meiningen, who achieved an ensemble that was carefully controlled, especially in crowd scenes. In the free theatres the naturalistic directors, from Antoine to Stanislavsky, retrained actors and chose properties to bring out the rich subtext of the play. At the beginning of the twentieth century, the great producer-director Max Reinhardt showed the world what it meant to give a particular character to each production. He often chose a different place for each play to be produced—*Oedipus* in a large circus in Berlin, *The Merchant of Venice* in a square along a canal in Venice, *Everyman* before the cathedral in Salzburg. For each play, he took an entirely different approach, making sure that actors, scenery, music, and the building itself would contribute to the one idea. He even anticipated the interest in "environmental theatre" as he rebuilt a large theatre or warehouse space for *The Miracle* into the interior of a medieval cathedral, with actors and audience inside the same space.

Filmmaking requires an even more complex organization, and it is even more difficult for one artist to leave his mark on a film. In the great days of Hollywood, besides the actors and technicians who carried out orders, dozens of people, from a whole battery of scriptwriters to the public-relations men, had a say on how the film should be made to appeal to the supposed taste of the mass audience. Only occasionally did the creative originality of the artist come through. It is no wonder that in the rebellion against the big studios during the forties and fifties filmmakers insisted on the *auteur* theory, which holds that even if many people work on a film, they should be carrying out the creative idea of one person, usually the director, who should not only exercise control over script and photography but also have "the final cut," that is, the final approval of the editing.

In the freer forms of theatre, the guidance of the director may be even more important than in the standard categories of plays, for loosely organized material easily gets out of hand and without a firm central control may become chaotic. Still, actors have often had a large part in shaping the production, as we have seen. Starting with no script or a very general sketch of the action, some experimental directors have liked to set the actors to improvising and then to incorporate their best efforts in the performance. The ingenuity of actors and director has often combined in working out the plan of the playing area and creating special effects in movement or sound, verbal or nonverbal. In the commercial theatre, however, as well as in most resident companies and college theatres, the director usually has a full written text to deal with and takes full responsibility for shaping it for the stage and interpreting it to the actors. Most plays can be worked out by long-established methods.

First the director, with help from the designer and sometimes from the actors, must decide just what variety of entertainment or exaltation, romance or reality is to be created for the audience, how to use the particular stage, what conventions of performance will be set up, and what the overall style will be. The director and his helpers must analyze the play for its elements of structure and texture and choose the appropriate method, knowing that the techniques that create a rich mood may not be the ones to make clear the theme or the action.

The actor learns lines alone or with others in small groups, tries improvisation both alone and at rehearsal, and continues his lifelong training in body, voice, and imagination outside the theatre, but in the long hours of rehearsal he has the director with him. The designer works separately, completing sketches and work drawings, building structures, and setting lighting instruments, but he checks repeatedly with the director at the critical stages, even though he does not expect to bring all parts of his contribution together until the later rehearsals. In an art theatre with control of its own space, the designer often has the main platforms and ramps and steps, and at least practice properties and sometimes practice costumes, available for rehearsal for several weeks before the opening of the show.

Convention and Style

Convention and style were no problem when a standard repertory of plays was presented by a company performing in one house, season after season, for a faithful audience. But today, when audiences are seeing plays in many different kinds of theatres or in club rooms and churches without the regular theatre arrangements, when playwrights are trying many new forms and directors are reviving old plays in mixtures of old conventions and new, when drama is overlapping with opera, the musical, and dance, it is very important that for each production one set of conventions and one consistent style be agreed on by all.

Convention

In the Prologue to this book we explained that conventions are theatrical customs, the accepted rules of the game, and that they may vary widely from one country to another, from one age to another, and from one kind of play to another. The newer forms of theatre have brought in whole new sets of conventions. Some of them have been puzzling to audiences, and this lack of familiarity often accounts for the failure of playgoers to understand "new" plays. A theatregoer, like an opera or symphony or dance buff, must be flexible, willing to accept an artistic experience with new rules.

Some of the more common conventions of the Western theatre in the twentieth century are dimming the house lights and raising a front curtain to indicate the beginning of each act of a play; the "fourth-wall convention," or the assumption that the side of the stage toward the audience is an invisible fourth wall with no furniture against it; the practice of having the actors speak to one another, ignoring the audience completely; the use of some lighting for the stage (or movie screen) even when the time is dark night. Such familiar conventions are not noticed at all, but audiences can adjust to any new convention or set of conventions if the unfamiliar methods are made clear near the beginning of the performance and are used consistently throughout. When, for instance, Wilder wanted the actors to break out of character and speak their own feelings at the climax of the third act of *The Skin of Our Teeth*, he created similar breaks in the first and second acts. His method was simpler in *Our Town*, where he used the Stage Manager to tell the audience from the beginning exactly what method to expect.

The more open forms of theatre set out to surprise the audience, to wake them up and invite them into the action by putting actors out in the audience and otherwise breaking expected relationships. In "happenings," a short-lived fad of the mid-sixties, the audience itself had to perform, with a few suggestions to start them off. Such group improvisation does not need a theatre but is better crowded into an old storehouse or some outlandish cave or tunnel. Guerrilla actors like to stage events in a crowd to provoke spontaneous audience reaction.

If the audience is separate from the play, the conventions must enable them to hear and see the actors. In the large theatres of the nineteenth century, when expansive emotions were popular, movements were large, and the sweeping gestures were always made with the upstage hand so that they never covered the speaker's face. Voices were projected with full tone, inflections were wide, and actors practiced long on consonants and vowels. In defending the old style of diction that often broke a word into parts, Shaw said that at least the old stock-company actor would be heard in the last row of the gallery when he screeched, "My chee-ild!" Few theatres now are so large that a well-trained actor cannot be heard, but

9–1 Realistic scene on a thrust stage. A strong sense of enclosed reality is created without walls, by the use of a low bench between actors and audience and by the actors' relationships to one another and to the properties. Chekhov's *The Three Sisters*. The Tyrone Guthrie Theatre, Minneapolis, 1963.

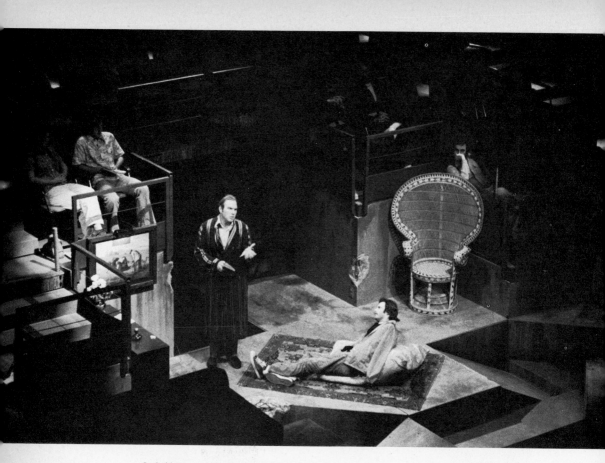

9–2 New conventions with new forms of theatre. An "environment." Audience and actors in the same space, the playing area broken into many small areas and different levels to make access seem difficult. John Ford Noonan's *The Year Boston Won the Pennant*. California Institute of the Arts production, directed by John Pasquin, designed by Ron Wilson.

actors and audience have grown accustomed to amplifiers, which often make the voices unpleasantly loud and mechanical and encourage the actors in lazy habits of speech. Even the conventions of realism allowed the furniture to be turned in an "open" position so that the actors would not stand in front of one another or turn their backs completely to the audience. Many details were made large and brightly colored to project to the audience. In costume materials only large, bold patterns were used.

The choice of the means of expression by playwright and director is also a matter of convention. In realism the actor rarely shows eloquence of voice or language, only suggesting, in broken tones, his inner feelings. Yet the theatre must find expressive intensities of some kind. In musical comedy we are not surprised when the actor bursts into song. Brecht and other advocates of total theatre make extensive use of masks, soliloquy, poetry, song, and dance and ask the audience to accept them in plays dealing with reality. *Waiting for Godot* calls for high skill in clowning, and Peter Brook's production of *A Midsummer Night's Dream* required skill in gymnastics.

Style

Style is the particular manner of expression, the way a writer puts his words and phrases together, the way an artist handles his lines and chooses his colors, the way an actor or actress moves and wears the costume. It is extremely important that one style be used throughout a production to unite words, movement, line, form, and color. Members of an audience may not be able to describe a style or know how it is achieved, but they are aware of incongruity when one actor stands out from the rest of the cast or when the costumes or settings do not fit in with other aspects of the production. The playwright partly determines the style; a play cannot be done in just any style. But every play permits considerable latitude as director, actor, and designer decide on a style that emphasizes some aspects and subordinates others.

The realists attacked all the old styles and announced that by presenting reality itself on the stage they were creating a theatre without any style or interpretation. When realists identified their restrained, implicit acting with reality, they had to describe any other style as an artificial and useless ornament superimposed on reality and distorting or obscuring it. They labeled the melodramatic style "ham" and delighted in revivals of melodrama that burlesqued the large emotional gestures and frank playing to the audience of the nineteenth-century theatre. Only gradually has it become clear that realism is itself one style among many and that in their individual ways all styles are theatrical.

The term *stylization,* which came into use when the expressionists began distorting scenery and dehumanizing characters with dreamlike and machinelike movements and voice inflections, implied something markedly different from realism; a director might be asked if he planned to stylize a production or play it straight. Stylization is not the same as style; there are a number of stylized—that is, deliberately artificial and unreal—styles. But a definition of style in its broadest sense must include much more than these.

In the broadest sense, style is the expression of an outlook on the world, a philosophy, a point of view. When many people have the same social, political, or philosophical attitudes, they choose similar ways of expressing themselves and create a style for a whole period. Thomas Jefferson and the revolutionaries in France and America wanted Greek

Revival public buildings because they wanted to recapture in all aspects of public life the dignified nobility of the Greek republic. The Victorians wanted for their churches and colleges the mysterious gloom of Gothic architecture and stained-glass windows, and something of their point of view can still be felt in the old buildings. Our kitchens, laboratories, and automobiles must not only be clean and efficient, but they must by their very style express newness, precision, power, and speed. When we revive an Elizabethan play, we may want a speed of movement and streamlining of setting that has some suggestion of modern living, or an imaginative director like Peter Brook may want to embody a concept that is neither "modern" nor "Elizabethan." Usually, however, we also want the rich splendor and dignity that we see too little of in the twentieth century. When we revive an eighteenth-century comedy, we may prefer light, free-standing screens to the picture backdrops of the period, and we may adapt the rococo costumes to twentieth-century fashions, but we seek to achieve, in the curved lines of the setting and the bold stance and bows and curtsies of the actors, an appropriate elegance and a crisp combination of assertion and politeness. Style in play production is usually an adjustment between the vision of the playwright, the expectation of the audience, and the particular tastes and wishes of director, actors, and designer.

Style is achieved largely by selection—the choice of certain conventions and techniques, the choice of certain qualities in the medium, and then limitation of the expression to those few qualities. If the colors are limited to a few pastel shades, the production will have a distinctive delicacy and softness, but the actors must then use soft, delicate movements, or they will not be in harmony with the setting. While each play must have its own particular style to express the exact nuances of what the director considers to be the play's meaning, it is useful to set up a half-dozen or so general classifications of common styles. In addition to period styles, there are several widely used styles that playwrights and producers are aware of as they plan. Although the Moscow Art Theatre has been known primarily for the realism of its style, one of the original directors, Nemirovitch-Dantchenko, taught his actors to consider six other styles which he called heroic, Homeric, epochal, comical, farcical, and lyrical. In the early days of the Yale Drama School, students tried to distinguish six major styles: classicism, romanticism, naturalism, realism, expressionism, and impressionism; but the distinctions seemed more theoretical than practical.

Style is not something added to a play as decoration; it is the basic manner of expression, and its control is one of the most powerful means of achieving unity in a production.

Structure and Texture

The structure of a play may be tight and compact or loose and episodic.
The tight structure will have one action or a series of actions closely related
by cause and effect, each a link in a firmly wrought chain. It is a climactic
structure, starting not at the beginning of the story but much later, near
the climax, when all the past stresses accumulate and lead to one climactic
confrontation. Unity is much more important than variety. The result is a
limited action of high compression, usually confined to one place and
concentrated into a short time, with a few characters. On the other hand,
the loose, or episodic, structure is guided more by variety than by unity
and offers a wider scope, with many characters and many episodes loosely
strung together. It often tells from the beginning a long story of the many
experiences of one picaresque character. The episodic structure is characteristic of most romantic stories, while the tight, compact form is appropriate to classic tragedy.

In either case, a play has six possible dramatic values, and all six may
help in different ways to give the play organization and unity. Aristotle
listed them as plot, character, theme, dialogue, music (interpreted in
modern drama to mean "mood" or "rhythm"), and spectacle. The first
three values concern the structure of the play, the last three the texture.
The *structure* is the form of the play in time. The *texture* is what is directly
experienced by the spectator, what comes to him through the senses, what
the ear hears (the dialogue), what the eye sees (the spectacle), and what is
felt as mood through the entire visual and aural experience. Texture, as we
have seen, has become increasingly important in contemporary drama.
Indeed, some playwrights and directors attempt to build theatre pieces
out of moving scenic objects, rhythms, sounds, and music, at the risk of
losing the conventional audience by the complete neglect of story and
character. (See Figures 8–6, 8–7, 8–11, and 8–12.)

Some plays are rich in all six of Aristotle's values, some in only one or
two. Sometimes a director may decide to emphasize and build up one
value that he or the audience could be interested in, even if it means not
exploiting fully some other value, giving attention, for instance, to mood
and rich characterization while letting the plot take care of itself.

Action or Plot

The Greek root of the word *drama* means "to do," "to act." In a drama
something happens before our eyes; drama portrays the present moment,
but that moment is full of promise and threat, pregnant with the future.
There is delay, but the critical moment does arrive and a fate is deter-

mined, a choice is made, a door is closed forever. The audience is caught up and carried from crisis to crisis in a rhythmic pattern of tension and relaxation, swept to a climax by an irresistible momentum, then left at the end changed and thrilled by the sense of having gone through a great experience.

Dramatic action is not just external movement. Thought and decision are also action, and the confrontation of two minds can create conflict as tense and exciting as a physical fight on the stage. The rebel Titan, Prometheus, chained to a rock from the beginning of the play, cannot move around the stage, but each of his visitors makes him all the more determined to defy Zeus.

Plot is the arrangement of the incidents that take place on stage. Much of the actual story may already have taken place. A complete narrative about the boy Alan in *Equus* would begin with events of his childhood and adolescence and proceed to his employment in the stable, his night rides on the horses, his blinding the horses, and his appearance in a magistrate's court. But Shaffer's play starts after all that; it shows how the psychiatrist delves into Alan's past and bit by bit finds the motivation of his shocking deed. Not what was done but why it was done makes the dramatic plot. In Ibsen's plays the plot is often the gradual revelation of some long-hidden truth about the past. Discoveries explode one by one like carefully placed time bombs, shaking and sometimes destroying those forced to hear. A drama is interaction, with each speech demanding a reaction from another character.

A plot may be a fight to the finish between a good hero and a villain, arousing our basic fighting instincts as well as our moral indignation. It may be a race or a contest between worthy opponents, creating suspense as first one side and then the other gets ahead. It may be an actual or metaphorical journey in which the young hero, like a medieval knight, searches for his Holy Grail, now getting closer, now distracted and delayed. Courtship is a variation of the journey. "Boy meets girl, boy loses girl, boy gets girl"—there is the structure of a three-act play. Another pattern is the invasion of the lives of stay-at-homes; an intruder or a guest in the house may disturb the peaceful equilibrium and cause all kinds of complications before peace is restored. We have seen this kind of plot, treated in a very individual way, in Pinter's plays.

The trial is one of the most powerful patterns for a play, concentrating deeds of the past into the suspense of the judgment—the long-awaited destiny. Sometimes it is in the formal setting of a courtroom, but there is much the same excitement when Oedipus serves as his own prosecuting attorney and his own judge, calling up witness after witness to find the murderer of the old king, only to discover that he himself was the murderer and the old king was his own father. Sometimes the conclusion of a play is a sudden revelation of that which was hidden: the discovery of the lost papers, the clearing up of the mistaken identity, the finding of the stolen child, the true heir, the real prince, the unknown benefactor. Many plays follow some pattern of nature—the rhythm of the day or the seasons or of a stormy night clearing before the dawn.

In making the ground plan for the structure of the play, the director outlines the plot. Sometimes he or she consciously divides the play into parts, which, for the benefit of the actors, are given conventional labels. The opening part is the *exposition,* which makes clear to the audience what has gone before and what the present situation is. Then at a certain *point of attack* the *inciting force* appears, followed by *complication* after complication. The tension increases in a *build,* or crescendo, to a *minor climax,* followed by a *let-down.* There is *anticipation* or *foreboding* of future conflict, and with delay or continued threat comes great *suspense.* Each confrontation of opposing forces creates a *crisis.* Usually there will be a point of no return when the fight comes out in the open in the *major crisis,* which may also be the point of highest tension, or the *major climax.* After that comes the *conclusion* or the *dénouement,* the French term for "untying" the plot. Aristotle gave us such terms as *discovery,* when that which was unknown becomes clear, and *peripeteia,* the reversal of the plot.

The plot is the basis for the overall rhythmic pattern of the play. Whether a play is broken up into acts and scenes by intermissions and scene changes, or whether it flows without interruption like an Elizabethan play or a movie, it is organized in time. Like a symphony, it must have a pattern of tensions and relaxations, of builds, climaxes, and let-downs, of units of different sizes and intensities. Like a river winding through a valley, a plot does not move in a straight line but pushes toward one side until its impulse is exhausted by the mounting resistance, and it is turned with new force against the other side.

Character

If the plot is what happens, character is why it happens. The motivation is the basis of the action. Plot may be what gives the play its immediate sense of excitement, but plays are remembered for their characters. Lear on the heath, Lady Macbeth rubbing blood from her hands, Cyrano helping his rival to win Roxane, the undefeated Amanda of *The Glass Menagerie,* the defeated Blanche of *A Streetcar Named Desire*—characters like these can never be forgotten. It is through the creation of character, the evocation of the nuances of personality, the immediate and the deeper motives of the soul, that actors win their audience. Even the minor characters come to life to give the play variety and vitality as the actors find a distinct personality and an inner meaning for each.

The director, both alone and with the actor, makes a careful study to create each character with a particular tone and quality—not just the recognition traits of age, size, occupation, appearance, dress, tempo, rhythm, roughness or softness, but characteristic attitude. Is he or she naturally a doubter, a kidder, joyful or morose, ardent or disdainful, playful or serious? Is he or she conceived according to the conventional idea of his or her role in society—father, mother, judge, pedantic school-teacher, or go-getting young executive? Or does the character violate the conventional picture, such as a mother who is an executive and smokes cigars? Perhaps the character can be explained by some of the Freudian concepts—repressions that burst out in unpredictable compensations, inferiority complexes, destructive obsessions and neuroses, nervous tics and compulsive gestures. The character may be introverted or extroverted; he or she may react appropriately or overreact. Most important are the deeper motives—what the character will fight for, what he or she ulti-mately respects. The actor may bring to the study of character personal observations from life or from research in books, newspapers, and other plays. Within the play itself director and actor note what the author says, what the character does and says, and how the other characters speak of and react to this man or woman. Does the character play a different role with each person? Is there a pattern of change as the character develops or discovers himself or herself in the course of the play?

Whether it is conscious choice, as Sartre and the existentialists demand, or unconscious natural bent that gives the outline of the charac-ter, that outline is filled in by the actor, who brings to the part his or her own natural tones and qualities, and according to skill and range, adds or emphasizes those qualities the actor and the director think the character should have. In rehearsal the director will help the actor enrich the part by finding unexpected moments when a strong character shows weakness and a weak character strength, and by giving an evil character some moments of sympathy and a good character contradictory moments when he or she seems not so good. People are not all of one piece and are all the more fascinating for their complexity.

In addition to understanding individual characters, the director and actors must see clearly the playwright's scheme of characters. A play is not a solo by one character but a complex composition. Not only do the characters change one another, but each character is defined by compari-son and contrast with all the others. The playwright has added other examples to reinforce, to explore variations of, to oppose and contrast with, the central characters.

Theme and variation is as important in theatre as in music. The situation of two brothers who are treated differently and who grow up in different ways was the subject of one of the earliest Greek comedies; it was then dramatized by the Roman playwright Terence in *The Brothers* and has been used in hundreds of plays since. Variation on a different level and in a different key is frequent in all kinds of plays, especially in romantic comedy. A comic pair of lovers sets off the serious pair, and obviously it is easier in any class-conscious society to make lower-class characters more comic. The humble characters are funny for seeming to repeat somebody else, but they serve another function in romance. The ancient Hindus regularly set a clownish servant as the companion to the romantic king. The servant could feel fatigue, hunger, fear, and pain—could suffer all the indignities of finite existence—but the king never could because he dwelt in the realm of ideal perfection.

As in all art, contrast is vital in drama. The hero and the villain enlist our interest in their fight because they are so different. Every protagonist is defined by the nature of the antagonist. Hamlet contends in quite different ways with the king, his mother, Ophelia, Polonius, and finally Laertes, and is provoked into a different role with each. Romeo is defined by contrast with his enemy, the hot-tempered Tybalt, but also by contrast with his close friend Mercutio, who is raucous, bawdy, and cynical about love. Prince Hal in *Henry IV* is defined partly by contrast with Hotspur, whose courage goads Hal into proving his valor; but he is defined even more, in his carefree moments, by his friendship with Falstaff.

Sometimes a more elaborate scheme of characters provides one character for each aspect of a problem. In Shaw's *Saint Joan*, each institution—the Church, the Inquisition, the feudal lords, the State of England—has a champion, and some more than one, to bring out the several attitudes in the debate at Joan's trial. To create a kind of epitome of New York as a melting pot, Elmer Rice in *Street Scene* brought into one New York block representatives of all the principal nationalities in that cosmopolitan city, just as O'Neill in several of his plays of the sea brought on shipboard all nationalities from both sides of the Atlantic. The character scheme may be as important for the theme of the play as what happens or what conclusion any of the characters reaches.

The way a character develops and changes may be the major action of a play. Growth, self-discovery, learning, and conversion can be fascinating to watch and very dramatic.

In planning an absurdist drama, the director and the actors need not discard all the concepts of motivation and development that have enriched the drama over the centuries. But for some plays they must be ready to plan a character who suddenly takes on an obsession, without continuity with previous motives. Actually, there is a great deal of continuity in most dramas of the absurd. Sabina is the same character throughout *The Skin of Our Teeth*, though she takes on a slightly different personality as she sets out to seduce Mr. Antrobus in Act II. In Ionesco's *The Lesson*, the Professor has a strong drive to teach the girl. There is no sudden change as the drive gradually becomes more intense and demonic until he attacks and stabs her. An absurdist play may require that the character be conceived as fragmented or distorted, but even in the most dehumanized or mechanized dance drama or in the plotless "operas" of Robert Wilson, the theatre deals with an image of the human race, and that image will always deal with some aspect of character.

In some contemporary plays the characters are not carefully individualized. They may be archetypal, as in a morality play. Often their motivation, as in a Pinter play, is not revealed; perhaps the playwright does not know it. The actor must then create a character with subtle undertones, enigmatic, not completely understood but still convincing as a human being. The actor trained only in the Stanislavsky "method" cannot meet this challenge. We will discuss the problem in the next chapter.

Theme

The theme of a play—its full underlying meaning—may not be clear until we have thought it over for some time. The theme may be so implicit in the characters, in what happens, in the rich texture of the actors, the setting, and the performance that it cannot be put into words, though we may know that the play stands for certain values of living and that we have learned more about life by seeing it. Sometimes a minor character states the theme, but the impact is stronger if the main character makes his own discovery. Only in a very few plays can the theme be called a moral, for a moral is a neat, external conclusion *about* life, rather than a complex, gradually developed attitude *toward* life.

We must be careful, however, not to mistake a single statement by one character for the meaning of the whole play. At one point in *King Lear,* the blinded Earl of Gloucester comes to the conclusion that "As flies to wanton boys are we to the gods. They kill us for their sport." But that is only the momentary conclusion of one character. Gloucester later finds a new patience and accepts his condition.

Sometimes the theme is indicated when what is said in the dialogue offers an ironical contrast with what actually happens. Soon after Portia of *The Merchant of Venice* delivers a splendid sermon on mercy, she shows something less than mercy when she has Shylock in her power. In *Hedda*

Gabler, Judge Brack seems a wise commentator, quietly watching Hedda, sure that he understands her and has her in his control. But he is the most surprised of all when she kills herself. He ends the play with the famous tribute to the unpredictability of human nature, "Good God!—People don't do such things."

Whether brought out by direct statement, by ironical contrast, or by implication, the theme is an essential part of a play. In epic theatre the theme is often the structure of the play. We have seen how both *Our Town* and *The Skin of Our Teeth* are organized by theme, and the same is true of *Kennedy's Children* and *Einstein on the Beach.* Even the most trivial farce implies certain philosophical attitudes, and the great playwrights from Aeschylus, Sophocles, and Euripides to Shakespeare, Moliere, Goethe, Ibsen, and Shaw have made significant contributions to human thought.

Dialogue, Mood, and Rhythm

Plot, character, and theme, as we have seen, are the elements of structure. Equally important are the elements of texture—dialogue, mood, and spectacle. Indeed, modern theatre people, like modern painters and musicians, are particularly interested in texture. The word is derived, like the word *textile,* from the Latin word for "weaving." Our strongest sensation of texture comes from touch, from feeling the difference, for instance, between a ribbed sweater and a silk shirt, but we extend the word to the other senses. In painting texture adds considerable surface interest as the artist achieves depth and vibrancy by interweaving brush strokes, smears, and spots of color in applying his oils or even by adding pieces of cloth, paper, wire screen, or rope to his canvas. In the theatre texture is created by the sounds and images of the language, by the subtle but powerful hold of the mood, and by the materials, color, and movement of setting and costume.

Most modern plays limit poetic language to local dialect and subordinate words to other elements such as background sounds or movements, clothes, and furniture to create a rich composite effect of local color. Lush language is left to romance, wit to high comedy, and poetry to the outdoor festival plays and a few dramas in verse. Even so, the director and the actor must study the dialogue of any play very carefully, for it is chiefly through the sound, and particularly the rhythm, of the dialogue that the playwright indicates the basic mood of the play and the changing moods of the scenes in sequence.

For his fifth dramatic value Aristotle used the term *music,* but most modern plays make little use of music as such. Hence we substitute the words *mood* and *rhythm* for *music.* Mood in the theatre depends upon a blending of many elements, including spectacle and language, but it is created chiefly by rhythm. For modern human beings, as for primitive man, rhythm is the great coordinating principle, as powerful and indispensable in the theatre as in dance or music. Movement without rhythm is clumsy, jerky. Rhythm creates a relationship between the parts of the body and between one person and another. Sailors pulling a rope or hauling a sail sing a chanty with a strong rhythm, in order to pull together. The coxswain coordinates the crew of a racing shell by calling out the rhythm. Spectators at a play follow the rhythm of the actors as closely as a crew follows the coxswain; the rhythm reverberates through the audience, binding stage and house together under one spell. Though the actor does not need to be conscious of the rhythm if he is thinking of the mood itself, the director must know exactly what mood he wants and what rhythm will be best able to produce it.

Many scenes in the theatre have as strong and definite a beat as a march or a dance. In *The Emperor Jones,* a driving, relentless rhythm is created by a drumbeat that at first is very slow, but gets faster and faster as the natives pursue Jones through the jungle and stops only with the pistol shot that kills him.

Most theatres in history have made rich use of music, at least as background if not in song and dance, and an orchestra was a regular attraction in commercial theatres until the Second World War. Even though the naturalistic directors banished conventional musical instruments, they used many other sounds, from nature, from human activities, or from the mechanized city. In a movie or television drama the voices are almost as richly supported by background music as the singers in a Wagnerian opera.

We have noted the important part music plays in *Marat/Sade* and some other plays of our time. Whether or not music is used in a play, director and actors make some use of the musician's vocabulary and techniques: suspension, pause, interruption, bunching and spreading out, and strong dynamic contrasts.

If there is no music in the play to build the rhythm and mood, the director often uses music in rehearsals to set the tone and rhythm for a scene and to help the actors get into the right mood. In period plays, this can be as helpful in creating a style and atmosphere as Cavalier boots and capes, eighteenth-century wigs and ruffled shirts, or Victorian ladies' tight bodices and high collars.

From dancers, the director learns how to devise practice exercises; for instance, to vary a walking movement by making it heavier as in marching and stamping, or lighter for swinging or lilting, then to go on to prancing, skipping, jumping, and leaping. Then the director may add an intention or emotion—responding to the sky and wind of a hilltop, strutting in front of someone in pride or defiance, tiptoeing around while someone else sleeps—or a special quality, tenseness or relaxation, smoothness or jerkiness. Or practice exercises may illustrate everyday words such as *punch, slash, press, flick, dab, float,* and *wring,* or involve analysis of movements, as light or heavy, quick or sustained, working against varying outer resistance or inner resistance. A few minutes of dance practice at the beginning of a rehearsal may help the actors get the right rhythm.

But more immediate to the theatre than rhythms suggested by music or dance are those supplied by the playwright, especially the poet-playwright. The rhythm of the phrases, the sounds of the words, and the rich suggestion of the images give the actor a chance to create a mood that may be the most compelling force of the play. Shakespeare's characters, without the help of scenery or lighting, cast a spell over the scene by the power of rhythms and words. Much of the dark anguish of *Hamlet* is created in the opening scene of the changing of the guard at midnight and the remark of the guard who is being relieved, "'Tis bitter cold and I am sick at heart." The moonlight balcony scene of *Romeo and Juliet* is built up in the phrases of Romeo, who sees Juliet as brighter than sun and moon, her eyes twinkling like stars. He addresses her: "Bright angel . . . thou art/ As glorious to this night, being o'er my head/ As is a winged messenger of heaven." He speaks of the blessed moon "that tips with silver all these fruit-tree tops," of "how silver-sweet sound lovers' tongues by night," evoking a spell of idealized love in the sustained light rhythms and sounds. For the violent scene of the fights and deaths, a hot noon atmosphere is quickly created with sharper rhythms and images:

> The day is hot, the Capulets are abroad,
> And if we meet we shall not scape a brawl,
> For now these hot days is the mad blood stirring.

—a passage in which the air is stabbed by short phrases, monosyllables, and seven accented syllables in the last line. For the storm scenes in the third act of *King Lear,* Lear answers the thunder with the trumpet tones and slow, heavy rhythms of "Strike flat the thick rotundity of the world." But in the next storm scene the mood is more quiet and eerie as Lear begins to go mad, and the new tone is set by the strange mock madness of the outcast Edgar: "Through the sharp hawthorn blows the cold wind."

We have noted Pinter's command of dialogue in which commonplace speech becomes hypnotic in its stresses and repetitions, interspersed with pregnant pauses.

The intent of the characters in a play may set the rhythm. Hope has a brighter, lighter rhythm than despair. A character will set different tones when he is dreading, teasing, urging, begging, or threatening; when he is weary, exasperated, suspicious, quizzical, or puzzled.

Spectacle

Spectacle is the most controversial of the six dramatic values; the purists repeatedly attack it, and the intellectuals despise it. We have seen how the neoclassicists and many of the realists cut it down to a few group effects that could be created by the actors themselves, and we remember that three of the greatest theatres in history—the Chinese, the Japanese Noh, and the Elizabethan—while making much use of poetry, dance, and song, had no painted settings and used colors only for splendid costumes and a few portable symbolic indications of place.

Yet spectacle does belong in the theatre. It is important to see Macbeth and Lady Macbeth in splendid robes, sitting on splendid thrones, with attendants, trumpets, banners, tapestries, and canopies—the full panoply of royalty—to mark their triumph. And the banquet scene must be made an impressive spectacle, showing Macbeth in a closed circle of friends and councilors when his hopes are dashed by Banquo's ghost. In order to know the magnitude of the desecration wrought by the Spaniards in Peru as Peter Shaffer conceived it in *The Royal Hunt of the Sun,* the audience must see the sun-king of the Incas splendidly enthroned in a huge sun-medallion and the glittering procession of his subjects bearing the golden treasure that is to fill the royal chamber. Both in such romantic dramas and in naturalistic scenes, we expect most characters to be shown in the larger world around them, the world of nature, history, or society. Yet we must add that in the last several decades there have been quite stark productions of Shakespeare that have depended successfully on Shakespeare's words and the actors' performance.

If we take spectacle in a broad sense as stress on the visual aspect of a play, we find much of it in the newer forms of drama. Intricate arrangements of iron framework and ladders, with various levels and projections, are plain, severe, yet they can create visual excitement. After seven decades of Chekhov in quiet, homey settings, it was quite startling in Andrei Serban's production of *The Cherry Orchard* in 1977 to see the back wall fade away, as though the movie camera were zooming in, to show us row on row of cherry trees. And Robert Wilson's elaborate visual effects are a new kind of imaginative spectacle, rich in design and color.

Spectacle has been important in motion pictures since the very early days, and the introduction of the wide screen in the 1950s gave it even more impetus. The camera can so easily bring in the wide sweep of mountains and valleys, of buildings and streets, of processions and

9–3

Meaningful spectacle. Gold, glory, and religious display of the Emperor of Peru, who is killed by the Spaniards. Shaffer's *The Royal Hunt of the Sun*. Directed by John Dexter and designed and costumed by Michael Annals. Photo © Angus McBean.

dances, of battles and holocausts, that many a director has let the spectacle overwhelm all other elements. But spectacle can be used more subtly to show how character is shaped by history and geography and can create symbolic overtones for the main action by the use of montage to cut in parallel examples, symbolic objects, or landscapes that invoke a particular mood. There have been a few epic films that made extensive use of spectacle but also had good plots, sound characterization, and a well-developed theme—among them *Gone with the Wind* (1939), *The Bridge on the River Kwai* (1957), *Lawrence of Arabia* (1963), *Becket* (1964), and *The Lion in Winter* (1968). We have noted *Barry Lyndon* (1975) as an example of beautiful romantic spectacle.

The overall texture is a blend of many elements: the dialogue, with its rhythmic phrases, suggestive images, and vibrant sounds; the mood, created by the qualities and rhythms of the actors; and the spectacle, with its colorful settings, changing lights, and moving masses of costumes.

10

Rehearsal
and
Performance

FORMAL, BALANCED COMPOSITION
ON A THRUST STAGE. CHARACTERS ARE
EVENLY SPACED FOR ARISTOCRATIC
STATELINESS AT A WEDDING THAT IS
SUDDENLY TURNED INTO A SCENE OF
VIOLENT ACCUSATION. SHAKESPEARE'S
MUCH ADO ABOUT NOTHING. THE
EUCLID-SEVENTY-SEVENTH STREET
THEATRE OF THE CLEVELAND
PLAYHOUSE PRODUCTION. DIRECTED
BY KIRK WILLIS AND DESIGNED BY PAUL
RODGERS.

When the director is sure what attitude of comedy or tragedy to aim for, what style is needed, what patterns to follow in plot, character, and theme, and what qualities to create in dialogue, mood, and spectacle, he or she starts to put the play on the boards. After director and designer have worked out the ground plan and know where the doorways, steps, and levels are to be and where the walls and furniture will shape the playing areas, the designer and his assistants go their own way for a time while the director concentrates on putting the actors on the stage. In working with the actors, the director makes use of five special techniques: composition, picturization of relationships, movement, pantomimic dramatization, and rhythm. The first two are techniques for controlling the picture in space, and the last three set the play into movement in time. The director considers how to make the play clear and meaningful to both eye and ear. In the early rehearsals each moment of the play must be looked at as though it were a still photograph, so that the composition may be clear and the relationships in the picture may be meaningful; later the director watches and listens as the large movements, the reading of lines, and the small reactions propel the play through its rhythmic patterns in time.

The principles of directing considered here were developed, for the most part, in productions of standard types of plays on a proscenium stage, but they are applicable also, with some adjustments, to plays of the freer forms presented on any type of stage. Plot and characterization are negligible in some plays of the last several decades, as we have seen, but the stage picture must still be meaningful and the action must flow rhythmically. On the open, thrust, or arena stage, with audience all around or partly around the playing area, the director must be sure that every character is seen part of the time by each section of the audience and that no character blocks another for any length of time. In the unusual places used for some experimental productions, special problems confront the director. But imagination and a sharp eye are requisites of directing in any circumstances.

Director and Actor

Controlling the Picture in Space

The director's first step in staging the play is to visualize it in space. The problem is not like putting a single orator on a podium or a preacher in a pulpit; the director must visualize an action involving people with other people and with the world they live in. If the actors were left to themselves, they would get in front of one another and muddle the composition, and each would move without regard to what the others were doing. The grouping would be meaningless, and the attention of the audience would be scattered. The composition of the picture and the picturization of relationships must be controlled by someone outside the picture; hence these two techniques belong very logically to the director.

The movie and television director has a camera with which to select and control what is to hold the attention, but the stage director has only the actor and the space of the stage for the picture. In placing and moving actors in the various areas of the stage, he or she has many ways of changing the picture to give different meanings and to shift the attention from one character to another. The director may subordinate one character by turning him away from the audience while giving prominence to another by asking him to "open up" (that is, turn more toward the audience), to stand up, to step out from a group, or to move from a weak area of the stage to a stronger one. Or the director can throw the emphasis on one character without moving him by moving the characters around him, so that they give him more space and contrast, and by having them turn their "eye-focus" on him. In deploying the actors, the director divides the stage into six areas (sometimes nine) and labels them *up right, up center, up left, down right, down center, down left,* and sometimes *right center, center,* and *left center* (Figure 10–1). Stage left and stage right indicate the sides as viewed by the actor facing the audience; upstage is away from the audience and downstage is toward it. For four centuries—in some places well into this century—upstage was actually higher than downstage, since the old picture stage had a sloping floor to give a forced perspective effect to the wing-and-backdrop setting.

Not only are some areas stronger than others, but different areas have different qualities. The soft, distant areas up left and up right are good for lyric moods, for longing, dreaming, brooding, and for some delicate love scenes. Scenes in those areas are so soft that they do not assure us that

10–1

Stage areas. The director divides the stage into at least six areas, which vary in quality and strength from the soft up left or up right to the very emphatic down center.

action will follow. For instance, a lonely, isolated person, hearing other people talking unfavorably about him, could smolder up left or up right in pain and anger, but not until he came into the area down left or down right would we believe him capable of taking revenge. Decisions and quarrels often need the strength of the down center position after a climactic move from one of the weaker areas. But scenes of violence are too shocking if brought downstage. A stabbing or strangling is usually played in a weak area; it will be strong enough upstage left behind a sofa, with other actors covering the body, and more convincing than it would be if the audience could see how the blow is faked. Even a film usually omits the final impact, showing only the arm or the shadow of the murderer and the horrified face of an onlooker.

The director devotes the first rehearsal to *blocking*; that is, going through each scene speech by speech, telling the actors when to come in, where to stand or sit, on what lines to move or carry out such "stage business" as handling the properties, and how to perform many of the small reactions that go with the lines. As they go through the actions, they write the directions down in their scripts. If a commercial acting edition of the play is used, the director tells them to disregard the printed stage directions, for usually he or she has worked out new movements and actions that will fit the particular stage, the setting, and the dramatic concept the director has in mind.

Blocking of the first act may take one three-hour rehearsal or longer, and three or four more rehearsals may be necessary to get the act set before the next act is blocked. Directors vary a great deal in the extent of their blocking, some giving full directions immediately, others leaving much of the detail to be worked out later as the actors try out their lines and their reactions to one another. Almost any director makes adjustments in later rehearsals as director and actors discover better ways of moving and reacting. It is necessary to make sure constantly that the picture has clarity, focus, and variety. The form of the composition, its formality or diffuseness, hardness or softness, will add meaning to the play.

A tense moment in a college production of *The Caine Mutiny Court Martial* appears in Figure 10–2. In considering the overall controls, the director has decided that this is a very strong situation play with romantic, even melodramatic, interest in conflict, threats, fears, and concern over justice. With the designer, he decided to bring the action far downstage but not actually to break the fourth-wall convention. Since the concern about justice is abstract and the people are removed from the actual ships and storms where the mutiny took place, the setting and composition can be rather abstract and formal. But since conflict is so important in the play and is not resolved into an unquestioned justice at the end, the ground

10–2 Trial scene with formal lines on a diagonal ground plan. Primary emphasis is on the officer on the stand, and secondary emphasis is on the prosecutor. Wouk's *The Caine Mutiny Court Martial.* Mankato State College production, directed by Ted Paul and designed by Burton E. Meisel.

plan is placed on the diagonal; the court is not square to the front, and the judge is not so dominant as in a civil courtroom. The designer has provided several levels for playing, and in this scene the director is making good use of them to give the prosecutor an uphill handicap in his assault on the witness. The isolation of the two figures at the front, with considerable free space, and their dynamic interaction make them stand out clearly from the seated figures. Of the two, the officer on the stand easily dominates, even without the special lighting, because of his higher position and because his face and body are turned more toward the audience than toward the others. Furthermore, in contrast to everybody else he is relaxed, and contrast, like isolation in space, adds a powerful emphasis. If attention should wander to the judge or his associates, it is sent right back to the officer because they are looking at him. The director constantly uses such eye-focus of the characters on stage to point to the center of interest. If the attention is to go to the judge or one of his seated associates, the director will need to turn several people to look at him and subordinate the forestage men by turning their faces away from the audience.

For a very informal composition, let us consider the scene from *A View from the Bridge* shown in Figure 10–3. Although the space used is fairly shallow, the characters are very much at home, and the environment is important. The play is a naturalistic drama that has strong conflict under the surface, but in this scene the little conflicts and changing interactions are more important than any one thread of action. Character and mood, at

10–3 Informal scene in naturalistic style. Curved lines hold the compact group together. Though the characters are emotionally isolated, the grouping indicates many potential loyalties and conflicts. Miller's *A View from the Bridge.* University of Oregon production, directed by William R. McGraw and designed by Karl Kaufman.

least for this scene, are more important than plot. The curved lines of the composition create informality and warmth and bring all the characters into a close circle. Yet the director keeps nearly all of them isolated from one another. All belong to one family, yet they cannot come together. There is a great deal of variety, with two people standing, two seated, and one sitting on the floor; the director has used this variety to create many different relationships. The boy sitting on the floor has one thought—his love for the girl he is with—and both his humble position and his eyes are begging for her love. He is safely enclosed between the two women, but he is isolated from the men, and the line of their faces, with conflict brewing, leads directly to him. The woman standing could easily take the attention—her position gives her a high level; she is near the center of the stage; and she is facing front in contrast with the two seated men. But she subordinates herself by dropping her eyes. At this moment she will not tie herself to anyone, though the lines of the picture tie her closely in three directions. The curved lines and her nearness to the young couple show her sympathy for them; her position at the table ties her to her husband sitting at the table, though she separates herself from what he is saying; her standing shows her implicit sympathy with the young man standing at stage left. The man sitting at the table is obviously the man of the house and all the others are closely tied to him, but he keeps his isolation and is slightly hostile to the young man at his left. Nobody is completely subordinated, and each could easily be given the center of attention. For instance, if the boy sitting turned his face more toward the audience, he would be stronger, and if one or more of the three other characters turned an eye-focus on him, he would be the center of action.

We see that bringing a character from the side toward the center or from upstage toward the audience will make him stronger. But it is easy to subordinate characters, even in strong areas, by turning the face and body partly away from the audience, for the actor whose face is turned more nearly to the front will hold the greater interest. A higher face will dominate a lower; a character standing will dominate one sitting; one on a step or platform will dominate one on a lower level. Eye-focus of the actors is one of the easiest means of controlling the attention of the audience, since we tend to look at what someone else is looking at. A single figure with space around him can, like a small weight on a long lever, counterbalance a large mass. An element of the scenery that repeats the line of the actor, or a guard or attendant, can give him more importance. Contrast is such a powerful element that it can counteract any of the other methods of controlling attention. One figure sitting, bent over, with his head turned away from the audience, is weaker than a figure standing and facing the audience, but if there are three or four straight standing figures, the weak, bent figure takes the attention by contrast. It is the whole picture that the audience sees, and each actor, each property, each part of the setting must take its place in the controlled context or it will distract the attention and destroy the illusion of the scene.

The audience is seldom aware of the composition in itself, unless it is cluttered or confused. What is seen is the story in the picture, told through the action and interrelation of the characters. This story-telling arrangement may be called "picturization of emotional relations." It is a visual language, a medium as powerful as words, by which the director communicates with the audience. It is one means by which a play, so short in comparison with a novel, can make as strong an impression, sometimes even stronger. The actor, the designer, and the director can show the audience at a glance complexities and qualities of relationship that would require many pages of a novel to describe or suggest. In a well-directed scene of an accident in the street, for instance, the audience can tell by the position of the actors which is the wife of the victim, which the mother, the father, the friend, the wife's friend, and which are mere passers-by, adding their own groupings and emotional reactions in the background. Characters on stage, as in real life, naturally turn toward and stay near those they like or trust or feel something in common with, and keep at a distance or turn away from those they dislike. Many other relationships of characters can be clearly indicated by the stage picture; for instance, one person asking, refusing, suspecting, accusing, protecting, or disdaining another. Farewells are different if someone is leaving for a long or a short absence, for a picnic or for war or for prison. If the director can give the scene a title that describes its basic action, he or she can see more clearly how to arrange the picture.

Moving the Play in Time

For the director, even more important than the control of the picture in space is the movement of the actors and the progression of the play in time. On the stage people don't just talk, they do something, and as they carry on daily business they are constantly changing their relations with one another. The playwright's dialogue is the surface expression. It is the director's job to find the inner life of the play and see that it, too, is expressed, in the changing moods, the larger movements, and the smaller business and reactions of the actor.

Movement is picturization in action. As relationships and attitudes change, the movements are as important as the words—indeed, often more important, since they can modify or even contradict the words and add other meanings and nuances. Hence the director makes sure that the actor understands the character's motivation and begins his action with the thought; then the movement will express his intention and the words will be part of a total response. It usually takes many rehearsals for the actor to achieve a good integration of intention, speech, and movement, and in the early stages improvisation may be helpful to bring movement and words spontaneously from the thought. The English director Joan Littlewood found that even professional actors needed preparatory exercises to get both the imagination and the muscles limbered up. In the opening scene of *A Taste of Honey*, a weary mother and daughter arrive at their squalid new lodgings. Miss Littlewood had the two actresses spend an hour dragging heavy suitcases around the stage, trying to get on buses, arguing with landladies, struggling with rain, even imagining they were dragging the suitcases down long, dark, filthy tunnels. They learned how to feel worn out and fretful.

No actor on the stage moves alone. Any movement is part of a readjustment that the other characters must at least acknowledge. The actors are all bound in one web of interrelationships as if invisible rubber bands were stretched between them. As they follow curved paths around one another and around the furniture, the actors create a sense of depth in a stage picture that otherwise looks rather flat.

Movement in the group is one of the director's ways of creating a build, sometimes more powerful in increasing tension than the rising speed, volume, and pitch of the dialogue. A long, talky scene needs some "breaking up," even if no great build is required. The first part of a scene will usually carry itself, and the director will conserve power, adding few movements and only those that are casual and related to the background. As the scene progresses, he or she will add more and more movements, timing them closer together and increasing their size and intensity, always making sure that they are so placed and motivated as to reinforce the scene and not distract from it. If one character is telling a long story to several others, the director may not want to give any noticeable movement to the teller, but the needed breaking up or build can be gained if some listeners, at first very relaxed, get excited and move in closer, while others interject audible reactions and nod in agreement at one another after vivid moments in the tale.

While guiding the large movements and the reactions of the actors to one another, the director must constantly be aware of the little "pantomimic dramatizations"—each actor's indication, by facial expression, stance, movement, the handling of properties, of what the character is thinking or feeling. The lift of an eyebrow, a sneer, a shake of the head, the tension of the body, can be a more vivid language than speech.

In the coaching rehearsals, directors differ widely in their ways of stimulating the actor. Those who follow the Stanislavsky or the Actors Studio methods spend a great deal of time discussing the motivation of the character, comparing the character's experience with previous experiences of the actor, becoming almost amateur psychoanalysts in hope of discovering and releasing the actor's inhibitions. Other directors believe there is nothing like simply rehearsing the play itself. Laurence Olivier expressed his impatience with the New York method in an interview for the *New York Times:*

> I'd rather have run the scene eight times than have wasted that time in chattering away about abstractions. An actor gets the right thing by doing it over and over. Arguing about motivations and so forth is a lot of rot. American directors encourage that sort of thing too much. . . . Instead of doing a scene over again that's giving trouble, they want to discuss . . . discuss . . . discuss. . . .

The final coordinating rehearsals are generally considered to be nightmares, and in the days when amateurs brought everything together—

costumes, scenery, properties, and lighting—at one last frantic dress rehearsal, they were just that. The performance could not possibly be as bad as that rehearsal, and the legendary saying was repeated: "A bad dress rehearsal means a good performance." But today school theatres and community theatres are much more serious and usually have from three to five dress rehearsals, besides working out many of the details before the first dress rehearsal. The company of an art theatre with its own building has a great advantage over casts playing in commercial theatres where they cannot get on stage until the last minute. It is a great help to actors to have platforms and steps, doors and windows to practice with and to have scene changes and much of the lighting worked out beforehand. For a period play, practice properties and parts of costumes, especially high heels and long practice skirts for the actresses, may be used for weeks. Then just before the dress rehearsal the director and the designer often have a dress parade, bringing all the actors on stage in costume and makeup to try the key moves and see what changes and adjustments are necessary.

After the strenuous, coordinating dress rehearsals, it is a good idea to have several full rehearsals that run through without interruption. Most of the director's suggestions are made to the actors after each act or after seeing the play as a whole. Free to watch the flow of the play, to feel the surges toward the climaxes, the director may make many notes, some of them on details that can be improved next time through, but at this point the chief thing to look for is the overall effect. Is the style maintained consistently? Is the plot clear? Are the characters believable? Do the important ideas come through in words and actions? Is the texture rich and controlled, not too soft or too harsh? And, finally, do all the elements—setting, lighting, movement, tones, words—move together to carry the play to its big climaxes and give it structure and shape? By this time the actor is free to follow without interruption the secret life of the play in the hundred and one little reactions that give the play vitality, ready for the one final spark that will set the performance aflame—direct contact with a live audience.

Actor and Audience

For all that modern theory calls for the domination of the director, the actor (man or woman) is still the center of the theatre. For all that modern theory calls for the subordination of the actor to the ensemble and the overall mood of the play, the best actors are remembered even more than the play. For all that many directors in the last two decades have been

10–4 Virtuoso acting. Irene Worth and Raul Julia in Serban's production of Chekhov's *The Cherry Orchard.* New York, 1977. Photo Sy Friedman.

fascinated by the choral group, the individual who possesses the secret magic of a primitive shaman still emerges as the great force in the theatre.

Acting is a paradox. The actor, like the singer, is both the instrument and the one who performs on the instrument. While the painter and the instrumental musician stand outside the thing they create and are involved only indirectly and symbolically, actors identify with the characters they portray and seem to be living the emotions they show to the audience. But it is only a seeming, a pretense, a make-believe, a "play-like," an illusion, a mirror image. Both actors and audience know perfectly well that what is seen on the stage is not actuality. Both may be "carried away," and children in the theatre sometimes cry out in imaginary participation. But a second person inside the actor is always watching, guiding, criticizing, adjusting the performance to the tension of the audience. When the actor is asked if he feels the emotions of the character, the answer is yes—and no. Especially in rehearsals and the first few performances, he may feel very involved, but later he sometimes feels merely carried along by technique and rote memory. He is never sure just what combination of warm heart and cool head may give the best performance.

Traditional Training of the Actor

Like other artists, actors can be trained. For many years that training was mostly in the theatre. A young man or woman who had shown promise in oratory and declamation in school would be hired for little pay to play small parts in a provincial stock company. There the elder actors would criticize the novice's work and prescribe voice and body exercises handed down for generations. An actor or actress who showed talent would get a chance at the longer parts and eventually be invited to join a company in a large city.

With this kind of training the actor developed a voice to be heard in large theatres and learned to build long speeches to ringing climaxes. He learned to move in the aristocratic deportment of bows and curtsies, to show skill in singing, dancing, and fencing. In high or "genteel" comedy, actors expected to play with elegance, pride, and teasing insinuation, and in low comedy with exaggerated anguish or glee. The real test was what they could do with Shakespeare. If they succeeded here, their prestige was established and they might find a following as ardent as that of a movie star in the twentieth century.

The nineteenth century had one of the most popular theatres in history. Yet as realism came in late in the nineteenth century and smaller theatres changed the expectation of the audience, the large style of acting seemed exaggerated and empty. A radical new approach to actor training was begun by Constantin Stanislavsky in Moscow in 1897.

The Stanislavsky Method of Actor Training

As director of the Moscow Art Theatre, Stanislavsky worked out a new method, which was adopted by most acting schools in the United States as well as in Russia. Assuming that his students were familiar with traditional techniques and were working many hours a week in courses in movement, dance, fencing, voice placement, singing, and diction, he concentrated on the inner preparation of the actor, which he has described fully in *An Actor Prepares,* the most admired book on acting in modern times.

First of all, Stanislavsky wanted to free the actor (man or woman) from distraction and false actions, to teach him to relax each part of the body from unnecessary tension, and especially to free him from conventional techniques of projection inherited from the nineteenth century. Instead of trying to convey to the audience a big general emotion, the actor was to concentrate on relations to the other characters, to the furniture around him, and especially to small properties and pieces of business, the specific details of everyday living. Give an actor something to do—hold a teacup, put out a cigarette, move a chair, hand something to another character—and both body and voice would come alive. The immediate triumphs of naturalistic acting are in the little reactions, the pantomimic dramatizations—the unconscious snarl on the lips, the half-clenched fist, the flinching shoulder—that give color to the spoken phrases and are a visible expression of the inner life of the character.

To create a consistent role in depth, the actor must analyze the character's "objective" in each scene and hence define the "spine" of the character for the whole play. He must visit the kinds of houses, streets, and neighborhoods associated with the character, absorbing the sights, sounds, smells, and moods of the environment. Using the "magic if," he must, alone and with the other actors, spend days thinking, feeling, acting, and speaking *as if* he actually were the character. With long practice and concentration, the actor might transform himself and make a complete new creation of each role.

Such acting requires only a very limited kind of body and voice training, for its power lies in the unconscious mind, which must be stimulated by "psychotechniques." Stanislavsky found that the actor had several ways of calling up deep feelings, of searching for the "inner flow," the "deeper content," the "inner musical score," or "subtext," that lay hidden behind the words of the play. Stanislavsky recognized, as Freud did, that although the subconscious could not be forced to reveal its secrets directly, there might be indirect ways of unlocking its treasures. Most important of the psychotechniques was the appeal to emotional memory. If the actor thought back to an experience of his own that had created a feeling similar to that of his situation in a play—a childhood experience, for example, perhaps trivial in itself but important to him at the time—he might rediscover the tone and texture that had accompanied the original experience. Another psychotechnique was improvisation. Treating the words of the play script as only a surface component of the full experience, the actor might go behind the words, imagining other moments in the life of the character and improvising appropriate actions and words for them. When the actor returned to the play itself, he or she would possess the inner flow, the hidden life, of the character and thus could present a whole person.

The "method" school of acting achieved its first triumph in America through the Group Theatre of New York. Starting work together in 1931, this group of young actors dedicated themselves to the serious year-round study of acting, to the development of good ensemble playing, and to the production of serious new American plays. They broke up in 1941, but after the war one of their directors, Lee Strasberg, founded the Actors Studio, an institution not for production but for actors both young and old to continue serious study. For the next three decades the Actors Studio and the Stanislavsky approach dominated the training of American actors.

Without deliberately raising the voice or asserting a gesture, the "method" actor can move an audience deeply by the dark, inarticulate tragedy that is held in. One among many fine examples of the application of this method on the American stage was the impersonation by Marlon Brando of Stanley Kowalski in *A Streetcar Named Desire* in 1947. Uneducated, crude in his treatment of his wife though genuinely in love with her, seething with resentment at the comments of his snobbish sister-in-law, Blanche Du Bois, Stanley suffered in silence or made brief, insulting replies, until finally he could bear no more and proved his power by attacking Blanche. By the actor's identification with the character, Kowalski came through to the audience not as the beast Blanche thought him but as a sensitive human being who must be pitied (Figure 10–5).

New Directions in Actor Training

Even in the 1950s not all productions were naturalistic, and gradually actors and teachers of acting realized that the Stanislavsky method was not enough. For one thing, when classics were revived, the superiority of English actors to American actors in plays of the past was evident. English

10–5
Superb acting in a naturalistic scene. Smoldering resentments lead to rape. Marlon Brando and Jessica Tandy in Williams' *A Streetcar Named Desire*. New York, 1947. Directed by Elia Kazan. Photo Theatre and Music Collection, Museum of the City of New York.

actors had not been limited to one method. One sign of a growing uneasiness was that the Institute for Advanced Study of Theatre Arts brought to New York directors from European and Asian theatres to teach their traditional techniques and to direct sample productions.

The limitations of the "method" have become more glaringly evident in the last two decades, when many of the most interesting productions have called not for the suggestion of an anguished soul but for the active use of a well-trained body, for varied movement on the stage, even for dance. Could it help the gymnastic fairies in Brook's production of *A Midsummer Night's Dream?* The choral group in *Hair* did not need Stanislavsky techniques but spontaneity, youthful energy, and some ability in singing and dancing. The parables in *Godspell* did not require a deep subtext but vivid, quickly drawn caricatures. In most productions of the avant garde of the 1960s, not psychological intensity but agility, speed, adaptability, quick change of role were required. American actors and teachers of acting began to doubt the universal validity of a kind of training they had accepted unquestioningly. It was certainly not in keeping with many aspects of current culture. How could young people be satisfied with the quiet underplaying of the Stanislavsky school when they were accustomed to electric guitars, loudspeakers, and a microphone at every performer's mouth? For many of them the "inner life" meant Yoga or Transcendental Meditation or some other popular Oriental teaching. They demanded full, sensuous experience to create altered states of consciousness. And for the prophets of the "theatre of cruelty," dreaming of actors in ritual groups carrying every emotion to the extreme, what inspiration was there in the "method"? Could the "method" help in portraying the many characters in plays and films who seem to have no past but to exist only in the present as they suddenly find themselves involved in complex relationships?

It is easier to see that something is wrong than to provide a remedy, and it has not been easy to replace the Stanislavsky method. No one has come up with a complete new theory, but a few trends are evident. In the first place, there is general recognition that actor training must take into account the wide range of demands the actor may encounter in many kinds of plays, in many forms of stage space, and in many styles of performance. Most followers of Stanislavsky paid little attention to formal voice training, assuming that one kind of vocal exercise would do as well as another. Teachers now insist upon careful training that is directly related to the use of the voice on a stage, especially to the development of deeper resonance. Similarly, it was assumed that any kind of physical exercise, in sport, gymnastics, or acrobatics would meet the actor's requirements. Now body training for the theatre has absorbed many of

10–6 Theatre of cruelty. Hidden hatreds erupt in a cruel ritual enacted before an audience of Negro actors in white-face masks. Genêt's *The Blacks*. New York Off Broadway production, 1961. Photo Martha Swope.

the traditional techniques of ballet and modern dance and several of the traditional Oriental techniques. By the 1960s the Actors Studio, the shrine of devotion to Stanislavsky, had added classes in Tai Chi Ch'uan, the traditional Chinese training for defense.

Central in recent training is group work, often combined with sensitivity training, to increase the actor's awareness both of himself alone and as part of an ensemble. Theatre games, involving a group of students, develop spontaneity through improvisation and also provide the discipline of group coordination. Classes in styles of acting take into account not only period styles but the requirements of different kinds of contemporary plays.

Any teacher of acting finds suggestions in the work of such directors as Peter Brook and especially Jerzy Grotowski. Grotowski developed a more complete system of training than most of the other directors of the avant-garde groups described in Chapter 8. His actors achieved a wild, almost terrifying intensity in mocking derision or anguished pain that seemed the opposite extreme from the quiet, subtle underplaying of the Stanislavsky school. They developed techniques for extending the range of body and voice—"plastiques," for instance, of rapidly flexing and rotating the joints to stretch the muscles, or locating resonances for the voice in unaccustomed parts of the head and body.

Besides both new and old Western techniques, Grotowski borrowed training methods from the Kathakali dance dramas of India, from Chinese opera, and from the Japanese Noh. Each actor was encouraged to seek the "root impulse" of any action in order to integrate the inner being with the outer expression. And, like Peter Brook and many contemporary idealists who seek a "global village" and communication among people of all races and languages, Grotowski hoped to achieve an objective expression so basic that it could appeal to the collective unconscious of all people without depending on the audience knowing the words—acts and gestures as specific as ideograms or hieroglyphs. Although no one has followed his theory and practice exactly, Grotowski has been an inspiration for many teachers seeking new approaches to the problems of acting.

Any imaginative director who has his own small performance group works out exercises that will develop the special qualities of voice, body, and imagination that his idea of theatre requires of his chosen actors. But no wise teacher of acting will forget the value of a modified Stanislavsky method in training actors for plays that require characterization in depth, and it is to be hoped that, no matter what directions the theatre takes, there will always be some of this kind of play.

The Actor as Virtuoso Performer

The most popular acting companies of the Renaissance had no playwright; they were the Italian *commedia dell' arte* troupes, who in the sixteenth century and for two hundred years afterward entertained Europe both at cultivated courts and at noisy street corners. Each performer was a star, perfecting one role in a lifetime of practice. Yet the troupe took great pride in the way they played together. They made up the words as they went along, following an outline of a plot tacked up behind the scenes by the manager to indicate what episode was to come next. They memorized witty sayings and retorts, and the lovers memorized songs and love sonnets and poems of complaint; but the good performers were well-read people who could improvise and adapt their dialogue to the immediate situation, making references to local affairs and taking advantage of any response of the audience or accident on the stage.

The company presented a whole family of stereotypes. The young lovers were constantly interrupted and thwarted by the two old masked fools, Pantalone, the rich *magnifico* from Venice, or the pedantic Doctor from Bologna with a gallimaufry of learned words. The two *zanni*, or comic servants, came to the rescue and at the same time created further complications. Even when the lover sang a charming serenade under his Lucinda's window, Pantalone was around a corner mocking him, waiting to rush out and beat him. Or perhaps it was not Lucinda at all but Harlequin disguised in her cape, showing his black, devil-like half-mask to the audience. Or Pedrolino, the country servant, jumped through a window and interrupted the lovers, or the Spanish captain came strutting and bragging down the street.

Commedia performers were acrobats, mime experts, singers, and jugglers as well as improvising actors, and even in foreign countries they could make their movements and gestures so vivid, their inflections so lively, that nobody needed a translator. Sometimes the plot was serious, but it did not remain so for very long before the comic performers started one of their famous running gags known as *lazzi*. Many of the *lazzi* were so well known that the manager would merely indicate in the scenario that at this point Pulcinella would try to delay the Doctor with the *lazzo* of the broken leg, or of suicide, or of "which would be better," "spill something on the cloak," or "pretend to see ghosts." Patterns of repetition were set, then broken, reversed, or interrupted. Doubtless some performances did not work—an entrance was made before another actor reached his gag line or the expected cues got jumbled. But when the teamwork was right and the comedians were in good form, the *commedia* was one of the highest delights in theatre history. The actor as performer, without playwright or director, was left as a goal and an ideal.

An extraordinary production, in the spirit of the *commedia*, was given in London and New York in 1974–75, with an English actor, Jim Dale, as the virtuoso performer. *Scapino*, based on Moliere's *Scapin*, which, in turn, had reflected *commedia* performances, was set in modern Naples. It was played on a wide stage without a curtain, much of the action well down front, even over the orchestra pit, very near the audience, to give the effect of a platform performance. The dialogue was set, not improvised, but there was continuous action, the movements were stylized, and the pace was extremely rapid. Dale was as agile, as light, as an acrobat or a dancer, with a perfect sense of timing. The plot was a tangle of intrigue, with Scapino now triumphant, now defeated, always knowing and merry, using, together with his fellow actors, some of the *commedia* gags. By clever wiles, for instance, the "old man" was persuaded to be tied in a sack, then beaten. The entire performance, played with the greatest ease, verve, and finesse, was a kind of complex dance of many figures. Such acting is extremely difficult for even the best-trained modern comedians. When *Scapino* played in New York and some replacements in the cast

10–7
A virtuoso comic performance. Jim Dale beating the old man who hid in a sack. *Scapino*, adapted from Moliere's *Tricks of Scapin*. New York, 1974. Directed by Frank Dunlop. Photo Martha Swope.

were necessary, it was very hard to find, among dozens of experienced actors who tried out, any who were equal to the demands of the style, and of course the perfect ensemble acting of the original English company was not duplicated.

The "stars" of stage and screen are the modern virtuoso performers, though they may not always show up at their best. We applaud them in the classics and in contemporary plays, in serious drama and in comedy. But the most thrilling performances are not necessarily those of the virtuoso stars. The theatregoer dreams of being present on one of those glorious evenings when audience and actors are in complete rapport, when every actor is captive in the web of the play, and when the principal actors, who may not be virtuoso performers, reach the peak of their power, and surpass themselves and create a masterpiece.

11

Design for the Theatre

MOUNTAIN TOP IN A SUPERNATURAL
REGION. SPACE STAGE, WITH
CHANGING PROJECTED IMAGES.
WAGNER'S *DIE WALKÜRE*.
METROPOLITAN OPERA PRODUCTION,
NEW YORK, 1967. PHOTO E. FRED SHER.

The design of a production creates an environment for the actor—a pedestal, a showcase, a picture, a machine for acting. It gives the actor form, creating a space in which he can move. It adds color, change, contrast, and mood as it shapes the play in both space and time. As we have seen, the designers of scenery, costume, and lighting must be in on the planning of the production. The locations of entrances and exits and the shaping of playing areas determine the patterns of movement the director can use. The kind of setting and the costume and lighting changes determine how one scene flows into the next and affect the play's rhythmic structure. As much as the playwright or the director, the designers are responsible for the unity of the production.

The Setting

In the nineteenth century the main function of scenery was to indicate time and place. The painted backdrops, along with the costumes, told the audience they were in ancient, medieval, or modern times, in Spain or China, prince's palace or peasant's kitchen, summer garden or winter snow. No matter whether the mood was comedy or tragedy, satire or fantasy, the designer brought on the stage the results of careful "research." Going to the theatre was as important a way of learning facts as a guided tour through a museum or a social survey of how the other half lived. The historian, the sociologist, the journalist, and the designer were equally interested in presenting local color. The designer used gaily colored landscape backdrops or box sets with realistic detail, according to whether the piece was a romantic opera or a realistic character play. He was glad enough if he created a mood, but mood was a byproduct. His first thought was of the actuality of time and place.

The modern designer, in protest, has gone to the other extreme. He insists that the design should not be a decoration separate from the actors but should be an integral part of the movement of the play. To indicate time and place is far less important than to create mood and atmosphere, to shape the movement of the actors, and to give a unifying idea; many modern designs do not indicate place at all but present imaginative, atmospheric abstractions or arrangements of pipes, ramps, platforms, and steps. In 1899 Adolphe Appia, in one of the most famous theatre books, *Music and the Art of the Theatre,* distinguished the "expressive" from the "symbolizing" functions in a work of art. He said that the symbolizing details that indicate the particular locale should be kept to a minimum—just enough to orient the audience, as a signboard might—in order to allow the expressive functions free play. By 1919 Kenneth Macgowan had defined the aims of the new stagecraft as simplification, suggestion, and synthesis: simplification to get rid of all Victorian ornament that might distract attention from the actor; suggestion to evoke a mood by simple means—"a single Saracenic arch can do more than a half dozen to summon the passionate background of Spanish *Don Juan*"; and synthesis to create a unity and consistency whereby actor, setting, lights, and action would express the essential inner quality of the play and would change as the play progressed.

In a sense the new ideal means the complete abdication of the designer, for the modern design must not stand out as a beautiful picture. Robert Edmond Jones described the new challenge in an inspired book called *The Dramatic Imagination.*

> A setting is not just a beautiful thing, a collection of beautiful things. It is a presence, a mood, a warm wind fanning the drama to flame. It echoes, it enhances, it animates. It is an expectancy, a foreboding, a tension. It says nothing, but it gives everything. . . . The designer creates an environment in which all noble emotions are possible. Then he retires. The actor enters. If the designer's work has been good, it disappears from our consciousness at that moment. . . . The actor has taken the stage, and the designer's only reward lies in the praise bestowed on the actor.

Kinds of Theatre

In the liberation of the performance from traditional patterns in the 1960s, many young rebels and experimenters found their greatest adventure in using a "found" place for their productions. No matter if there were no comfortable seats—the adventurous audience could stand, or sit on the floor, or on part of the platforms and steps used by the actors. All the better if the place were a run-down warehouse, store, or garage. The environment could unite audience and actor in one room. But the novelty soon wears thin unless the room is completely rebuilt for each production.

The flexibility of the "found" place or a specially built room has been incorporated into our theatre institutions through an experimental room, sometimes called "the little black box," where playing structures can be built and chairs for the audience can be rearranged in many different ways (Figures 7–5, 9–2). It can have good sound and lighting equipment, and best of all a floor cut up in modules which can be lowered or raised to different levels by the touch of a button, between scenes or even during the performance.

The search for new relations between actor and audience has led not only to the flexible room, which we do not call a theatre, but to two new-

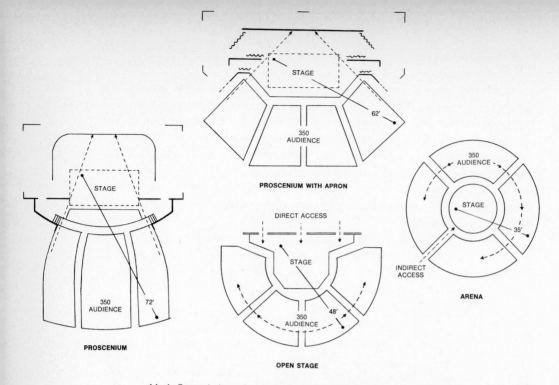

11-1 Ground plans showing the relative distance of the last row of an audience of 350 from the actor in four kinds of theatre—regular proscenium, proscenium with apron, thrust or open stage, and arena. Drawn by Don Creason after a drawing by James Hull Miller.

old forms of theatre: the *thrust* or *apron* stage, with audience seats three quarters of the way around the playing platform, and the *arena* or *theatre-in-the-round,* with the audience on all four sides of the playing area. Even when we use the traditional proscenium stage, we like to bring the action forward nearer the audience. Hence the designer must consider four possible patterns of actor-audience relationship. His problem differs according to whether he is putting the audience in the same environment as the actor, building a few suggestive sculptural forms for a thrust or arena stage, or building a complete scenic picture back of a proscenium, where he can use elaborate stage machines for hanging and changing scenery and lighting.

The great advantage of the arena stage, or theatre-in-the-round, is that it brings the actor and the audience very close together. Audiences that are used to closeups in film, with a face filling the whole screen, like to feel near the actor. The ground plans of Figure 11–1 show that the last row of an audience of 350 will be more than twice as close to the actors in an arena theatre as in the proscenium type. Glenn Hughes, who started the in-the-round movement in college theatres in the 1930s, planned his arena stage primarily for drawing-room comedy, with only three rows of seats—

170 in all—and a playing area little larger than a 12-by-18-foot rug. But the splendid Arena Stage in Washington has a stage 30-by-36 feet and seats 752 in eight steeply banked rows. The Lambertville Music Circus in New Jersey seats 1,300, and Casa Mañana, the music circus in Fort Worth, seats 1,832 under its aluminum dome.

More scenic decoration is possible in theatre-in-the-round than might be guessed. Low hedges, fences, flower boxes, and so on can give a touch of local color below the line of sight, and lightweight scenic elements may hang from above (Figure 11–2). At the corner entrances, and even in the middle of a side section, realistic segments of walls, windows, and doors may be used if they are indispensable to the action. Columns, arches, pavilions, and other light outline forms can be used in the center and still allow action to be seen. The Arena Stage in Washington has trap doors in the floor for trenches, openings, entrances, or even an orchestra pit (see Figure P–1).

The thrust stage may be used with elaborate scenic effects or with very little. Some plays can be presented almost as in the round, as we see

11–2 Arena staging with the rich texture of local color suggested by fragments of scenery. A small-town yard and back porch are suggested by the flowers and the low board fence built into one corner. The steps and platform give a variety of levels. Inge's *Picnic*. Eastern Illinois University production, directed by E. G. Gabbard and designed by John E. Bielenberg.

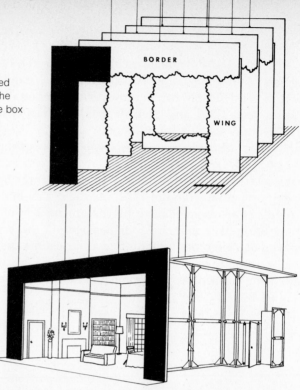

11–3
The two scenic formats inherited from the nineteenth century—the wing-and-backdrop set and the box set. Drawn by Don Creason.

in *The Three Sisters* at the Guthrie Theatre in Minneapolis (Figure 9–1). Both the living room and dining room furniture is in place on the forestage, with only window seats to suggest walls. On the other hand, for *Tamburlaine,* the opening production at the Olivier Theatre of the National Theatre complex in London, several three-dimensional, towerlike structures on wheels were brought on in turn, to suggest the exotic Eastern kingdoms Tamburlaine was conquering.

The most interesting challenge of the thrust stage is to design a three-dimensional structure either of steps, platforms, and arches, or of plastic shapes which the actors can walk on or under or through and even sit or lie on. It can be merely an abstract shape or it can be textured and painted to look like stone or grass. In one year the Guthrie produced both *King Lear* and *Love's Labor's Lost* using plastic forms that did not change throughout the play. In *King Lear* the stonelike levels and terraces were slightly modified as actors brought on a few simple seats and added a piece of fabric here and a hanging there.

It is the *proscenium* stage, the standard Western form since the early Renaissance, that offers the great opportunity for the designer. It puts the actor in a framed picture, or directly in front of the picture. The framed setting not only creates mood and style, it shapes the movement and the action of the whole play. (See Figures 11–3 and P–3.)

The Design Format for the Proscenium Stage

In using the proscenium stage, the first task of the designer is to find a format—a scheme of settings and transitions that will give the play a smooth and meaningful progression from one scene to the next. Suppose the designer is to plan a production of *Boris Godunov,* a grand opera of many colorful, spectacular scenes. He could follow the pattern of the classic Greek and Elizabethan stages, with one splendid formal architectural structure for the entire play, making a few changes of curtains and properties serve to indicate many localities. But it would be more exciting to plan a complete change of setting for each change of place in the story. A realistic approach would fill the stage picture with walls and houses, ramps and platforms, then remove the whole setting in sections and replace it with another realistic set for the next scene. Such a change takes several minutes. Even when the theatre has an elevator stage to lift a section or an entire setting from a lower level or a wagon stage to roll in scenery from the side, the shift usually means letting the curtain down for several minutes and interrupting the flow of the play.

The old wing-and-backdrop arrangement was simple. The drops could be lifted up into the flies by ropes and pulleys, and the side wings could be slid out in grooves to show another set of drops and wings already in place—a change quickly made before the eyes of the audience. Nowadays most productions use some combination of the two formats, making scene changes in sight of the audience by raising and lowering drops, turning small turntables, or rolling in small wagon stages, and hiding some upstage changes with a curtain or painted drop while another scene is playing in the shallow downstage area. To plan such a format for *Boris Godunov,* the designer first makes a chart showing which are interior and which exterior scenes; which are Russian and which Polish and what differences the two must show; which are intimate scenes and which crowd scenes; what contrasts must set the palace scenes off from the church and inn scenes; how the crowd can be shown off; how and to what degree the coronation scene should be made a climax to the others. He examines pictures of the architecture and decoration of the period and listens to the music of the opera to catch the mood. He constantly considers how his ideas would work on the stage. If he plans to fly several painted backdrops or sections of wall, he must find out whether the theatre has enough lines to hold these and still leave lines for a few rows of lights. He must decide whether there is enough space at the sides to move more solid structures; whether the same platforms, steps, and ramps can be used in several scenes; whether some small scenes can be set in front of the larger scenes that are not moved; whether the format can show a meaningful sequence in the order of the scenes.

Epic theatre, as we have seen, demands a format that permits easy flow from one scene to another. Brecht's Mother Courage pulls her peddler's wagon, like a medieval pageant wagon, on and off the stage as she follows the soldiers of the Thirty Years' War. In *Our Town* the Stage Manager brings on the few suggestive properties needed. For *Death of a Salesman,* Jo Mielziner, the designer, decided not to try to change settings for the thirty-five scenes Miller had written but to borrow from the Elizabethan stage the idea of a permanent symbolic structure at the back, with many small scenes brought onto the forestage. Then he used an expressionistic technique. Back of Willy's house he put a transparent gauze painted with sky and cool green leaves for the scenes when Willy dreamed of the happy past. When Willy felt caught by the ugly present, the gauze scene faded out and the lights back of it caught up a backdrop painted with threatening brick apartment buildings.

The most interesting format of the early part of the twentieth century is called a *space stage*. It came in when the development of the spotlight made it easy to show a limited area in a pool of light. Since the space can be brought out of complete darkness, the front curtain was no longer needed. Since the pool of light is independent of the lighting of the background, the old painted wings and backdrop became obsolete. Since one pool can be dimmed out as another is brought up, it was possible to put several centers of action on the stage simultaneously and move the attention from one to another. The space stage could be put before dark curtains, but it was better before the vast lighted heavens of the sky cyclorama or "cyc"—the sky that so brilliantly shows the rounds of day, twilight, and night, and the changing moods of the play. A space stage often has several acting levels, to which may be added simple scenic pieces that are lightweight enough to be brought on by hand or let down from above.

The triumph of the space stage is the projection. With light we can add scenic details to, or even replace, the built and painted scenery. We are all familiar with the slide projector and the movie projector, which use a lens to focus an image on a light-reflecting surface. Even without lenses, transparencies and cut-out silhouette forms set before a small source of light, as from a shadow-box, will project an image on the cyclorama or any other surface in or around the stage. If the surface is translucent and there is room, the image can be projected from the rear, or both front and back projections may be used. The image can move, as in showing clouds drifting across the sky. It can dim in or out quickly, or two projections can cross-fade or be superimposed.

The projection may be realistic, as in the Seattle street scene in Figure 11–4, where the building seems to be just behind the men on the platform.

11–4 Realistic background projected on a screen. *The Dream and the Deed*, a civic pageant-drama of Seattle, designed by John Ashby Conway.

Or it may be an ideogram or symbol: we often see a picture of the White House projected on a screen in the broadcast studio behind a newscaster reporting White House news.

We have seen that epic theatre often uses projections to enlarge the scope of the main scenes, using now slogans, titles, or quotations, now pictures of people, buildings, or events to remind the audience, out of the corner of the eye, of other ideas and people related in a direct, or sometimes an ironic, way to the central theme (see Figure 6–9). Audiences can combine different impulses, and the mixed media can add a great deal of power and variety. The reflecting surface does not have to be flat and fixed. In the ballet *Astarte,* the Joffrey Ballet presented a dance of two lovers before the projection of a movie of the same two dancers with enlarged closeups, and the screen itself billowed and stretched and took different shapes. The Laterna Magica of Prague achieved fascinating effects by showing living actors on the forestage who seemed to move into the screen, and screen images that suddenly took three-dimensional form as the same actor moved in relation to the movie images on the screen.

11-5 Multi-media in light, form, and movement. The human image as part of the flow of the universe. The moving dancers in abstract costumes are caught up in the moving patterns of projected light. Nikolais' *Somniloquy*. Photo © 1975 Milton J. Oleaga.

Alwin Nikolais not only uses strange shapes of costume for his dancers but sometimes projects still patterns of light and movies onto his performers, cutting and breaking one kind of movement by another.

Projections are indispensable for catching attention and getting across ideas in the spectacular commercial and industrial shows that are put on mostly in large convention and exhibition halls. Thousands of dollars may be spent on equipment, and hundreds of slides and movies may be used. Many kinds of material may be shown—abstract designs, slogans, landscapes, people, events. The new equipment and ideas developed in such productions can be very useful for theatre production (see color plate).

The most startling new development in projection is the hologram. Holography is an alternative to photography. Instead of recording the flat focused image of an object, the film of the hologram records the interference pattern when the object is lighted by a coherent light from a laser beam and that light is cut across by a different beam of coherent light at a controlled angle. When the hologram is lighted by coherent light of the same wavelength (color) as the second beam, an image of the original object in three dimensions is formed either on a screen or in the smoky or dusty air. As in color photography, the image can be created in a combination of three colors. It is startling to see an image that someone can walk right through. Holograms are already used in Disneyland and doubtless will be used soon in the theatre. One thinks of many possibilities— Banquo's ghost, for instance.

Four Methods of Design

There are four ways of creating a design. Sometimes it is obvious which method has been followed, but often a good design looks as if several approaches might have been used at once.

One method is to start with the real place, the full actual scene, and select from it, cut it down, and reshape it for the particular stage, building materials, methods of changing scenery, and moods needed. By leaving off the ceiling and most of the side walls and cutting down the back wall, the designer can suggest a room without overwhelming the actor in naturalistic detail and can create a simple sculptured form that is a welcome change from the splashy backdrops and ponderous box sets inherited from the nineteenth century. A pool of light from spotlights above the stage can concentrate the attention on the actor almost as intensely as a camera closeup. By lighting the cloth or plaster cyclorama at the back of the stage instead of filling out the picture with a painted backdrop or painted walls, the modern designer can show the actor and the streamlined setting against the expanding space and hypnotizing lighting of the sky. As Oliver Smith put it, "Design is principally the elimination of everything which is not absolutely necessary. A beautiful set should be a skeleton allowing air for the other participants of the theatre to breathe in." (See Figures 5–5, 5–6, and pages 256–57.)

A second method is to start with the actors and the few most important events of the play and then add space, platforms, shapes, and voids around them. Mordecai Gorelik told his students to start with the action of the play, ignoring locale, season, weather, time of day or night, and time lapses; all of that can be put in later. What the actors are doing must come first. He had his students write an outline of the action in two hundred words, then boil the outline down to sixty words, then choose the most important moments of the action and draw that action, using stick figures and including props only when they are important—a suitcase if someone is leaving, a boy outside a door with a bouquet of flowers and a box of candy, the girl inside the door. When the student sees clearly what the actors are doing, he can start designing. Norman Bel Geddes was sure that, no matter what the nature of the play, the designer should disregard any period concept of architecture or locale and think only of abstract "solids and voids." "The voids," he explained, "are spaces where entrances from nowhere to within the sight of the audience can be made," while "the solids are the areas between these voids."

A setting designed with close attention to stage movement is sometimes called a machine for acting. Lee Simonson calls it a plan of action, as important in controlling the movement of the actors as the architect's ground plan for a kitchen or a railway station is in creating and shaping lines of traffic. A design can suggest which relationships are possible and which are not likely to occur. Juliet on her balcony is an object of worship just out of Romeo's reach. Some groups should be completely separated, like a jury set apart by a railing from the others in the courtroom. Other groups may be only partly separated, with easy passage up or down steps or between the pieces of furniture that often mark the separation. A row of arches is often used for a ballroom scene to allow small groups to come forward into sharp focus while the dancing continues more quietly behind the arches (Figure 11–7). The Capulets' ball in *Romeo and Juliet* is often

11–6 Setting as a "machine for acting" in which levels suggest a ship. Coxe and Chapman's *Billy Budd*. University of Minnesota production, directed by David Thompson and designed by Lyle Hendricks.

11-7 Formalism. An architectural screen of large Renaissance arches gives dignity and unity to the play. Slight changes are made behind the arches by letting down simple elements such as leaves for an orchard or a panel for an altar. Shakespeare's *Much Ado About Nothing*. University of Arkansas production, designed and drawn by Don Creason.

staged with such a scene. Or the director may prefer to give full display to the dancers in a large open area, then take most of them offstage or stop the dancing while, in a separate alcove, Romeo whispers his poem to Juliet and takes his kiss.

The ultimate in the machine-for-acting approach was *constructivism*, which was popular among some Russian producers in the 1920s. Using no walls and little or no indication of location, the designer broke the stage floor into different levels with platforms, ramps, steps, and ladders to allow the actors many positions. The supports were frankly exposed, adding the interest of posts, beams, towers, scaffolds, pipes, and guide wires (see Figures 7–5 and 11–8). The constructivist sculptors had led the way in abstract compositions, using wire, string, glass, and metal and borrowing from both mathematics and machine structures. Vsevolod Meierhold, who introduced constructivism to the theatre, brought his lighting instruments into view and even worked out a machinelike, acrobatic approach to acting, which he called biomechanics. He liked to make his props and scenery move, with beds flying through the air and walls sliding, and to have real automobiles and motorcycles run down the aisles, up over the orchestra, and onto the stage. We have Norris Houghton's description in *Moscow Rehearsals* of how a lover expressed his abandonment and joy at a reunion with his love: "Meierhold places the lady at the foot of a tin slide, the lover climbs up a ladder to the top of the

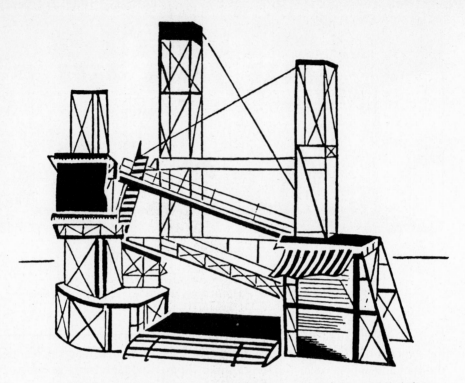

11-8 Constructivism. An abstract structure of pipes, girders, towers, and platforms that suggests the skeleton of a machine provides the actors with a "machine for acting." Setting for Tairov's adaptation of *The Man Who Was Thursday*. From Mordecai Gorelik's *New Theatres* for *Old*.

slide, zooms down it feet first, knocks the lady off onto the floor, and shouts something that sounds like Russian for 'Whee!'''

Such extremes, useful for satires on the machine age, have not often been seen. Far more popular were the styles called *formalism* and *abstractivism*. Remembering that the Greek, the Elizabethan, and the Chinese classic stages used permanent architectural structures with little or no realistic scenery, designers have turned to modern abstract structures which, with flexible lighting and a few portable cloths and props, can serve for many different scenes. For a number of years Jacques Copeau at the Vieux-Colombier in Paris put on a variety of productions, with slight additions and changes, in a basic architectural form of steps, platform, and upper level. The Festival Theatre in Stratford, Ontario, is now the best-known theatre that uses one architectural structure for all plays.

A third method of design is to start with the mood of the play, forget the details of actuality, and find the lines, shapes, and colors that will create the mood desired. Of course, both the remantic picture setting and the naturalistic scene sought to create mood, but they did so by borrowing directly the moods of reality—the flowers and clouds of a sunny day, the texture of the slum kitchen. The modern designer wants to make more direct use of the expressive power of line, form, texture, and color.

Line, as it outlines shapes and masses, can have qualities and associations. It can be thick and coarse or light and delicate. Horizontal lines suggest stability, with the peace of the horizon and the repose of lying down. Vertical lines are as active as standing up, as strong as lifting and reaching. Vertical and horizontal lines together can give strength, security, and equilibrium. Diagonals are more dynamic, with the threat of falling and the effort of preventing the fall. Sharp angles suggest pain, constriction, and the sharpness of a point. Curves can suggest warmth, lushness, smoothness, and even playfulness. In movement, lines can explode out from a center with power and speed (Figure 11–9), or, conversely, move together to a point of emphasis. Lines can have rhythms, now bumpy, now jerky, speeding up or slowing down.

From the beginning of the century, Gordon Craig called on designers to search for the inner soul of the play. First of all, he wanted a bold shape.

11–9 Idea and mood in an expressionistic setting. The platform for the confession suggests both a cross and a gallows. The broken fragments of houses suggest anguish and disintegration of personality. The high central figure and the bright light and radiant lines expanding from the center create an exciting release and exaltation. Kaufman's opera *The Scarlet Letter*. Design by C. M. Cristini for an Indiana University production.

It might be a stripped-down abstraction; it might include steps, platforms, and doorways for the actors; it might even include beds, balconies, fountains, and the few properties necessary for the action. But above all, the design must create a single dominant image. In a famous passage in his first book, *On the Art of the Theatre,* he suggested how the designer might go about deciding on a design for *Macbeth:*

> We take *Macbeth*. . . . I see two things. I see a lofty and steep rock, and I see the moist cloud which envelops the head of this rock. That is to say, a place for fierce and warlike men to inhabit, a place for phantoms to nest in. Ultimately the moisture will destroy the rock; ultimately these spirits will destroy the men. Now then, you are quick in your question as to what actually to create for the eye. I answer as swiftly—place there a rock! Let it mount up high. Swiftly I tell you, convey the idea of a mist which hugs the head of this rock. Now, have I departed at all for one eighth of an inch from the vision which I saw in the mind's eye?
>
> But you ask me what form this rock shall take and what color? What are the lines which are the lofty lines, and which are to be seen in any lofty cliff? Go to them, glance but a moment at them: now quickly set them down on your paper; *the lines and their direction,* never mind the cliff. Do not be afraid to let them go high; they cannot go high enough; and remember that on a sheet of paper which is but two inches square you can make a line which seems to tower miles in the air, and you can do the same on the stage, for it is a matter of proportion and nothing to do with actuality.
>
> You ask about the colors? What are the colors that Shakespeare has indicated for us? Do not first look at Nature, but look in the play of the poet. Two; one for the rock, the man; one for the mist, the spirit.

Craig warns of the dangerous attempt to "tell of the moss of the Highlands and of the particular rain which descends in the month of August." But this is no mere picture independent of the actors. He continues, "You have to consider that at the base of the rock swarm the clans of strange earthly forces, and that in the mist hover the spirits innumerable . . . clearly separate from the human and more material beings."

Early in this century, Joseph Urban decided in designing Wagner's *Die Meistersinger* that it was less important to show the whole of Nuremberg with all its Gothic details than to give the impression of joy, of the radiant splendor of sunshine as the people greeted Hans Sachs. The pagan element in *King Lear,* so strong in the imagery and in Lear's oaths and curses, would be enormously reinforced by the setting, designed by Bel Geddes but never used, of an arc of Stonehenge rocks bursting into flames at the top (Figure 2–6). Different interpretations of Hamlet may be achieved as much by the setting as by the acting. Before dark curtains and shapeless cloths, Hamlet is a lone existentialist wanderer in a nightmare world. Before a throne-tower and a Christian altar, he has ample reason, in his respect for political order and his Christian conscience, for hesitating to murder the king. In the London production of *Waiting for Godot,* the desolate wasteland and the forlorn stick of a tree left the two tramps in an empty universe. In the University of Iowa production, bright-colored puffs of smoke from behind the earth-banks punctuated every pause. That universe was not empty at all: a bright demon was just out of sight, laughing at mankind. Craig, who craved nobility, would not have liked the "confrontation" or "junk sculpture" style of recent years. The rusty stovepipes and wheelbarrow were quite appropriate to Grotowski's production of *Akropolis,* in which old European idealists are confronted with a gas chamber, and musty, decaying, cobweb-covered Gothic arches were effective for the bitter mood of *Rosencrantz and Guildenstern Are Dead;* but some designers like to set up for any play bold structures with the rough textures so sought after by some recent artists, whether or not the play has a bitter or mocking tone.

The fourth method of design is metaphor—scene as idea. The scenic metaphor was an obsession of the expressionists. They not only distorted natural lines to indicate the nightmares of the disturbed mind and to make lines express mood directly, but constantly searched for some symbol, some visual image, to catch the inner meaning of a play. A tree could not just be barren and desolate; it had to look like a skeleton, or, in O'Neill's *Desire Under the Elms,* to let down grasping fingers from brooding heights. For Andreyev's *Life of Man,* Lee Mitchell designed geometrical forms with opening lines for the birth scene and with closing lines for the death scene, while he symbolized the crowning scene of worldly success by a gilt-edged screen with a large dollar sign on it. Lee Simonson's *The Stage Is Set* describes two famous productions of *Richard III* in the 1920s.

> I have seen Richard III storm up and down the blood-red stairway provided for him by Jessner and Pirchan at the Berlin State Theatre, but his malignity was as successfully dramatized by Arthur Hopkins and Robert Edmond Jones in New York where a reproduction of the gate of the Bloody Tower backed every scene like a fanged jowl that alternately menaced and devoured. The single background of the prison that was the background of every character's fears and ambitions became as effective a symbol as a single stairway.

Even when the designer does not resort to such an obvious image, he often has some visual metaphor in mind. Albee wanted the setting for *Who's Afraid of Virginia Woolf?* to suggest a cave or a womb, but the designer, William Ritman, created the impression of a cavelike enclosure in a real room. Gorelik describes his own need for a metaphor, whether the audience is conscious of it or not. While telling all the necessary facts of locale and atmosphere, the setting must suggest the essence of the action. Thus, as Gorelik put it:

> The attic bedroom of *The Three Sisters* is not only an attic, not only a bedroom, not only a girls' room, not only a European room, not only a room of the period of 1901, not only a room belonging to the gentlefolk whom Chekhov wrote about. On top of all that, it may be, for the designer, the scene of a *raging fever*.

This search for an image of action takes the designer right back to the director's analysis of the basic action of the play. Even when the play requires that the setting and costumes emphasize the period or the local color, the designer can make sure that the appropriate mood is created and the theme clarified. The design becomes much more than a decoration to cover the backstage void or to indicate time and place. It creates mood, style, and metaphor. It must shape the action, reinforce the meaning, and propel the play to its conclusion.

The Costumes

The costumes continue the design into the characterization and movement of the actor. Even if they seem like everyday clothes, they must be given a theatrical flair, a boldness, simplicity, and brightness that can make an impact at a distance. They must create a world of the imagination. Today in the resident theatre and the college theatre, the costume shop is a major part of the building, and the design and making of costumes is considered as much a creative art as the writing of the plays or the acting or singing.

The nineteenth-century tradition of costuming, like that of set design, put great emphasis on historical and geographical authenticity. The producer and designer spent great effort in research, and the costume sections of large libraries and of Hollywood studios made large collections of books with pictures and descriptions of the costumes and accessories of all ages and countries. Costume rental houses grew up as every repertory theatre or amateur club or high school production expected to show the audience an authentic costume for King Henry V or for a Palestinian shepherd in the time of Christ. With the same point of view that he held on setting, Craig told us not to try to put a costume museum on the stage but to create imaginative costumes that suggest character. In *On the Art of the Theatre*, he urged:

> Make a barbaric costume for a sly man which has nothing . . . historical and yet is both sly and barbaric. Now make another . . . for a man who is

bold and tender. Now make a third for one who is ugly and vindictive . . . it is no easy thing to do. . . . Then go further: attempt to design the clothing for a divine figure and for a demonic figure.

Even for a historical play like *Henry IV*, Hotspur's costume may tell us that the time is the beginning of the fifteenth century, but still more it must tell us that here is a proud, fiery rebel who despises elegance, subservience, and compromise.

If modern costumes for historical scenes shock us by having too little aesthetic distance, a really authentic costume would distress us by having too much. A good historical costume is a compromise, adapted to the taste of the audience and to their idea of the period. The good designer has always instinctively made that adaptation, and we can tell at a glance whether a medieval dress for the stage was made for an audience that wore bustles or bell-bottoms.

In planning the costumes, the designer is aware of five things costuming can do: it can enhance the actor, create the character, set the style, tie the individual into the scheme of characters, and show the progress of the play.

Just as the scene designer starts with the moving actor and the stage space, creating the areas, levels, and shapes that enhance the action, so the costume designer starts with the moving actor and the costume material, creating new shapes, colors, and movements that enhance the actor. Material may be fitted or draped. Some dancers' costumes are entirely fitted, with color and texture but with nothing added to the shape, allowing the movement of the body to be seen in its simplest form. Most Greek and Roman costumes are entirely draped, as are some ceremonial robes today. But more often the designer combines fitting and draping: a tight bodice leading into a flowing skirt, a tight upper arm leading into a flowing sleeve, a fitted body partly covered by a cape, arms and legs partly seen between the panels of sleeves and skirts. An accent such as a belt, a band, or a ruffle is most interesting at the transition from a fitted to a draped section. Accents sometimes mark the joints of the body, especially the shoulders and sometimes the hips, but, except for comic effects, not the elbows and knees.

Whether fitted or flowing, with accent or accessory, the costume transforms the appearance, the movement, and indeed the soul of the actor. An actor in his underwear or a dancer in a leotard is a very different person from a performer in makeup and costume. A warrior in plumes and war paint and a chieftain in mask and ceremonial decorations take on roles already shaped by the design. In Brecht's *Galileo*, the Pope receives the scientist in his dressing chamber with sympathy and understanding.

But as the attendants dress him, adding robe after robe, he is transformed into an official representative of the Church, with a very different attitude.

Psychologically the costume is very important. Looking in a mirror, the actor gets a vision of what he is supposed to be; he must live up to that vision. Some directors say that in many situations no makeup is needed. But what actor would be willing to plunge into a role without watching himself transformed into a different being as he puts on the costume and makeup? Dance teachers find that a mask is a stimulation to a dancer, giving him a vision of the character he is to create in movement. In sophisticated society an impersonal mask is worn at a ball to hide the identity, but in primitive societies a mask is the embodiment of identity. Like a primitive tribesman, the actor must put on his *persona*, or mask, before he can become the personality to play his role.

In movement the actor soon learns why the designer gave him a cape or a long sleeve. As he turns his shoulders, lifts his elbow, or raises his

11–10 Fantasy costumes: monkeys with painted faces and masks. *The Wiz*. New York, 1975. Directed and costumed by Geoffrey Holder and designed by Boris Aronson. Photo Martha Swope.

11–11
Costume for characterization. A draped ceremonial costume turns the soldier Joan of Arc into a more dignified leader at the coronation, yet the scallops suggest vulnerability. The king's long cloak and fur cape and his sceptre and crown are a little too large, suggesting that he is scarcely equal to the position. Anouilh's *The Lark*. University of Texas production, directed by Francis Hodge, designed by John Rothgeb, and costumed by Lucy Barton.

arm, the cape or sleeve sweeps on beyond, extending the movement and accenting it. The longer and heavier the cape, the slower the sweep. That extra material is not a hindrance but a tool he can use if he learns its feeling and makes the costume act. At the end of a speech he can swing the cape across his body with an impressive gesture of finality as he turns to walk away. The actress learns to give her full skirt a swing that expresses the character and just what she is thinking. A cane, a pipe, or an umbrella in the hand becomes a telling extension of the personality, and no one has exhausted the possibilities of the fan for indicating changes of thought or feeling.

If the costume makes the actor, it is no less true that the actor makes the costume. No amount of beautiful fabric or dashing style can affect the audience until the actor feels and projects the beauty and the dash.

But the costume designer not only enhances the actor, he creates the character. The costume must tell the audience at a glance if the character is young or old, rich or poor, doctor, beggar, or thief, brassy barmaid or kind old grandmother, if he is arriving from a cold journey or off to play tennis in the sun. It can show character change. The shabby, hard-working clerk of the first act becomes a well-dressed corporation president in the second. The eager girl in her plain clothes and simple makeup blossoms into an elegant society leader with chic evening clothes and sophisticated hairdo.

The dashing young spendthrift becomes a drunkard in untidy clothes. The costume may characterize by not fitting. The king's garments on Macbeth "hang loose about him like a giant's robe upon a dwarfish thief." Not only the traditional insignia—the king's crown, the bishop's mitre, the priest's collar, the scholar's dark-rimmed glasses—but the whole range of caps, canes, fans, gloves, and other accessories indicate immediately who the character is or what impression he is trying to make. The little man in a plain costume bursts forth proudly with a new hat, or Cinderella wears rough, itchy stockings with her unaccustomed new clothes—who can say how much is suggested by costume and how much by the pantomime of the actor?

The third function of costuming is to help establish the spirit and style of the play. Costume can add dignity to tragedy, charm to romance, and playful variety to light comedy. The designer can learn as much about the style of a period from an artist as from a history book—for instance, from Watteau's soft, satin-clad aristocrats in gentle landscapes or from Hogarth's robust, comic caricatures of boorish types.

Selection is a very powerful means of creating style. To limit the color scheme for the entire cast to pastels, to earth colors, to two or three primary colors, or to black and white makes a strong, unified impression. To choose within a range of heavy, dull textures, or of shiny taffetas and satins, creates a particular feeling and style while allowing for considerable adaptation to individual characters.

Sharp contrast is startlingly comic. That is why stripes and bright spots are so often used in comedy. Incongruity is even more comic: the small vertical hat over the big round face, the sleeve or cape that is too small or too large, out of proportion to the rest of the costume, the color or texture that does not match. The costumer may emphasize the peculiarities of the character—the fat stomach of Sir Toby Belch and the thin lines of his companion, Sir Andrew Aguecheek—or he may accent an awkward place such as an elbow or a knee. Droopy, baggy, and floppy parts of the costume are as comic as a limp wrist, a sagging chin, or a defeated gesture.

The fourth consideration of the costume designer is the scheme of the characters. The costumes must give harmony to the picture by a unified color scheme and must be closely related to the setting yet stand out from the background. The costumes must look good together, and they must be so planned that in large scenes the colors are well distributed. Yet the costumes must control the spread of attention, indicating which are subordinate characters and which important, and must make many fine distinctions within the overall picture.

The designer can do more than the actor or director in making clear how the characters line up in loyalty or opposition, in similarities and

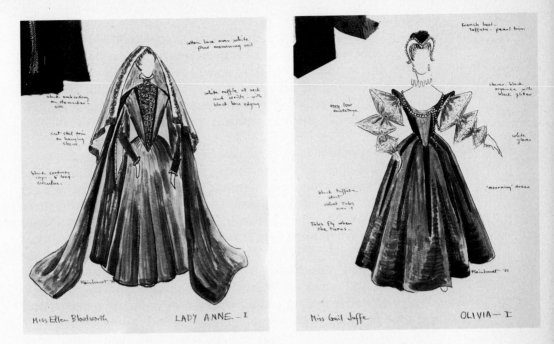

Miss Ellen Bloodworth   LADY ANNE - I

Miss Gail Jaffe   OLIVIA - I

11–12 Two costumes for women in mourning. The costumes are based on the same period, but one is designed for tragedy and one for romantic comedy. Soft flowing lines and heavy corduroy material convey the dignity and sorrow of Lady Anne in Shakespeare's *Richard III*, while the shiny taffeta bodice and skirt, the crisp glittering sleeves, and the low decolletage suggest that bright energy is more important than mourning for Lady Olivia in Shakespeare's *Twelfth Night*. Designs by Paul Reinhardt.

differences. The scheme is simple in *Romeo and Juliet,* where the feud sets two groups apart. The audience should know at a glance who belongs to each group; Mercutio should be in a mixed costume and the friar and the prince should be seen to be completely above the quarrel. Some designers use two quite different colors for the two sides. Similarly, in the back-and-forth fighting in *Macbeth,* it is important to know at a glance who is fighting for Macbeth and who for Macduff. *King Lear* is more complex. Not only are there two families—the king's and Gloucester's—but there are good and bad children in each family. Lear's two wicked, flattering daughters are united against the honest, plain-spoken Cordelia. The costumes can make that clear even if the designer does not go quite as far as a Munich production in which the wicked daughters were in identical scarlet dresses and Cordelia was in pure white. The costumes of the servants reflect the same opposition between flattery and honesty. Lear's plain-speaking servant (Kent in disguise) is plainly dressed and Goneril's sycophantic servant, Oswald, is elegantly dressed. We know they will clash. In any play the characters must be vivid enough to stand out from the environment, but those who are at home will be in close harmony with it and with one another, while intruders will be set apart. If a son brings a noisy girl into a dignified home, the costume should signal the conflict as she enters. In the next act the costumes and setting should indicate immediately whether the environment has changed her or she has changed it.

The fifth approach to costume design concerns the progression, the change and development in the course of the play. Katherine in *The Taming of the Shrew* is transformed from a high-tempered, aristocratic girl to a disheveled, almost defeated wife and then to a gracious, compliant wife who is knowing in her gesture of obedience. Her costumes should show the changes; at the end they should be softer and more matronly but still have some lines and colors of assertion and self-reliance. Sometimes the tone of the play must change when it is impossible to change the set. Carnival hats and streamers at a party can quickly add gaiety, while putting on or merely closing and buttoning dark raincoats can cover and dampen the previous brightness.

Like the setting, the costume should be more than charming or spectacular decoration, more than style and mood. As an instrument for each actor to play on, it becomes part of the action. The costuming helps organize and clarify the group on stage.

The Lighting

> Now the dark stage begins to burn and glow under our fingers, burning like the embers of the forge of Vulcan, and shafts of light stab through the darkness, and shadows leap and shudder, and we are in the regions where splendor and terror move.
>
> Robert Edmond Jones, *The Dramatic Imagination*

The audience is held spellbound as the house lights go down, the curtain disappears, and the lights bring form out of nothingness. Both the actor and the setting emerge in bold relief, creating highlights and shadows in the controlled, plastic light of the spotlights. Then, as the action moves from one part of the stage to another, the light gets stronger at the point of action and the rest of the stage recedes into the margin of attention. Lighting, even more than setting, shapes the action and exerts a hypnotic control over the interest and emotions of the audience. As Norman Bel Geddes described it, "Good lighting adds space, depth, mood, mystery, parody, contrast, change of emotion, intimacy, fear."

In theatrical lighting, the age of electricity can boast of its superiority to all other ages. While the Greeks and the Elizabethans used the open sky and most medieval performances took place in the daytime, many kings and princes knew the impressive effect of a processional entry into a city at night, with torches and pageants sparkling with lights. When the Renaissance princes created the first modern stages in their palace ball-rooms, they started a tradition of bright chandeliers for the well-dressed audience, bright chandeliers for the actors, and lights behind the scenery for stunning effects of moving clouds and sunrises and sunsets.

Gas lights, introduced at the beginning of the nineteenth century, concentrated much brighter light on the stage and permitted some degree of control because the footlights, the border lights above the actors, and the house lights could be turned down separately. But still stage lighting consisted of the flat general glare from long rows of open flames. Only when the limelight and the carbon electric arc were introduced in the middle of the century was it possible to concentrate a strong light in a narrow space by the use of a lens. When it was discovered that a piece of calcium or lime heated to incandescence in a gas flame produced a very strong, concentrated light, *in the limelight* became a new term in the English language. Even brighter is the light from the spark that arcs between two rods of carbon when a strong electric current is sent across the gap. If a metal box is placed around that arc with a lens at the end, it will send down a bright spot to make one or two actors stand out from all the rest. This "follow spot" is still sometimes used for specialty numbers in a revue, though it is rather crude in comparison with the subtle equipment possible today.

It was with the invention of the incandescent lamp in 1879 that the real development of modern lighting began. The incandescent lamp is safe and noiseless, available in many sizes, and easily controlled by a dimmer. The filament is so concentrated that a spherical or ellipsoidal reflector and a lens create a pool of directional, not diffused, light. It is easy to put a sheet of colored gelatin, acetate, or glass in front of the lens. Today light has shape, direction, and color and can easily be changed from bright to dim.

Light not only gives the actor and setting shape but also gives the picture a new dimension in time. By the end of the nineteenth century, London and New York were being impressed by the changing moods of twilight, sunset, moonlight, and dawn of Sir Henry Irving's Shakespeare and David Belasco's ultrarealistic, sensational scenes of the Wild West, exotic foreign lands, and city slums. Important developments in the last several decades have provided smaller instruments with more powerful sources of light. In the 1930s the reflector lamp was invented, a light that has the whole spotlight—reflector, lens, and filament—built into the bulb. Too small for the main lighting of a large stage, it is extremely useful in smaller areas, and it is the main instrument for window displays and most architectural and landscape lighting. More recently the quartz lamp and several other lamps have been developed to produce a very intense light from a concentrated source, increasing the flexibility of both stage and outdoor lighting.

The great prophet of the new art of lighting was Adolphe Appia, whose *Music and the Art of the Theatre* has been invaluable to stage designers. He might have called it *The Music of Light,* for light was the new element to express the soul of the drama that was so well created in Wagner's music but impossible to express with the painted backdrops and flat lighting of the nineteenth century. "Light is to production," Appia wrote, "what music is to the score: the expressive element in opposition to the literal signs; and, like music, light can express only what belongs to 'the inner essence of all vision!'" The new use of light meant a radically new approach to the plastic form of the stage. Instead of drawing the third dimension on the backdrop, Appia wanted to set the actor moving in three dimensions on ramps and platforms and to create the third dimension by catching both the actor and the plastic setting in highlights and shadows. That required sculptural forms with very little painted detail and little color; the form, the intensity, and even the color were to be created by the mobile, focused light.

Appia made the first analysis of the kinds of light to be derived from the different instruments. He defined the basic difference between "general" and "specific" lighting, or "diffused light" and "living light," in the four kinds of lights and lighting:

1. The fixed border lights, which light the painted flats, supplemented in the wings and on the stage floor by the movable striplights.
2. The "footlights," that peculiar monstrosity of our theatres, designed to light both the scenery and the actors from in front and below.
3. Spotlights that throw focused beams of light on playing areas or projections on flat screens.
4. Light within the settings, that is, light intended to reveal the transparent parts of the setting by lighting from behind.

The third type, which Appia called "living light," was most important, for it could create form-giving shadows. The first two, giving general or diffused light, could have only a subordinate function, that of softening and blending the sharp contrasts of the living light.

To create and control this dynamic, revealing light, the lighting designer works out a *light plot,* a chart of the placement of all the lights and a list of all the changes. The light plot is actually a complete lighting score comparable to the musical score or the text of the play.

The spotlights are planned first. Since the general lighting will be only supplementary, consisting of striplights used mainly for blending and for lighting the background and the cyclorama, the main lighting will be by spots—spots from the light bridge or a pipe just behind the curtain and spots from the beams in the auditorium. Since evenly diffused lighting would take away shadows and hence form, the spotlights are not spread everywhere but grouped to form pools of light. The stage is divided into areas, either the six playing areas defined by the director or whatever areas the setting suggests. Usually two spotlights are focused on each area, aimed from the two sides about ninety degrees apart and casting light down at an "angle of throw" of about forty-five degrees. Each side of an actor's face will get some shadowing, but not too much. If one light is stronger than the other, or, better yet, if one is of a warm color and the other cool, the plastic effect will be richer. Sometimes, if a director uses strong movement in a particular direction, up a ramp or stairway, for instance, the designer may meet the moving actors with shafts of light rather than lighting by the more static pools.

Sidelights and backlights are used for special effects. Light from the side or from straight above gives very sharp shadows, far too strong for most realistic scenes unless subtly blended with some front lighting. Back lighting, from above but from upstage of the actors, adds a highlight on head and shoulders, a halo effect frequently used in television lighting to make an actor stand out from a dark background. For most plays only the more subtle tints of colors are used: flesh pinks and very light ambers if the scene is warm and sunny, lavender or light blue if a colder mood is needed. But for dance and for less realistic plays, strong colors and sharp angles of throw from the sides, which produce extreme shadows, can give excitement.

General illumination for the cyclorama usually comes from standard strips both above and below, wired in three circuits. In lighting, the three primary colors that mix together to produce other colors are not the red, yellow, and blue of the painter but red, green, and blue. Dimming these three colors up or down will produce almost any sky effect, from night to sunrise to daylight to fire, as well as all the unnatural colors of red and purple.

Appia's fourth kind of lighting, from inside the setting itself, has had very little use in the theatre so far, though it has long been used for commercial signs and juke boxes that glow from within. Architects have

11–13 Back lighting in two consecutive, related scenes. A strong light from above and upstage of the actors catches the top of their heads and shoulders with a halo effect, while they are left dark enough to be silhouetted against a bright background. *Rain*, from a story by Maugham. University of Wyoming production, directed and designed by Richard L. Scammon, lighted by Scammon and Soller, and costumed by Charles Parker.

begun making use of it to illuminate buildings at night; more exciting than general illumination from floodlights is the effect produced when a building is treated like a piece of sculpture, with sequences of dark and lighted spaces set against the darkness through the use of luminescent panels and alcoves and ledges lighted from hidden sources. The theatre has the same opportunity. Not all the light has to come from far above the stage area. In an age of transistors, of miniature control and illumination units, and of three-dimensional sculptural forms on the stage, a revolutionary, very exciting lighting could be built into the setting.

The nerve center of the lighting is the switchboard that controls the dimmers. The early kind of dimmer was the resistance dimmer, a long handle that pulled the contacts around a heavy plate-shaped coil to put more resistance into the circuit. The early dimmer board might occupy a whole wall and need several strong-armed workers to manipulate, though master handles and large master dimmers were developed so that several circuits could be dimmed together by one handle. Basic and dependable, the resistance dimmer is still used in many places. But many new systems have been invented, each making the last seem old-fashioned and clumsy. The auto-transformer, especially a neat model called the Variac, was the rage in the 1930s. Then electronic systems of control captured the interest of designers. But they now seem enormous, clumsy, and very expensive in comparison to the small silicon-controlled rectifier invented in the late 1950s. This "solid state" instrument has no moving parts and hence is long-lasting. It enables a very small current at the switchboard console to control the full current near the lamps. One silicon rectifier modifies one phase of the sixty-cycle-a-second alternating current, while a second rectifier modifies the other phase. They will not work on direct current. Since the designer has available small, sensitive dimmers and small spotlight lamps, each with its own reflector built into the bulb, it has become common practice to supplement the large spotlights with numerous sources of light around the stage, with many circuits, all controlled from a console smaller than an organ console. At the board an expert operator follows the light plot and at each cue moves small levers or punches small buttons that control a number of changes, bringing various sets of lights up or down at various controlled speeds. Many switchboards now have some kind of memory system by which a complex series of changes can be preset, recorded on an IBM card or a tape, and stored until needed. As with a computer, it takes time to set the program, but once set the system handles far more changes than an operator could write down on a cue sheet. Most lighting designers feel that the human element must never be lost, however, and that the man at the switchboard must make fine, intuitive adjustments as he watches the play; so the switchboard should be located where the operator can see the entire stage.

Like setting and costuming, lighting is an integral part of the play, serving many functions. It highlights the center of action and subordinates the less important areas. It reveals form, giving plasticity to each actor and each background structure and shaping the playing areas to reinforce the composition of the director. It not only suggests local color and time of day but also creates mood through color, intensity, shape, and angle. Perhaps most important of all, dynamic changes of light do as much as the dialogue, the plot, the actor's movement, and the incidental music and sound to propel the play to its goal.

Epilogue

The Pleasure of Your Company

THE LAURENCE OLIVIER THEATRE,
LARGEST OF THE THREE THEATRES IN
THE NATIONAL THEATRE COMPLEX.
ACTORS IN A SCENE FROM
TAMBURLAINE STAND ON THE THRUST
STAGE, VERY CLOSE TO THE
AUDIENCE. NOTE THE CIRCLE OF
LIGHTING INSTRUMENTS ABOVE THE
CIRCLE OF THE ACTING AREA. PHOTO
© DENYS LASDUN & PARTNERS,
LONDON.

> Our revels now are ended. These our actors,
> As I foretold you, were all spirits, and
> Are melted into air, into thin air;
> And, like the houseless fabric of this vision,
> The cloud-capp'd towers, the gorgeous palaces,
> The solemn temples, the great globe itself,
> Yea, all which it inherit, shall dissolve
> And, like this insubstantial pageant faded,
> Leave not a rack behind. We are such stuff
> As dreams are made on, and our little life
> Is rounded with a sleep.
> Prospero in Shakespeare's *The Tempest*

Is the play—any play—a dream? An insubstantial pageant that fades, leaving not a rack behind? Are the words, the poetry, the work of the creative imagination all that will endure after the actors have disappeared, the great globe itself has dissolved, and our little life is rounded with a sleep? As it was in Shakespeare's Globe Theatre, itself an image of the cosmos, so now, at the end of a good play, the spellbound tension of the audience is relaxed in applause and we seem to wake as from a dream. Call it hypnotic trance, illusion, imagination, willing suspension of disbelief, a higher state of consciousness—it is a transcendent experience, a symbolic journey into the sacred realm. It takes us out of local time and place into *ille tempus,* that time that was before us and will be after we are gone, the other world of visions, meanings, of the gods and our ancestors, who bequeathed us language and all the arts, who enlighten our path with purpose.

We leave the theatre feeling more friendly than before with the rest of the audience, for these individuals have shared our journey. We have seen deep into the lives of characters so like ourselves yet so different—lives lived more intensely than our own, focused, framed, complete, clear, whole. Our journey has widened our sympathy and deepened our compassion. We are more civilized.

The more literal-minded pilgrim, returning from his journey to the ideal, immediately gets busy reforming the world, hoping to build the Kingdom on earth as it is in Heaven. What better tool than the theatre? Do not classroom teachers use dramatization to teach children the facts of geography and even manners and morals? Do not television commercials use actors in character to call attention to products and to suggest action? Marxists, seeing the world in terms of class warfare, insist that art is a weapon and that if it is not used directly for the revolution it is a defense of the bourgeois status quo or mere empty "formalism." Such earnestness provokes the opposite theories of art for art's sake or art as entertainment.

A more balanced view is that, of course, art will reflect in various ways the conditions of the artist's time and place but that the relation between art and action is rarely direct, that the greatest satisfaction in art is the understanding of human relations on a symbolic level.

Theatre as Therapy

The psychologically oriented pilgrim who returns from his theatre journey sees it as a journey into the mind. This is Hamlet's point of view: that art is an excellent tool for diagnosis of inner guilt and one that can be used to purge or relieve guilt. Hamlet believes he can use the players to make the king show his guilt in public.

> I have heard
> That guilty creatures sitting at a play
> Have by the very cunning of the scene
> Been struck so to the soul that presently
> They have proclaimed their malefactions;
> . . . .
> . . . . The play's the thing
> Wherein I'll catch the conscience of the King.

Hamlet's plot does have an effect, though not exactly what Hamlet planned.

The therapeutic function of all the arts is fully recognized, first of all for the artist himself. We have had in the painter Vincent Van Gogh and the playwright Eugene O'Neill examples of artists, disturbed to the point of destruction, who nevertheless held off disaster for decades by relentlessly creating new artistic forms to give order to their feelings. And the paintings of Van Gogh and the plays of O'Neill have been of tremendous help to other people in meeting the disturbances of the modern age.

Psychodrama has had striking success in the treatment of mental illness. With a partner, each patient acts out, with improvised dialogue, scenes of his relationships to members of his family or whoever is the focus of his disturbance. By reenactment of scenes in the past where he took the wrong turn, the patient discovers the right turn.

The theatre is one of the world's greatest therapeutic agencies, but the therapy it provides is more often abstract and generalized, whereas psychodrama is specifically derived from, and pointed to, a particular person. Hamlet had to add a speech to make the play touch the king. It is not the individual quirk that the theatre may offer to cure, so much as a general malaise. All the arts, but especially the theatre, point to the strains in a society and sometimes help prevent disaster. Great religious leaders insist that the most ineffable joy is enlightenment, which relieves human beings from the agony of confusion and provides a light in darkness, a path through chaos, a place in time and space.

The modern world offers excellent means for orientation in space. People can go to, or get a message to, almost any spot on earth. But in time they are dangerously disoriented. They fear the future because they have no past and do not know where they are or how they got there. They try to run a society without reading the minutes of the previous meetings. The early Christians did not need history; they were sure that the Second Coming of Christ—when history would cease to exist—was imminent. Since 1945 the promise of the second coming of the atomic bomb has been so paralyzing that history has seemed to lose all meaning. But such works as *Roots,* the book (and television film) by Alex Haley, who dug deep into dusty records and traced his family to their African origins and down through the slave years to his own time, demonstrate that the present can be linked to the past. Several popular British television series broadcast in the United States, particularly *The Forsyte Saga* and *Upstairs Downstairs,* have also provided a compelling view of the past. An increased understanding of our place in history and of how our ancestors changed through the years is one of the great healing pleasures of the theatre. Perhaps therapy for a disturbed society is as important as therapy for an individual. It is supplied in the many forms of theatre.

The Commercial Theatre

At the top of all types of theatre organizations is the "legitimate" theatre, the professional theatre of the cities, the favorite institution of the establishment. It includes Broadway in New York, the West End in London, and the Boulevard theatres in Paris. It thrives on a fashionable, well-dressed audience, who have parties before and after the show and meet friends in the intervals between acts to discuss the play and the actors. Most Broadway theatres have so little corridor room that the intermission audience has to spill out into alleys and streets. But the subsidized theatres of Europe and the recent theatres of London and America recognize that the parade of people watching and greeting other people is an important part of the theatrical occasion.

The commercial theatre, theatre dependent on the box office, started in the sixteenth century a generation before Shakespeare, when, with the expansion of the free-enterprise system, London, Paris, and Madrid became cities large enough to support sizable acting companies. These companies had a precarious living, especially in plague years, but by alternating plays of a wide range and being invited to perform at court during the Christmas season, several companies in each of the three cities survived.

For four hundred years the commercial theatre has worked, after a fashion, paying fantastic fees to the great personalities who can draw crowds. When in the twentieth century film, radio, and television drama took the popular audience, it seemed that Broadway was doomed. Actually the quality of live theatre has improved since it has not had to furnish mass entertainment and has been able to include new, creative kinds of drama.

But the speculative pressures have increased. A hit comedy or musical may bring in millions of dollars at the box office, and millions may be lost on the flops and the near hits. Starry-eyed investors, or "angels," in hope of large gains, in the spirit of horseracing, seem ever ready to pour in more money. Newspapers and television gossips spread the word of the latest success, and out-of-towners want to see what the sophisticated crowd is talking about. A hit is often sold out a year in advance, and scalpers make big money by peddling scarce tickets. Patrons who want to see only the most fashionable hits tend to overwhelm the more perceptive theatregoers who are interested in a wide variety of dramatic fare.

Yet Broadway, in spite of the chaos and the frightful waste, still puts the final stamp of approval on an American play or actor. Hence thousands of young hopefuls descend on New York each year looking for a chance to break into the theatre. Very few make it, and even those who get established in New York average only a few weeks of work a year; so many productions close after one night or a very short run. On the other hand, an actor who gets into a Broadway hit may be stuck in the same part for months or years, with no chance for further development. It is no wonder there is a strong drive to find a wider base for the top professional talent of the country.

The concept of how a theatre is related to a society has undergone a change. A century ago the great actors played a long season in New York, alternating several plays in a system called "repertory." For the rest of the year they took to the road, sometimes for a year or two. The star was what people paid to see and they paid well, no matter if the play, the scenery and lighting, and the acting of the minor characters were all very poor. The commercial star system, at least in London and New York, was a success in terms of what it offered.

By accepting much more limited goals, two kinds of commercial theatre have made a go of it: the dinner theatre in the smaller cities and the "straw hat" theatre in reach of the summer resorts. Dinner theatre appeals to families and groups of friends, who can hold their own parties at tables around the buffet platform. When the meal is over the food is removed and the stage is moved forward. The audience knows what to expect: a light comedy or occasionally a musical that can be done with limited cast and scenery, certainly nothing experimental or difficult. Summer theatre is often of a higher quality than dinner theatre, for a featured player of Broadway, film, or television fame may play a summer season, trouping from one playhouse to another, presenting a recent popular success or sometimes a new play announced as "prior to Broadway."

For the winter season in large cities, standards are much higher and theatregoers demand good quality in settings and lighting, a carefully rehearsed cast, and, in some places, a wider range of new and old plays than Broadway provides. The theatre is now regarded as far more than "entertainment," as an art with psychological, social, humanistic, and spiritual values. Such a theatre requires subsidy.

The Subsidized Theatre

European countries have subsidized the theatre since the sixteenth century. Even before Shakespeare, Italian dukes and French and English kings paid for elaborate productions for the guests at their coronation and wedding festivities. When opera and ballet gained wide audiences in the seventeenth century, the typical European theatre became the royal theatre built and partly supported by the king but open to the public. In many European cities the royal theatre is still one of the most splendid public buildings, with spacious setting and an imposing design. The most impressive building in Paris is the opera house built under Napoleon III. It is approached by the long, wide Avenue de l'Opéra, and the older, more modest national theatre, the Comédie Française, is at the other end of the avenue. In all Western countries theatre is increasingly recognized as a public institution no less important than church, museum, or library, and one that should be no more dependent on entrance fees than those institutions.

Only the two great English-speaking nations have been slow to subsidize the arts. England started some national help for drama groups during World War II, and in the 1960s set up two national companies and started a splendid National Theatre building on the south side of the Thames River. The United States, the richest country in the world, has been the laggard. When in the 1950s Cold War competition was sparked by the Russians' putting the first Sputnik into orbit around the earth, Congress voted an enormous subsidy for scientific research. More than a

E–1 The National Theatre complex, London, on an impressive site on the south bank of the Thames. A splendid building, housing three theatres of different types and many workshops and rehearsal rooms. Symbol of the importance of theatre in the life of a nation. Denys Lasdun, architect. Photo © Denys Lasdun & Partners, London.

decade later came a modest beginning in national subsidy of the arts. Even into the seventies, the appropriations of the United States government for the performing arts were less than those of the city of Hamburg, Germany, for its opera company.

Yet there have been major achievements in contemporary American theatre. As early as 1927, the Cleveland Playhouse, which had been staffed by amateurs, became a professional company. With the help of private donations, a beautiful building with two theatres was opened. In the 1960s Minneapolis and Houston took the lead in building regional thea-

E–2 One corner of the informal lobby of the National Theatre, where the audience can relax before the play, between acts, and after the play. Besides a restaurant, there are bars, snack bars, and bookstands, and often music or other live entertainment is presented for an hour or so before the play. Photo © Denys Lasdun & Partners, London.

tres for resident companies, and in the seventies New York and Washington each finally finished a splendid center for all the performing arts: Lincoln Center and Kennedy Center. Other civic theatres have begun to fit the same nonprofit image: a building paid for by private and corporate gifts and by city, state, and federal grants, usually located not in the crowded commercial area but near other nonprofit institutions, like art museums and concert halls.

The Resident Theatre

The best resident companies operate on a repertory system, offering a different play every day or every few days—and thus allowing the playgoer on a brief visit to the city to catch several plays. Each actor may be in three, four, or more plays in a season but will not play every night and will have a variety of roles and be able to come back fresh to a play after performing in others. Playgoers can subscribe for a whole season at good prices, simplifying the problem of getting tickets and assuring the management of a dependable audience. London has two such repertory companies, the National Theatre Company and the Royal Shakespeare Company, which produces both in Stratford and in London, bringing many Stratford productions to London in midwinter and presenting also a repertory of modern plays.

On a modest scale, several resident companies in the United States have been quite successful, among them the Guthrie Theatre in Minneapolis and the American Conservatory Theatre in San Francisco. The Kennedy Center in Washington does not have a resident company but has been successful in presenting productions that originate elsewhere and has fostered a number of new productions that have gone on to New York and other cities. The hope of the Lincoln Center in New York was to have a permanent resident company, but five regimes at the center's Beaumont Theatre have failed to establish such a company. When Joseph Papp, who had been very successful at presenting free Shakespeare in Central Park and at running a half dozen theatres in his Public Theatre building, tried for two years and gave up in 1977, it seemed clear that to get a resident company going in the city of chaotic Broadway would take a genius in creative planning and more money for subsidy than anyone knew how to find.

An efficiency expert might ask why we should subsidize local live theatre when most people seem satisfied with television drama. But activities like theatre, which are creative and relate each participant to the community, are worth supporting, whether they are "efficient" or not.

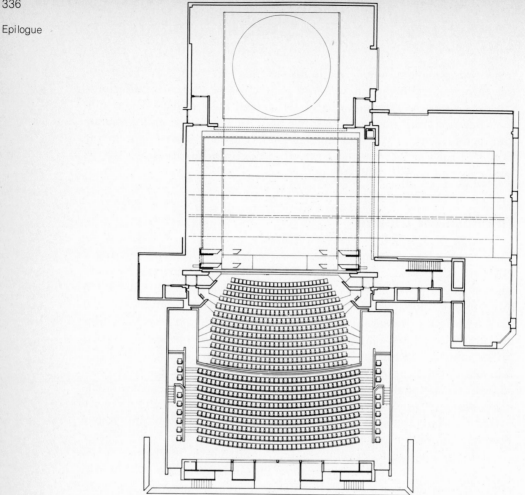

The fact that many impersonal needs can be satisfied efficiently by mass production offers a great opportunity: citizens can afford to subsidize those more personal needs, the arts, where there can be local distinction and creative joy. Mass marketing and mass communication tend to make all towns, all regions, exactly the same. It is worthwhile to foster local creative activity, both amateur and professional.

The College Theatre and the Community Theatre

If the United States has been slow in providing support for noncommercial professional theatre, it has led the world in public support for theatre in the schools. Many high schools, and some elementary schools, give some opportunity for creative improvisation and dramatic performance. College theatres have expanded from a few dozen in the 1930s to several

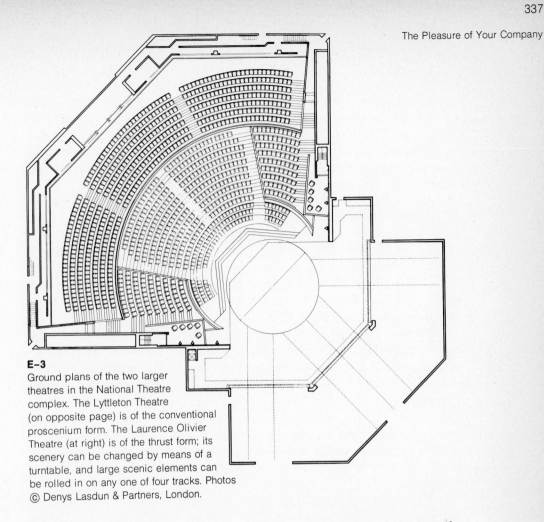

E-3
Ground plans of the two larger
theatres in the National Theatre
complex. The Lyttleton Theatre
(on opposite page) is of the conventional
proscenium form. The Laurence Olivier
Theatre (at right) is of the thrust form; its
scenery can be changed by means of a
turntable, and large scenic elements can
be rolled in on any one of four tracks. Photos
© Denys Lasdun & Partners, London.

thousand in the 1970s. Although some of the buildings are clumsily designed, many are among the best theatre buildings in the world, better than many of the older commercial theatres in London and New York. Colleges usually have a competent trained staff, and some give professional training.

This impressive academic theatre program has several goals. Among these, and as important as the training of actors and directors, is the creation of interested and knowledgeable audiences. To this end theatre departments offer courses in introduction to the theatre and present a wide range of exciting plays. Many students who have never seen a live performance beyond the senior class play in high school are surprised at the quality of college productions. Often there are college actors of considerable experience and training, and, as on the football field, youthful zest and enthusiasm can go a long way.

The resident theatre is like an adult, professional extension of the college theatre. The two cooperate closely, and in several instances a resident company has been developed by a university department. Both forms of theatre are planned on concepts delineated at the beginning of this century by Gordon Craig: that the theatre is not a show place for star actors but a creative art uniting many skills and that workers in the theatre must see that every detail down to the last button and the last offstage sound makes its creative contribution to the production.

Another goal of college theatre departments is to train for the community theatre. The community theatre is basically nonprofessional and the actors are amateurs, though the director and designer are usually professionals. An "amateur" is one who works without pay for the pleasure of creative activity. Many a good actor has given up the New York rat race to make a living in some other way and act in one or two plays a year with a good community theatre. Two lead roles in a year are two more than most actors can count on in New York.

Theatre makes an ideal community activity: each play lasts just the right length of time for workers who usually have jobs and other responsibilities outside the theatre. The performers quickly become a team of comrades. For from four to six weeks, they work together intimately yet impersonally, with new tasks each day. The excitement gradually increases and leads to a tremendous climax: the performance itself, shared by friends who have heard only hints of the conspiracy. Opening night becomes a gala occasion, with the audience in dress-up clothing and a reception in the foyer presided over by members of the theatre organization.

For college and community actors, the excitement is not over with the last performance: it must be carried on to a celebration. More than a farewell to the companions of the voyage, there must be some recognition of achievement. More than the applause and curtain calls, the flowers and telegrams, the flutter of friends backstage before and after the performance—more than all these, the actors need a kind master of ceremonies, preferably not the director, who gently and wittily brings up the mistakes and near-disasters and gives awards of praise and recognition. In amateur theatre, as in sports, shining trophies for excellence in everything from acting to backstage help may be given.

The Critic and the Review

Ideally, the event should be concluded with a critic from outside carefully delineating the strengths and weaknesses of the performance for the public record. But what is usually found in the college newspaper is an irrelevant literary discussion of the play, or meaningless praise of every-body, or the witticisms of a smart-aleck who attempts to show superiority by condemning the play entirely. Such harsh judgment puts an end to discussion: the most interesting criticism is sparing in judgment and lavish in description. A critical review with good description can make the playgoer see the play more clearly, and it should enable someone who has not seen the play to know what it was like and to join in the discussion.

Students should be warned that no critic, amateur or professional, can write a completely just review. Critics usually write in haste, and, although probably better informed than most playgoers, they also have prejudices and hangups. They often seem to expect a play to be either a masterpiece or a disaster, and it is seldom either. The worst sin is to attack a play for not being what it was never intended to be. Goethe once said that one should determine what a playwright is trying to do and how well he does it, and only then ask why the play was or was not worth doing.

The tradition of a skeptic-critic, often a hostile critic, belongs with the commercial, free-enterprise age of the theatre and seems less pertinent to a time when resident, college, and community theatres are considered part of the cultural life of any community. A very naive audience may need a skeptic-critic to sort out the good from the shoddy, but when much of the public is blasé from a glut of television entertainment, as well as bewildered by modern experiments in live theatre, a different kind of critic is needed. An advocate-critic can explain and comment on what theatre artists are trying to do. A national company in Europe regularly has on the staff a *dramaturg*, usually the holder of a doctorate in drama or theatre history, to help select the plays to be produced, prepare translations or adaptations, and give public lectures. The national theatre companies of Japan and England have similar "literary advisors."

The advocate-critic has a special opportunity with the resident or regional theatres away from New York. In this day of nationally publicized personalities, someone is needed to help citizens recognize the good qualities of their own companies, which do not get the attention given to Broadway or Hollywood productions.

In the Long Run

In a sense, every play is a complete experience in itself, and when we have had the pleasure of its company, we say, "That's that. When do we go to the next play?" Yet we do like to see some plays a second time, or to read at leisure the script we heard in the heat of performance. We like to compare plays by the same author, roles played by the same actor, and films made by the same director. A revival of a play of some years ago, or the autobiography of a famous actor, invites comparison of the attitudes of an earlier generation with those of our own time. Though we may laugh at the outdated manners and morals, we soon get a feeling of history and an understanding of our place in time.

Let the actors return to their spirit world and let the great globe itself dissolve: now we know our true nature. As Shakespeare's Prospero says, "We are such stuff as dreams are made on." The world of dreams is the world of knowledge, imagination, values, understanding—the timeless world that endures after "our little life is rounded with a sleep." The theatre shocks, diverts, and entertains us. It makes us look closely at the world we live in and perhaps consider what we can do to improve it. It rouses our sense of justice, purifying our motives and hopes, and warns us against over-simplification. As we are stirred by compassion for the stage characters, we feel a kinship with all mankind. And in theatre experiences, as actors or audience, we find ourselves as we create a *persona,* an identity, a role in relation to other people, indeed in relation to the universe. We know who and where we are. May our revels be never ending.

Bibliography

Bibliography

Theatre History

George Altman et al., *Theatre Pictorial* (1953). Margaret Berthold, *A History of World Theater* (1972). Oscar G. Brockett, *History of the Theatre* (3rd ed., 1977). Sheldon Cheney, *The Theatre* (rev. ed., 1952). Barrett H. Clark, *European Theories of the Drama* (1918; 2nd ed., with American theories, 1947; 3rd ed., with later European theories, 1965). Edwin Duerr, *The Length and Breadth of Acting* (1962). Bernard F. Dukore, *Dramatic Theory and Criticism: Greeks to Grotowski* (1974). George Freedley and John Reeves, *A History of the Theatre* (rev. ed., 1955). Bamber Gascoigne, *World Theatre: An Illustrated History* (1968). John Gassner, *Masters of the Drama* (3rd ed., 1953). Gassner, ed., *A Treasury of the Theatre,* Vol. I: *From Aeschylus to Ostrovsky* (3rd ed., 1967). Gassner and Ralph S. Allen, *Theatre and Drama in the Making* (1964). Gassner and Bernard F. Dukore, *A Treasury of the Theatre,* Vol. II: *From Henrik Ibsen to Robert Lowell* (4th ed., 1970). Phyllis Hartnoll, ed., *The Oxford Companion to the Theatre* (3rd ed., 1967). Barnard Hewitt, *Theatre USA, 1668–1957* (1959). James Laver, *Drama: Its Costume and Decor* (1951). Richard Leacroft, *The Development of the English Playhouse* (1973). Kenneth Macgowan and William Melnitz, *The Living Stage* (1955). Cesare Molinari, *Theatre Through the Ages* (1975). Daniel C. Mullin, *The Development of the Playhouse: A Survey of Architecture from the Renaissance to the Present* (1970). Alois M. Nagler, *Sources of Theatrical History* (1952). Allardyce Nicoll, *The Development of the Theatre* (5th ed., 1966). Nicoll, *History of English Drama, 1660–1930,* 7 vols. (1955–73). Nicoll, *World Drama from Aeschylus to Anouilh* (1949, 1976). Richard Southern, *The Seven Ages of the Theatre* (1961). J. L. Styan, *The Elements of Drama* (1960).

343

Chapter 1

Greek Tragedy

Peter D. Arnott, *The Ancient Greek and Roman Theatre* (1971). Arnott, *Greek Scenic Conventions in the Fifth Century, B.C.* (1962). Margarete Bieber, *The History of the Greek and Roman Theater* (2nd ed., 1961). James R. Butler, *The Theatre and Drama of Greece and Rome* (1972). Gerald F. Else, *The Origin and Early Form of Greek Tragedy* (1965). Edith Hamilton, *The Greek Way* (1937). George R. Kernodle, "The Fifth-Century Skene: A New Model," *Educational Theatre Journal, XX* (December, 1968). H. D. F. Kitto, *Greek Tragedy* (1950). Gilbert Murray, *Euripides and His Age* (1913).

Chapter 2

Middle Ages

Richard Axton, *European Drama of the Early Middle Ages* (1974). Grace Frank, *The Medieval French Drama* (1954). O. B. Hardison, *Christian Rite and Christian Drama in the Middle Ages* (1965). Stanley Kahrl, *Traditions of Medieval English Drama* (1974). V. A. Kolve, *The Play Called Corpus Christi* (1966). F. M. Salter, *Medieval Drama in Chester* (1955). Richard Southern, *The Medieval Theatre in the Round* (1957). Jerome Taylor and Alan Nelson, *Medieval English Drama: Essays Critical and Contextual* (1972). Glynne Wickham, *Early English Stages, 1300–1660*, 2 vols. (1959–1962). Wickham, *The Medieval Theatre* (1974). Rosemary Woolf, *The English Mystery Play* (1972). Karl Young, *The Drama of the Medieval Church* (1933).

Renaissance, 17th and 18th Centuries

John C. Adams, *The Globe Playhouse: Its Design and Equipment* (1961). Margarete Baur-Heinhold, *The Baroque Theatre* (1967). Bernard Beckerman, *Shakespeare at the Globe, 1589–1609* (1962). Gerald E. Bentley, *The Jacobean and Caroline Stage*, 5 vols. (1941–56). E. K. Chambers, *The Elizabethan Stage*, 4 vols. (1923). Alfred Harbage, *Shakespeare's Audience* (1941). Barnard Hewitt, ed., *The Renaissance Stage: Documents of Serlio, Sabbattini, and Furttenbach* (1959). C. Walter Hodges, *The Globe Restored* (2nd ed., 1968). Hodges, *Shakespeare's Second Globe* (1973). George R. Kernodle, *From Art to Theatre: Form and Convention in the Renaissance* (1944, 1964). T. E. Lawrenson, *The French Stage in the XVIIth Century: A Study of the Advent of the Italian Order* (1957). Allardyce Nicoll, *Masks, Mimes and Miracles* (1931). Nicoll, *Stuart Masques and the Renaissance Stage* (1937). Irwin Smith, *Shakespeare's Blackfriars Playhouse: Its History and Design* (1964). Richard Southern, *The Georgian Playhouse* (1948). Roy Strong, *Splendor at Court: Spectacle and the Theater of Power* (1973). Martin Turnell, *The Classical Moment: Studies in Corneille, Molière, and Racine* (1948). Enid Welsford, *The Court Masque: A Study in the Relationship Between Poetry and the Revels* (1927). Welsford, *The Fool* (1935). Frances A. Yates, *Theatre of the World* (1969).

Chapter 3

Comedy

Robert W. Corrigan, ed., *Comedy: Meaning and Form* (1965). Bonamy Dobrée, *Restoration Comedy, 1660–1720* (1924). J. C. Enck, Elizabeth T. Porter, and A. Whitley, *The Comic in Theory and Practice* (1960). Marvin Felheim, ed., *Comedy: Plays, Theory and Criticism* (1962). George R. Kernodle, "Excruciatingly Funny; or, the 47 Keys to Comedy," *Theatre Arts, XXX* (December, 1946). Walter Kerr, *Tragedy and Comedy* (1967). Arthur Koestler, *The Act of Creation* (1964). Louis Kronenberger, *The Thread of Laughter* (1952). Joseph W. Krutch, *Comedy and Conscience After the Restoration* (1949). Paul Lauter, *Theories of Comedy* (1964). Katherine Lever, *The Art of Greek Comedy* (1956). Kenneth Macgowan, *An Essay on Comedy and the Uses of the Comic Spirit* (1951). Erich W. Segal, *Roman Laughter: The Comedy of Plautus* (1968). Wylie Sypher, *Comedy* (1956).

Chapter 4

Romance and Melodrama

Harry Birdoff, *The World's Greatest Hit: "Uncle Tom's Cabin"* (1947). Michael R. Booth, *English Melodrama* (1965). Booth, *Hiss the Villain* (1964). Marvin A. Carlson, *The French Stage in the Nineteenth Century* (1972). Carlson, *The German Stage in the Nineteenth Century* (1972). Maurice Disher, *Blood and Thunder: Mid-Victorian Melodrama and Its Origins* (1949). Disher, *Melodrama: Plots That Thrilled* (1954). Marvin Felheim, *The Theater of Augustin Daly: An Account of the Late Nineteenth Century American Stage* (1956). David Grimsted, *Melodrama Unveiled* (1968). Barnard Hewitt, ed., *The Renaissance Stage* (1959). Richard Moody, *America Takes the Stage: Romanticism in American Drama and Theatre, 1750–1900* (1955). Hugh F. Rankin, *The Theatre in Colonial America* (1965). George Rowell, *The Victorian Theatre* (1956). Nicolas A. Vardac, *Stage to Screen: Theatrical Method from Garrick to Griffith* (1949).

Opera and Musical Comedy

Edward J. Dent, *Opera* (1949). Lehmann Engel, *Planning and Producing the Musical Show* (1957). Albert Goldman and Evert Sprinchorn, *Wagner on Music and Drama* (1964). Gordon Jacob, *The Composer and His Art* (1955). Joseph Kerman, *Opera as Drama* (1956). Abe Laufe, *Broadway's Greatest Musicals* (1973). Stanley Richards, *Ten Great Musicals of the American Theatre* (1973). Cecil Smith, *Musical Comedy in America* (1950). Stephen Williams, *Come to the Opera* (1961).

Dance

See bibliography for Chapters 7 and 8.

Chapters 5 and 6

Realism

André Antoine, *Memories of the Théâtre Libre* (1964). John Mason Brown, *The Modern Theatre in Revolt* (1929), reprinted in his *Dramatis Personae* (1963). Robert Brustein, *The Theatre of Revolt* (1964). Harold Clurman, *The Fervent Years: The Story of the Group Theatre in the Thirties* (1957). John Gassner, *Form and Idea in the Modern Theatre* (1956). Gassner, *The Theatre in Our Times* (1954). Mordecai Gorelik, *New Theatres for Old* (1940). Morgan Y. Himelstein, *Drama Was a Weapon: The Left-Wing Theatre in New York, 1929–1941* (1963). Robert Lewis, *Method—or Madness?* (1960). Lise-Lone Marker, *David Belasco's Naturalism in the American Theatre* (1975). Erika Munk, ed., *Stanislavski and America* (1968). Gerald Rabkin, *Drama and Commitment: Politics in the American Theatre of the Thirties* (1964). Duncan Ross, "Towards an Organic Approach to Actor Training: A Criticism of the Stanislavski Scheme," *Educational Theatre Journal, XX* (special issue, August, 1968). Constantin (Stanislavsky, *An Actor Prepares* (1936). Stanislavsky, *Building a Character* (1949). Stanislavsky, *Creating a Role* (1961). Stanislavsky, *My Life in Art* (1923). Edward Stone, *What Was Naturalism? Materials for an Answer* (1959).

Oriental Theatre

Rewi Alley, *Peking Opera* (1957). Kay Ambrose, *Classical Dances and Costumes of India* (1950). L. C. Arlington, *The Chinese Theatre* (1930, repr., 1965). Peter D. Arnott, *The Theatre of Japan* (1970). Faubion Bowers, *Japanese Theatre* (1952). James R. Brandon, *The Theatre of Southeast Asia* (1967). Jack Chen, *The Chinese Theatre* (1922). Earle Ernst, *The Kabuki Theatre* (1956). Ernst, "The Influence of Japanese Theatrical Style in Western Theatre," *Educational Theatre Journal, XXI* (May, 1969). Balwant Gargi, *Theatre in India* (1962). Chandra B. Gupta, *The Indian Theatre* (1954). Francis Haar, *Japanese Theatre in Highlight: A Pictorial Commentary* (1952). Kalvodová-Sís-Vaniš, *The Chinese Theatre* (1959). Donald Keene, *Bunraku: The Art of the Japanese Puppet Theatre* (1965). Keene, *Major Plays of Chikamatsu* (1961). Keene, *Nō: The Classical Theatre of Japan* (1966). P. G. O'Neill, *A Guide to Nō* (1953). *Performing Arts of Japan*, 5 vols. (1972): Tsuruo Ando, *Bunraku: The Puppet Theatre*; Yasuji Toita, *Kabuki: The Popular Theatre*; Masakatsu Gunji, *Buyo: The Classical Dance*; Yasuo Nakamura, *Noh: The Classical Theatre*; Masataro Togi, *Gagaku: Court Music and Dance*. Leonard Pronko, *Theatre East and West: Perspectives Toward a Total Theatre* (1967). A. C. Scott, *The Classical Theatre of China* (1957). Scott, *The Kabuki Theatre of Japan* (1955). Arthur Waley, *The Nō Plays of Japan* (1922). Adolf E. Zucker, *The Chinese Theatre* (1925).

Epic Theatre

Eric Bentley, *The Playwright as Thinker* (1946). Bertolt Brecht, *Brecht on Theatre* (1965). Brecht issue, *Tulane Drama Review*, T13 (Autumn, 1961). Martin Esslin,

Brecht: His Life and Work (1967). Hallie Flanagan, *Arena* (1940). Ronald Gray, *Brecht* (1961). Mordecai Gorelik, *New Theatres for Old* (1940). Gorelik, "An Epic Catechism," *Tulane Drama Review,* T5 (Autumn, 1959). Leo Kerz, "Brecht and Piscator," *Educational Theatre Journal, XX* (October, 1968). Maria Ley-Piscator, *The Piscator Experiment: The Political Theatre* (1967).

Chapters 7 and 8

Disruption, Reconstruction, and Liberation

Adolphe Appia, *Music and the Art of the Theatre* (1899, 1963, repr. 1975). Appia, *The World of Living Art* and *Man Is the Measure of All Things* (1960). Antonin Artaud, *The Theatre and Its Double* (1938). Eric Bentley, *In Search of Theatre* (1953). Bentley, *Theatre of War* (1973). Bentley, *The Theory of the Modern Stage* (1968). Faubion Bowers, *Broadway, USSR: Theatre, Ballet and Entertainment in Russia Today* (1959). Oscar G. Brockett and Robert R. Findlay, *Century of Innovation: A History of European and American Theatre and Drama Since 1870* (1973). Peter Brook, *The Empty Space* (1968). Robert Brustein, *The Theatre of Revolt: An Approach to Modern Drama* (1964). Sheldon Cheney, *Expressionism in Art* (1948). Ruby Cohn, *Currents in Contemporary Drama* (1969). Edward Gordon Craig, *On the Art of the Theatre* (1911). Margaret Croyden, *Lovers, Lunatics, and Madmen: The Contemporary Experimental Theatre* (1974). Martin Esslin, *The Theatre of the Absurd* (1961). Genêt and Ionesco issue of *Tulane Drama Review,* T19 (Spring, 1963). Mordecai Gorelik, *New Theatres for Old* (1940). Jerzy Grotowski, *Toward a Poor Theatre* (1968). Al Hansen, *A Primer of Happenings and Space/Time Art* (1966). Norman James, "The Fusion of Pirandello and Brecht in *Marat/Sade* and *The Plebeians Rehearse the Uprising,"* *Educational Theatre Journal, XXI* (December, 1969). Lawrence Kitchin, *Drama in the Sixties: Form and Interpretation* (1966). E. T. Kirby, ed., *Total Theatre: A Critical Anthology* (1969). Michael Kirby, *Happenings* (1965). Richard Kostelanetz, ed., *The Theatre of Mixed Means* (1967). Jan Kott, *Shakespeare Our Contemporary* (1964). Henry Lesnick, *Guerrilla Street Theatres* (1973). Bonnie Marranca, ed., *The Theatre of Images* (1977). Brooks McNamara, Jerry Rojo, and Richard Schechner, *Theaters, Spaces, Environments: 18 Projects* (1975). Loften Mitchell, *Black Drama: The Story of the American Negro in the Theatre* (1967). Robert Pasolli, *A Book on the Open Theatre* (1970). Leonard Pronko, *Avant-Garde: The Experimental Theatre in France* (1962). James Roose-Evans, *Experimental Theatre: From Stanislavsky to Today* (1970). Steven J. Rosen, *Samuel Beckett and the Pessimistic Tradition* (1976). Richard Schechner, *Essays on Performance Theory* (1977). Schechner, *Public Domain: Essays on the Theatre* (1969). James Schevill, *Breakout! In Search of New Theatrical Environments* (1972). Lee Simonson, *The Stage Is Set* (1932). James M. Symons, *Meyerhold's Theatre of the Grotesque: The Post-Revolutionary Productions, 1920–32* (1971). John Russell Taylor, *Anger and After* (1965). Walther Volbach, *Adolphe Appia, Prophet of the Modern Theatre* (1968). John Willett, *Expressionism* (1970).

Dance (Ballet and Modern)

Dolores K. Cayou, *Modern Jazz Dance* (1971). Anatole Chujoy, *The Dance Encyclopedia* (1949). Leon Dallin, *Techniques of Twentieth Century Composition* (1957). Agnes de Mille, *The Book of the Dance* (1963). De Mille, *Dance to the Piper* (1952). Lois Ellfeldt and Edwin Carnes, *Dance Production Handbook* (1971). Ellfeldt, *A Primer for Choreographers* (1967). Margaret H'Doubler, *Dance: A Creative Art Experience* (1957). Louis Horst and Carroll Russell, *Modern Dance Forms in Relation to Other Modern Arts* (1961). Doris Humphrey, *Making Dances* (1959). Boris Kochno, *Diaghilev and the Ballets Russes* (1970). Joan Lawson, *Classical Ballet: Its Style and Technique* (1960). Lawson, *History of Ballet and Its Makers* (1964). Gertrude Lippincott, ed., *Dance Production: Music, Costumes, Staging, Decor, Lighting, Photography, Make-up, Planning and Rehearsing* (1956). Aileene Lockhart, *Modern Dance: Building and Teaching Lessons* (2nd ed., 1957). John Martin, *Book of the Dance* (1963). Fannie Helen Melcer, *Staging the Dance* (1955). Rachel Percival, *Discovering Dance* (1964). Elizabeth Sherbon, *On the Count of One: A Guide to Movement and Progression in Dance* (1968). Bernard Taper, *Balanchine* (1963). Mary Wigman, *The Language of Dance* (1966).

Chapters 9 and 10

Planning and Directing the Play

H. D. Albright, W. P. Halstead, and Lee Mitchell, *Principles of Theatre Arts* (2nd ed., 1968). Bernard Beckerman, *Dynamics of Drama* (1970). Eric Bentley, *The Life of the Drama* (1965). James H. Clay and Daniel Krempel, *The Theatrical Image* (1967). Harold Clurman, *On Directing* (1972). Toby Cole and Helen K. Chinoy, eds., *Directing the Play: A Source Book of Stagecraft* (1953). Alexander Dean, *Fundamentals of Play Directing* (rev. ed., 1965). Bernard F. Dukore, *Bernard Shaw, Director* (1971). Northrop Frye, *Anatomy of Criticism: Four Essays* (1957). John Gassner, ed., *Producing the Play* (1953). Nikolai Gorchakov, *Stanislavski Directs* (1954). Francis Hodge, *Play Directing: Analysis, Communication, and Style* (1971). George R. Kernodle, "Style, Stylization and Styles of Acting," *Educational Theatre Journal*, XII (December, 1960). Suzanne Langer, *Feeling and Form* (1953). John Howard Lawson, *Theory and Technique of Playwriting* (1960). Frank McMullan, *The Directorial Image* (1962). Michel Saint-Denis, *Theatre: The Rediscovery of Style* (1960). Richard Schechner, *Public Domain* (1969). George Bernard Shaw, *The Art of Rehearsal* (1928). Lee Simonson, *The Stage Is Set* (1932). J. L. Styan, *The Elements of Drama* (1960). Alexander Tairov, *Notes of a Director* (1969).

Acting

Joseph Bertram, *Elizabethan Acting* (2nd ed., 1964). Bertram, *The Tragic Actor* (1959). Bertolt Brecht, "On Chinese Acting," *Tulane Drama Review*, T13 (Autumn, 1961). Michael Chekhov, *To the Actor: On the Technique of Acting* (1953). David

Cole, *The Theatrical Event* (1975). Toby Cole and Helen K. Chinoy, eds., *Actors on Acting: The Theories, Techniques, and Practices of the Great Actors of All Times as Told in Their Own Words* (1949). Alan S. Downer, "Nature to Advantage Dressed: Eighteenth Century Acting," *PMLA* (1943), 1002–37. Downer, "Players and the Painted Stage: Nineteenth Century Acting," *PMLA, LXI* (1946), 522–76. Edwin Duerr, *The Length and Depth of Acting* (1962). Lewis Funke and John E. Booth, *Actors Talk About Acting* (1961). Michael Goldman, *The Actor's Freedom: Toward a Theory of Drama* (1975). Arthur Lessac, *The Use and Training of the Human Voice* (1967). Ted Shawn, *Every Little Movement Has a Meaning All Its Own* (1963). Viola Spolin, *Improvisation for the Theatre* (1963). Constantin Stanislavsky, *An Actor Prepares* (1936). Stanislavsky, *Building a Character* (1949). Stanislavsky, *Creating a Role* (1961). Lee Strasberg, *Strasberg at the Actors Studio* (1965). Garff Wilson, *A History of American Acting* (1966).

Chapter 11

Scene Design

Howard Bay, *Stage Design* (1974). Willard F. Bellman, *Scenography and Stage Technology: An Introduction* (1977). Ned Bowman, *Handbook of Technical Practices for the Performing Arts* (1972). Nicholas L. Bryson, *Thermoplastic Scenery for the Theatre,* Vol. I: *Vacuum Forming* (1972). Jarka Burian, *The Scenography of Josef Svoboda* (1971). Harold Burris-Meyer and Edward C. Cole, *Scenery for the Theatre* (rev. ed., 1971). Irene Corey, *The Mask of Reality: An Approach to Design for Theatre* (1968). A. S. Gillette, *An Introduction to Scenic Design* (1967). Gillette, *Stage Scenery* (rev. ed., 1960). René Hainaux, ed., *Stage Design Throughout the World since 1935* (1956). Hainaux, ed., *Stage Design Throughout the World since 1950* (1964). George C. Izenour, *Theater Design* (1977). Robert Edmond Jones, *The Dramatic Imagination* (1941). Orville K. Larson, *Scene Design for Stage and Screen* (1961). Jo Mielziner, *Designing for the Theatre* (1965). Thelma R. Newman, *Plastics as an Art Form* (rev. ed., 1969). Oren Parker and Harvey K. Smith, *Scene Design and Stage Lighting* (3rd ed., 1959). Darwin Ried Payne, *Design for the Stage: First Steps* (1974). Lynn Pecktal, *Designing and Painting for the Theatre* (1975). Herbert Philippi, *Stagecraft and Scene Design* (1953). James Scholz, *Baroque and Romantic Stage Design* (1962). Samuel E. Selden and H. D. Sellman, *Stage Scenery and Lighting* (3rd ed., 1959). Selden and Tom Rezzuto, *Essentials of Stage Scenery* (1972). David Welker, *Theatrical Set Design* (1969).

Periodicals: *Theatre Crafts,* Rodale Press Inc., Emmaus, Pa. *Theatre Design and Technology,* U.S. Institute of Theatre Technology, New York.

Auditorium Forms

American Theatre Planning Board, *Theatre Check List: A Guide to the Planning and Construction of Proscenium and Open Stage Theatres* (1969). Walden P. Boyle, *Central and Flexible Staging* (1956). Harold Burris-Meyer and Edward C. Cole, *Theatres and Auditoriums* (2nd ed., 1964). Margaret Cogswell, *The Ideal Theatre: Eight Concepts* (1962). Margo Jones, *Theatre in the Round* (1951). Stephen Joseph, *New Theatre Forms* (1968). Jo Mielziner, *Shapes of Our Theatres* (1970). Horace W. Robinson, *Architecture for the Educational Theatre* (1970). Hannelore Schubert, *Modern Theatre Building: Architecture, Stage Design, Lighting* (1971). Maxwell Silverman and Ned Bowman, *Contemporary Theatre Architecture: An Illustrated Survey* (1965). Richard Southern, *The Open Stage* (1959).

Costume and Makeup

Lucy Barton, *Historic Costume for the Stage* (1935). Herman Buchman, *Stage Makeup* (1971). Irene Corey, *The Mask of Reality: An Approach to Design for Theatre* (1968). Richard Corson, *Stage Makeup* (5th ed., 1975). Motley, *Designing and Making Stage Costumes* (1965). Berneice Prisk, *Stage Costume Handbook* (1966). Douglas Russell, *Stage Costume Design: Theory, Technique and Style* (1973). Serge Strenkovsky, *The Art of Make-Up* (1937).

Lighting

Adolphe Appia, *Music and the Art of the Theatre* (1899, 1963, repr., 1975). Willard F. Bellman, *Lighting the Stage: Art and Practice* (2nd ed., 1974). Frederick Bentham, *The Art of Stage Lighting* (2nd ed., 1968). Edward F. Kook, *Images in Light for the Living Stage: A Survey of the Use of Scenic Projection* (1963). Stanley R. McCandless, *A Method of Lighting the Stage* (4th ed., 1958). Richard Pilbrow, *Stage Lighting* (1971). Jean Rosenthal and Lael Wertenbacker, *The Magic of Light* (1972). Thomas Wilfred, *Projected Scenery: A Technical Manual* (2nd ed., 1965).

Epilogue

Theatre and Society

William J. Baumol and William C. Bowman, *Performing Arts—the Economic Dilemma* (1966). A. L. Bernheim, *The Business of the Theatre* (1932). David Cole, *The Theatrical Event* (1975). Christopher Davis, *The Producer* (1972). Donald C. Farber, *From Option to Opening: A Guide for the Off-Broadway Producer* (1970). Farber, *Productions on Broadway* (1969). Robert E. Gard and Gertrude Burley, *Community Theatre, Idea and Achievement* (1959). William Gibson, *The See-Saw Log: A Chronicle of the Stage Production with the Text of "Two for the See-Saw"* (1959). Susan Jacobs, *On Stage: The Making of a Broadway Play* (1972). Siegfried Kienzle, *Modern World Theatre: A Guide to Production in Europe and the United States Since 1945* (1970). Jo Mielziner, *Shapes of Our Theatre* (1970). Henry Lee Munson, *Money for the Arts: The What, How and Why of Government Aid to the Arts in Seven Free Countries of Europe* (n. d.). Julius Novick, *Beyond Broadway: The Quest for Permanent Theatres*

(1968). Jack Poggi, *Theatre in America: The Impact of Economic Forces, 1870–1967* (1968). Julia Price, *The Off-Broadway Theatre* (1962). Rockefeller Panel on the Future of the Theatre, Dance, and Music in America, *The Performing Arts: Problems and Prospects* (1965). Glynne Wickham, *Drama in a World of Science* (1962). John Wray Young, *The Community Theatre and How It Works* (1957).

Index

Index

Note: *page numbers in italics refer to material in illustrations or captions.*

A 7
B 8
C 9
D 0
E 1
F 2
G 3
H 4
I 5
J 6